'… another great read … no complex narrative, just pure storytelling …'   5* Kindle review

'Filled with compassion and love'   Victoria Goldman,
                                                              Lovereading

'Never disappoints and brings a tear to my eye'   Hannah,
                                                          book blogger

'Simply yet eloquently told … Cathy's years of fostering experience shine a beam of light across the pages'
                                                      Liz Robinson,
                                                         Lovereading

'Amazing writing from an incredible lady'
                                                  5* Amazon review

'Wonderfully written book'   5* Kindle review

'A captivating insight into the life of a foster carer'
                                                Victoria Goldman,
                                                      Lovereading

'I have read all Cathy Glass's books and none disappoint'
                                                 5* Amazon review

'Great job, Cathy Glass. Keep doing what you do and I'll keep reading'   Goodreads review

Innocent

ALSO BY CATHY GLASS

THE MILLION COPY BESTSELLING AUTHOR

CATHY GLASS

Innocent

The true story of siblings
struggling to survive

HARPER
element

Certain details in this story, including names, places and dates, have been changed to protect the family's privacy.

HarperElement
An imprint of HarperCollins*Publishers*
1 London Bridge Street
London SE1 9GF

www.harpercollins.co.uk

First published by HarperElement 2019

1 3 5 7 9 10 8 6 4 2

A catalogue record of this book is available from the British Library

ISBN 978-0-00-834198-5

Printed and bound in Great Britain by CPI Group (UK) Ltd, Croydon

MIX
Paper from
responsible sources
FSC™ C007454

FSC
www.fsc.org

This book is produced from independently certified FSC™ paper to ensure responsible forest management.

For more information visit: www.harpercollins.co.uk/green

ACKNOWLEDGEMENTS

A big thank you to my family; my editors, Carolyn and Holly; my literary agent, Andrew; my UK publishers HarperCollins, and my overseas publishers who are now too numerous to list by name. Last, but definitely not least, a big thank you to my readers for your unfailing support and kind words. They are much appreciated.

CHAPTER ONE

TRAUMATIZED

Thank goodness I didn't have to witness their anguish and upset, I thought. I was sure I wouldn't have coped. It was bad enough knowing it was happening – two young children about to be taken from their parents and brought into care. During the twenty-five years I'd been fostering I'd seen a lot of changes, but the raw grief of a family torn apart didn't get any easier. I could imagine the children screaming and crying and clinging to their distraught parents as they tried to say goodbye. My heart ached for them. I also had sympathy for the social worker who was doing a very difficult job. No one wants to take children from their parents, but sometimes there is no alternative if they are to be safe.

It was now nearly two o'clock in the afternoon and I was standing in what would shortly be the children's bedroom. I could have put the cot in my room, but I was sure Kit, only eighteen months old, would be happier sleeping with his sister Molly, who was three and a half. Doubtless she too would find comfort in having her younger brother close. Fostering guidelines on bedroom sharing vary slightly from one local authority to another, but generally siblings of the opposite sex can share a bedroom up to the age of five.

Molly and Kit were coming to me as an emergency placement. Stevie, fifteen (whose story I told in *Finding Stevie*), had left at the end of August and now, a few days later, at the start of September, I was preparing myself and the house for the arrival of these two little ones, who were certainly going to be distraught. Sometimes taking children into care can be done with the cooperation of their parents, voluntarily, which is known as 'accommodated' or a Section 20. It's usually considered the better option, as the parents retain legal responsibility for their children and the process is less distressing for all involved. But that couldn't happen here, so the social services had gone to court that morning to ask the judge for a care order to remove the children from home and bring them to me.

Edith, my supervising social worker, had telephoned at 11 a.m. to tell me to expect the children if the care order was granted. The reason for the social services' application was that one of the children (she didn't know which one) had suffered what was thought to be a non-accidental injury. That meant that someone – presumably one or both of the parents – had harmed the child. Apart from this and their ages, Edith didn't have any more details. I would learn more when their social worker brought the children to me later today.

As soon as I'd finished speaking to Edith I'd gone into the loft and brought down all the early-years equipment I'd stored away there, including a cot, pushchair, car seats and boxes full of toys, all of which I'd wrapped in polythene to keep them clean after the last time I'd used them many years before. I'd struggled to get them down and to assemble the cot on my own, but my family were all out and I didn't dare leave it until they returned in the evening. Adrian, aged twenty-four, and Lucy, twenty-two, were at work, and Paula, twenty, was at college. I was a single parent, my husband having run off with a younger work colleague when the children were little. Very upsetting at the time but history now.

Having made up the bed and cot with fresh linen, I set a toy box at the far end of the room and came out. Hopefully Molly and Kit's parents would feel up to packing some of their children's clothes and toys, as it would help them settle with me to have familiar things around them when everything else in their lives had changed.

Downstairs, I quickly made a sandwich lunch, which I ate at the table with my mobile phone beside me. I was expecting Edith or the children's social worker to phone at any moment – as soon as the care order had been granted and they'd left court. Of course, there was a chance the order wouldn't be granted. If so, then preparing the room would have all been for nothing. It had happened to me in the past – I'd been put on standby to receive a child or children, and plans had changed at the last minute, which is why foster carers have to be flexible. It's unusual for a care order not to be granted, but what happens more often is that a relative steps in at the last minute to look after the children so they don't have to go to a foster carer they don't know.

I'd just finished eating my sandwich when my mobile rang.

'Cathy Glass?' a female voice asked.

'Yes, speaking.' I could hear traffic noise in the background.

'It's Tess Baldwin, social worker for Molly and Kit. I believe Edith spoke to you this morning and you're expecting Kit and Molly.'

'Yes, that's right. Their room is ready.'

'Good. We're on our way to collect them. We should be with you by five o'clock. The children have never been away from home before so are likely to be very upset.'

'Poor dears.' My heart clenched. 'I don't have any information about them other than their ages.'

'I'll explain more when I see you. The family only came to the notice of the social services on Monday. The decision to remove the children was made by us yesterday afternoon.' It was only Thursday now, which showed just how urgent they considered it to be to bring the children to a place of safety.

I had a couple of hours before Molly and Kit arrived. I texted Adrian, Lucy and Paula to let them know the children were coming so it wouldn't be a complete surprise. I then went quickly into the High Street where I bought a trainer cup, nappies and baby wipes for Kit (I assumed he was still in nappies), and some snack food that might tempt them both if they were too upset to eat – for example, corn and carrot sticks, little packets of dried fruit and fromage frais in brightly decorated pots. If the children didn't come with their own clothes, I'd be back here tomorrow to buy them what they needed. We'd get by tonight with the spares I kept in the ottoman in my bedroom. I had most sizes, from newborn to teens, all washed and pressed and ready for emergency use.

An hour later I was home again and, having unpacked the shopping, I began to make a cottage pie for dinner later. There wouldn't be much time once the social worker arrived with Kit and Molly, and most children enjoy cottage pie. I didn't know yet if Kit and Molly had any special dietary requirements, allergies or special needs, and it would be something I'd ask Tess when they arrived. If this had been a planned move, I would normally have received background information like this in advance of the children arriving, but this was an emergency, so everything was happening quickly.

Shortly after four o'clock my phone rang and it was Tess, the children's social worker. 'We're in the car with the children,' she said. 'We should be with you in about twenty minutes. Molly will need a change of clothes, she's just wet herself.'

'I'll have some ready,' I said. 'Tell her not to worry.' I knew how children fretted if they had an accident. It wasn't surprising she'd wet herself, given the trauma of being taken from home.

'See you shortly,' Tess said, and ended the call.

I went straight upstairs to my bedroom where I searched through the ottoman until I found a new packet of pants marked 'Age 3–4 Years', and a pair of jogging bottoms and matching top that should fit Molly. I took them into the children's bedroom and returned downstairs, my heart thumping loudly from nervous anticipation.

Waiting for a new child or children to arrive is always nerve-racking for the foster carer, regardless of how many times they've done it before. We worry if the children will like and trust us enough to help them, if we can meet their needs and work with their family – very important. Now I had the added challenge of fostering not one child but two, who were both very young. I hadn't fostered little ones in a long while. As a specialist foster carer with lots of experience, I was usually asked to look after older children with challenging behaviour, who, to be honest, I felt more confident in dealing with. Would I remember what to do with two little ones?

My crisis of confidence continued until the doorbell rang, when common sense and instinct kicked in. I answered it with a bright smile. 'Hello, I'm Cathy. Come in.'

Two female social workers stood before me, each carrying a child.

'I'm Tess, and this is Molly,' Tess said, introducing the child she was holding. 'And this is my colleague Preeta, with Kit.'

'Hello,' Preeta said as they came in.

I smiled at both children. They looked petrified – large eyes stared out from pale faces and they clung desperately to their social workers. Kit had a plaster cast on his left arm, his cheeks were bruised and there was a red bump on his forehead. 'Hello, love,' I said to him, and swallowed hard.

He drew back from me further into Preeta's shoulder.

'I've put some toys in the living room,' I said, and led the way down the hall, although I guessed it would be a long time before either child felt like playing. Their little sombre faces suggested they were very close to tears.

In the living room, Preeta sat on the sofa with Kit on her lap, still clinging desperately to her. Tess put Molly down. The child grabbed her hand for comfort. 'It might be a good idea if you changed her now,' Tess said to me. 'She's sopping wet, and can I use your bathroom to wash my hands?'

'Yes, of course. This way.' I could smell stale urine.

Leaving Preeta with Kit, we went upstairs to the bathroom, with Molly still clutching her social worker's hand.

'Help yourself to whatever you need,' I said to Tess, referring to the soap, towel and antibacterial hand wash. 'I'll change Molly in her bedroom.'

'Thanks. I don't suppose you have a change of clothes for me too?' Tess joked, sniffing the sleeve of her blouse.

'I'm sure I could find you a top,' I offered.

'No, it's fine,' she said with a smile. 'I've had worse than a bit of pee on me.'

I bent down to talk to Molly. 'I've got some nice dry clothes for you ready in your bedroom,' I said. 'Let's go and get you changed.' She stared back at me, bewildered. I gently took her hand and, leaving Tess washing her hands and forearms, I led Molly, silent and expressionless, around the landing and into her and Kit's bedroom.

I spoke brightly and positively as I pointed out the toy box, her bed and Kit's cot close by, trying to put her at ease. I held up the clothes I'd put out ready. 'You can wear these for now,' I said. She stared at the clothes. 'Can you change yourself or shall I help you?' Most children of Molly's age can make a good attempt at dressing and undressing themselves, although they still need help with fiddly things like buttons and zips. Molly just stood there, looking lost and staring at the clothes.

'I'll help you,' I said.

I began taking off her damp clothes. She was like a doll and only moved to raise her arms as I took off her dress and vest over her head. I then helped her out of her pants and socks. They were all wet and smelt of urine and I put them to one side to go in the washing machine. I wiped her skin with baby wipes. Her body was very pale like her face, as though she hadn't seen much sun, but thankfully I couldn't see any bruises or other marks on her as there were on Kit. 'That will do for now,' I said, throwing the wipes in the bin. 'You can have a bath tonight.' I dressed her in the clean clothes.

Tess appeared. 'Anything I should be aware of?' she asked, meaning injuries.

'No, I can't see anything. I'll give them both a bath this evening, though.'

'I'll arrange medicals for both children,' Tess said. This was usual when children came into care.

Molly still hadn't said a word, but while she looked very sad, she wasn't crying; indeed, I hadn't heard a sound from her since she'd arrived. 'Does she have communication difficulties?' I asked Tess. I knew so little about the children it was possible she had a hearing and speech impairment.

'No. She was talking to her parents at home,' Tess said. Then to Molly, 'You can hear me, can't you?'

She gave a small nod. It therefore seemed it must be the trauma of coming into care that was responsible, and possibly what had been going on at home. I'd seen it before in abused children – sometimes it was days before they were able to speak.

'Let's go downstairs and I'll tell you what I know,' Tess said to me. 'I haven't got the Essential Information Form, it's being completed now. I'll email it to you, and the placement agreement form.' In a planned move, this paperwork arrived with the social worker when the child was placed and gave their background information and the reasons they were in care.

We returned downstairs to the living room where Kit was as we'd left him, sitting on Preeta's lap. She had taken a toy fire engine with flashing lights and a siren from the toy box and was trying to interest him in it, but he wasn't even touching it – another indication of how traumatized the children were. Molly sat on the sofa beside Preeta and Kit and put her hand on his arm. Tess sat next to her. I asked both social workers if they would like a drink, and they wanted coffee. I also asked Molly and Kit if they'd like a drink, but they just looked at me. 'I'll get you some water and you can have it if you want,' I told the children with a reassuring smile.

In the kitchen I made two coffees and filled the trainer cup with water for Kit and a child's plastic beaker for Molly. I put some biscuits on a plate and then carried everything on a tray into the living room where I set it on the occasional table. As Tess and Preeta took their coffees – keeping the hot liquid away from the children – I offered Molly and Kit their drinks, but they didn't want them. 'OK, maybe later,' I said. 'Would you like a biscuit?' I showed them the plate but got the same response.

At that moment I heard a key go in the front door and the door open. Molly started. 'Don't worry,' I said. 'That will be my youngest daughter, Paula, returning from college.'

'Who else lives here?' Tess asked. Setting down her coffee, she took a pen and notepad from her bag. I guessed in all the rush she had as little information about me as I did about the children.

'As well as Paula, there is Adrian, my son, and Lucy, my other daughter. And Sammy the cat,' I added, smiling at Molly. 'He must be in the garden. You'll meet him later.'

'And your children's ages?' Tess asked. I told her.

'Do you like cats?' Preeta asked Molly, but she didn't reply.

'They don't have any animals at home,' Tess said as she wrote.

Paula appeared at the living-room door and smiled a little self-consciously. 'Oh they're sweet,' she said. The children shifted their gaze to her.

'This is Molly and Kit,' I said. 'Can you join us? I think it might help them.' So often, looked-after children take to the carer's children before they feel relaxed enough to begin to form a relationship with the carer.

'Sure,' Paula said, coming further into the room. 'Shall I play with them?'

'Yes, please.' I took some of the toys out of the box as Paula sat on the floor beside them.

'Do you want to play with these farm animals?' she asked the children. Molly stared at her, but Kit scrambled down from Preeta's lap and sat near Paula.

'Well done,' I said to her.

'You've hurt your arm,' she said to Kit, referring to the plaster. Molly, wanting to stay close to her brother, now left the sofa and sat beside him.

I smiled, relieved. It was a start.

'I'll give you some background information, then perhaps we can go into another room for the rest?' Tess suggested, so I knew that some of what she had to tell me she didn't want the children to hear. While Kit at eighteen months would have a limited understanding of what he heard, Molly at three and a half would probably understand most of it. Bad enough to have witnessed whatever had happened at home without having to hear it discussed.

'The parents are called Aneta and Filip,' Tess began. 'Filip is forty and fifteen years older than his wife. They have been married five years and these are their only children. They live in Eastwood.' It was a new housing estate on the edge of town. 'Aneta is a full-time mother and homemaker, and Filip is a warehouse manager who works very long hours. The family hadn't come to the attention of the social services before the start of this week. Aneta took Kit to the hospital in a lot of pain, and he was found to have a fractured arm. The mother is claiming he fell down the stairs, but the doctor had doubts.'

I saw Molly look over. Tess and Preeta saw it too. 'Why don't I go somewhere private now to talk to Cathy,' Tess suggested to Preeta, 'while you stay here with the children?'

'Yes, I think that's best,' Preeta replied.

'Are you OK to stay here too?' I asked Paula, aware that she would have college work to do.

'Yes.'

'We'll be in the front room,' I said.

Preeta joined Paula and the little ones on the floor with the toys as Tess quickly finished the last of her coffee and stood. I showed her into the front room where she closed the door so we couldn't be overheard. Away from the little ones, her professional reserve and composure dropped and she sank into one of the armchairs. 'Who'd be a social worker?' she said with a heartfelt sigh. 'It doesn't get much worse than this.'

CHAPTER TWO

CHAOS

'The children's mother, Aneta, was hysterical,' Tess continued as we sat in the front room. 'It was dreadful. She was clinging to the children, screaming and crying, trying to fight us off and stop us from taking them. The father – Filip – had to restrain her so we could leave with the children. Only he was in court; she stayed at home with the children. I've told him to call their doctor. I'll phone him after we've left here. He managed to pack a case with a few things for the children. Aneta couldn't. It's in my car – don't let me drive off with it.'

My heart ached from the scene Tess had just described. 'So the parents had no idea the children would be coming into care?' I asked.

'They knew we were going to court this morning. We advised them to get legal representation, but they didn't think it would be necessary. They will contact a solicitor now,' Tess said, and I nodded. 'Aneta insists Kit fell downstairs. Filip was at work and is standing by his wife and maintains she would never harm the children, that she loves them too much.' She paused to check her phone, which was on silent. I knew there must be more to it than this, as the judge would never allow the social services to remove the children because of one accident. 'That visit to the hospital', Tess continued, returning the phone to her pocket, 'was the sixtieth time she'd been with Kit.'

'What?' I gasped. 'He's only eighteen months old. That makes a visit nearly every week!'

Tess nodded sombrely. 'Questions will be asked as to why the social services weren't involved sooner. True, many of the previous visits were for ailments and minor injuries, but even so. Aneta was turning up regularly, saying the child had tripped and fallen, was sick, had ingested something they shouldn't, had a cough, rash or high temperature. She was clearly anxious about her children's health, but it was only on Monday when it was found that Kit had a broken arm that the history of her visits was thoroughly reviewed and the alarm raised. Now it seems similar had been going on at their doctor's. I'm applying for the children's medical records, but the doctor I spoke to said that Aneta was there most weeks – first with Molly and then with Kit. Her visits with Molly were initially put down to new-mother anxiety. It's not unusual for first-time mothers to be anxious about their baby's health and to keep seeking medical advice about minor ailments. But it continued with Kit and then the term "accident prone" started to be used. However, the children always appeared clean and Aneta was very attentive towards them. They were quiet while in the doctor's and well behaved.' She let out another heart-felt sigh. 'Kit's injury on Monday, plus the record of accidents for both children, crossed the threshold, so we felt they were at risk of significant harm and applied for the care order.'

'And it's a hundred per cent certain the injuries the children sustained were non-accidental?' I asked.

'You can never be a hundred per cent sure, but it is the most likely explanation and the judge agreed with us.'

I gave a small nod and sincerely hoped they were right, for the alternative – that the parents had been wrongly accused and had lost their children – was too awful to bear. 'And contact?' I asked. 'Kit and Molly will be seeing their parents?'

'Yes. I'll set up supervised contact, probably three times a week to begin with.'

'And the long-term care plan?'

'A full care order. I can't see them returning home.'

When Tess had finished telling me what she knew about the family we returned to the living room where Paula, Preeta and the children were still on the floor by the toy box. Kit now had a toy shaker in his hand, but neither child was playing. Molly had her thumb in her mouth and was snuggled close to her brother. The room was unnaturally quiet considering two children were there, but at least they weren't crying.

'We'll just have a look around and go,' Tess said to Preeta. Then to me, 'Do you have everything you need for tonight?' She crossed to the patio window and looked out.

'Yes, I think so,' I said.

'Nice garden,' she remarked, then went over to Molly and Kit. 'We're going to look at the other rooms now. Would you like to come and see where you are going to sleep?'

Kit kept his eyes on Paula, carefully watching her to see what she was going to do, while Molly had her head down, quiet, withdrawn and expressionless.

'Would you like to come with us to see your bedroom?' I tried, offering my hand to Molly. She shook her head, which was at least some response. 'OK, stay here, you'll see it later,' I said positively. While it was usual for the children to look around the house with their social worker when they first arrived – or before, if it was a planned move and they had a chance to visit – it wasn't essential, as it was for the social worker.

'I'll stay with them while you go,' Preeta said to Tess.

Tess nodded.

'This is the living room,' I said to everyone. 'It's where we spend most of our time in the evenings and weekends.' Tess then came with me into the kitchen-diner where I'd already put the children's seats ready at the table. 'Do you know if either of the children has any special dietary requirements?' I asked her as she looked around.

'No, I don't. I'll ask their father when I speak to him later and phone you.'

'Can you also ask him if they have any allergies?' It was worrying how little I still knew about the children, and I was responsible for them now.

'Will do,' Tess said. 'Apparently their mother often told the doctor she thought the children were suffering from allergies, but they changed on each visit, so if the child had a slight rash, upset tummy or cough, Aneta put it down to an allergy.'

'The doctor didn't agree?'

'I don't think so, but I'll check with the father.'

'I've made a cottage pie for dinner. I hope that's all right,' I said. 'I assume Kit is on solid food?'

'I would think so at his age,' Tess said. She sniffed the air. 'I thought I could smell something good. I'll ask about food when I phone Filip. He wasn't in any state to talk about that this afternoon.'

'Please also ask him about any likes and dislikes the children may have, and their routine,' I added. While Molly was old enough to tell me what she liked or didn't like – when she finally began to talk – Kit wasn't, so it was important Tess found out as much as she could from the parents. I couldn't do anything about the children actually being in care, but I could at least make their lives as comfortable as possible while they were with me.

'Do you want to see down the garden?' I asked Tess. She was looking through the window at the far end of the kitchen, which overlooked the back garden.

'No, I can see it from here. Let's have a quick look at the children's bedrooms and then we'll need to get going.'

I looked at her, concerned. 'Bedroom,' I said. 'I hope Edith told you I only have one spare room. I've put a cot in there so the children will be sleeping together.'

'Yes, that'll be fine,' she said, and we headed out of the kitchen-diner and down the hall. It was still very quiet in the living room. No sound of the children talking or playing. I didn't show Tess the front room as we'd just been there, so we went upstairs to the children's bedroom. 'There's not much space, but they can play downstairs,' she said, voicing her thoughts. 'It's nice and light. How long have you been fostering?'

'Twenty-five years.'

She nodded and headed out. I quickly showed her the other bedrooms and bathroom. 'You'll need to cover Kit's plaster to keep it dry when you bath him,' she said.

'Yes, is there a follow-up appointment at the hospital?'

'I would think so. I'll ask Filip.'

We returned downstairs. Sammy, our cat, must have let himself in through the cat flap, for he was now sitting in the hall, trying to decide if it was advisable to go into the living room with strangers there.

'Hopefully, the children aren't allergic to cat fur,' Tess remarked as we passed him.

'I hope so too!' For if they were, there was little I could do beyond what I did already: keep Sammy out of the bedrooms, comb him each day and regularly hoover. I couldn't make him disappear.

'You've got a nice bedroom,' Tess told Molly and Kit as we entered the living room.

Molly looked at her, worried and confused. Suddenly she jumped up from where she was sitting on the floor and cried, 'I need a wee!' But it was too late. A puddle formed at her feet. She burst into tears.

'It's OK, don't worry,' I said, immediately going to her. 'I'll mop it up and we'll find you some more clean clothes.'

'We'll leave you to it,' Tess said. 'I'll phone you as soon as I've spoken to their father.'

She and Preeta said goodbye to the children and headed out.

'Don't forget the suitcase in your car!' I called after them.

'I'll leave it in the hall,' Tess replied.

Seeing his sister upset, Kit now began to cry loudly. They both needed comforting, Molly needed changing again, and I had to mop up the wet before it soaked into the carpet. I heard Tess and Preeta open the front door and then my daughter Lucy's voice. She must have been about to let herself in. 'Hi,' she said, surprised. Then, 'What a noise!'

'In here, Lucy, please!' I called. 'We could do with your help.'

She came into the living room and, surveying the chaotic scene, threw her jacket onto a chair. 'And I thought I'd left work!' she exclaimed with a smile. She was a qualified nursery nurse.

'Meet Molly and Kit,' I said over their cries. 'Can you help Paula calm them down while I get a bucket and cloth?'

'Come on, it's OK,' she said, taking Molly's hand. Paula was holding Kit. I went quickly into the kitchen where I ran hot water into a bucket and added disinfectant. I took a cleaning cloth from the cupboard under the kitchen sink and returned to the living room.

'I'm leaving the case here!' Tess called from the hall. 'Everything OK?'

'Yes,' I replied. I knew they needed to go. The front door closed behind them.

I knelt down and set to work on the carpet. 'Shall I change Molly?' Lucy offered.

'Yes, please. Hopefully there is a change of clothes in the case in the hall.'

'I'll take the case upstairs with me.'

'Thanks, love.'

Having seen his sister disappear, Kit began to cry more loudly and point towards the door. 'Best go with them,' I told Paula. She carried Kit out of the living room and joined Lucy and Molly in the hall as I continued to clean the carpet.

At the same time I heard the front door open and my son, Adrian, call, 'Hi, Mum!'

Then Paula's voice, 'Hi, how are you, Kirsty?'

Oh no, I thought. We were hardly prepared for visitors. Kirsty was Adrian's long-term girlfriend and I really liked her, but she'd walked into chaos. He usually let me know when he was bringing her home for dinner. 'Hi, Mum. Kirsty's here. Did you get my text?' he called from the hall.

'I expect so,' I said, still on my knees. 'I haven't had a chance to check my phone. Come through.'

He appeared in the living room with Kirsty just behind him. 'A little accident,' I said, glancing up and smiling grimly. 'Nearly done. Nice to see you, Kirsty. How was school?' She was a teacher.

'They had to switch off the water to repair a burst pipe so we were given the afternoon off.'

'Very nice,' I said. I patted the patch dry and stood. The crying upstairs had stopped.

'Kirsty and I can eat out, Mum,' Adrian offered.

'No, It's fine. I've done plenty. We'll eat soon. As you saw we've got two little ones come to stay.'

'Is there anything I can do to help?' Kirsty kindly offered.

'No. Make yourselves a drink. I'll check on Kit and Molly and then we'll have dinner.'

Adrian took the bucket into the kitchen to tip away the water and put the cloths in the washing machine, while I went upstairs to see how Lucy and Paula were getting on. My daughters were my nominated carers. Foster carers are encouraged to nominate one or two family members or close friends to help them out and babysit when necessary. They are assessed by the carer's supervising social worker for suitability, and police-checked (now called a DBS check – Disclosure and Barring Service). Lucy had the added advantage of being a nursery nurse and the experience of being in care herself. She'd come to me as a foster child, stayed, and I'd adopted her. It was as if she'd always been my daughter.

'How's it going?' I asked as I went into Kit and Molly's bedroom. It was cramped now with Lucy, Paula, Kit and Molly all in there and the case open on the floor. The girls had found a dress for Molly, and Lucy was now helping her out of her wet clothes. There appeared to be a change of clothes in there for Kit too, pyjamas, some socks and a soft toy each, but nothing much else. The soft toys would be useful. Kit had spotted his and was now trying to get to it.

I smiled and took the toy from the case and gave it to him. He snuggled his face against its soft velvety fabric. I took out the other soft toy, which I assumed was Molly's, and placed it on her bed. Similarly styled, it had big loving eyes and soft fur. Hopefully, having these would bring comfort to the children when they had to sleep in a strange room tonight.

'We're doing OK here, Mum,' Lucy said as she changed Molly's clothes.

'Thanks. I'll go and see to dinner. Come down when you're ready, please.'

I gathered up Molly's wet clothes and went downstairs, where I put them in the washing machine with her other soiled clothes and the floor cloths, and set it on a wash-and-dry program. Kirsty came into the kitchen. 'Adrian's gone to change out of his suit. Can I help you?'

'You could lay the table, love. You know where everything is. There's a child's cutlery set for Molly in that drawer, and a toddler spoon for Kit. I don't know if he can feed himself, but he'll struggle anyway with the plaster on his arm.'

'I didn't know they were coming,' Kirsty said as she opened the cutlery draw. 'Are you sure it's OK for me to stay?'

'Yes, of course.' I smiled. 'I didn't know they were coming either until this morning. It's an emergency placement.'

'What happened to Kit's arm? And he's got bruises on his face.'

'He took a tumble down the stairs,' I said.

'Oh dear.' She knew I couldn't say much more because of confidentiality.

As she laid the table she told me about a boy in her class whose family was having help from the social services. While Kirsty and I would never break confidentiality by divulging names or discussing the details of cases like this, as a young teacher she sometimes shared her worries with me. If a child kept arriving at school dirty, late and hungry, or had unexplained injuries, she sometimes mentioned it as well as informing her head teacher. Teaching is now so much more than simply imparting knowledge; it involves a large pastoral role too.

Adrian, Paula, Lucy and the little ones all came down together with Adrian now carrying Kit. As Adrian sat Kit in his seat at the table and fastened the belt, I had the briefest glimpse of what a good father he'd make when the time came. I think Kirsty did too, judging from the look in her eyes. We settled around the table and I served dinner. I'd just sat down to eat when the house phone rang.

'I'll take it in the living room,' I said, standing. 'It's probably their social worker.'

It was. 'I've spoken to Filip,' Tess said. 'He doesn't think the children have any allergies, although Aneta worries about them a lot. He'll tell you more tomorrow. I've set up a meeting for one o'clock at the council offices so the parents can meet you. If you have any questions, you will be able to ask them then.'

'OK. I take it I'm not to bring Molly and Kit to the meeting?'

'No. I'll be arranging supervised contact at the Family Centre for the children to see their parents.'

'All right, thank you. I'll have to get some cover for Molly and Kit.'

'How are they?' Tess asked.

'Having a bit of dinner.'

'Good. See you tomorrow then.'

I scribbled 1 p.m. in my diary for the following day. I would need to find someone to look after Kit and Molly at very short notice. Lucy would be at work and Paula at college, and I didn't feel I could ask them to take time off. I knew other foster carers who could help me out as I had helped them in the past, but that would need to be arranged through Edith, my supervising social worker. I couldn't just do it by myself. I made another note in my diary to call Edith at 9 a.m. the next morning, and then returned to the dinner table.

CHAPTER THREE

DISTURBED NIGHT

Molly and Kit were quiet and subdued throughout dinner. They looked very sad and showed none of the natural exuberance you'd expect from children of their age, which was hardly surprising. Their world – the one they'd always known – had just come to an abrupt and traumatic end. They'd been taken from their hysterical mother in tears and had lost the only family they'd known and everything they held dear. Only in the worst cases of abuse had I ever seen a child happy to be in foster care, to begin with at least. It would take time, love, care, patience and lots of reassurance before they began to relax and were able to trust and smile again.

With encouragement from Lucy and me, Molly fed herself, while Paula and I – we had Kit sitting between us – popped spoonfuls into his mouth. Both children ate a little of the main course but didn't want any apple crumble and custard for dessert. I didn't know if Kit could feed himself. Apart from being hampered by the plaster cast, he was clearly too over-whelmed to make any attempt, and it didn't matter. If the children were staying with us long term, as Tess seemed to think, there'd be plenty of time to teach him to feed himself. That was the least of my concerns at present. It was eight o'clock by the time we'd finished and I needed to bath the children and get them into bed.

Paula apologized and said she had college work to do. I thanked her for her help, and she went upstairs to her bedroom. Lucy offered to help bath Kit and Molly, and Adrian and Kirsty said they'd clear away the dishes and wash up. I was grateful for their help. I was already worrying about how I was going to manage alone tomorrow when everyone was out. You've done it before and you can do it again, I told myself as another crisis of confidence loomed.

I thought it would be easier to bath the children separately to avoid Kit's plaster becoming wet. However, it was clear that Molly didn't want to be separated from her brother, so she came with Lucy, Kit and me into the bathroom. Lucy and I talked brightly to both children, trying to put them at ease, as we explained the bedtime routine and what we were doing. Kit just stood there as I undressed him, then put a plastic bag over his plaster cast and secured it at the end. Most toddlers would have shown some interest, perhaps laughed or tried to pull off the bag, but he stared at me, wide-eyed and lost. It broke my heart.

I carefully lifted him into the bath. He was heavy with the weight of the plaster cast. 'Sit down, love, but try to keep your arm out of the water,' I told him. 'We need to keep it dry.'

Neither child spoke. Molly was holding Lucy's hand and watched in silence as I gently wiped Kit's bruised face with a facecloth, and then sponged his little body. His skin was pale and he had some bruises on his shins and one on his other forearm, but I couldn't see any other marks – scars, cuts or cigarette burns, as I'd seen before on children I'd fostered. I'd let Tess know, although of course the bruises could have been from playing. Toddlers are always tripping, falling and bumping into things as they explore their surroundings with little sense of danger.

Once washed, I lifted Kit out of the bath and into the towel Lucy held out ready. I took the plastic bag from his arm and Lucy dried him as I bathed Molly. Children of her age can usually wash themselves a little, so I gave her the sponge and she drew it across her chest and legs. I washed her back. Her skin was pale too and she had one small bruise on her shin, which I'd noticed before when I'd changed her and was likely to be the result of a fall while playing. Thankfully there were no other signs of injury. I helped her out of the bath, wrapped her in a towel and then dressed her in the pyjamas I'd taken from their case. Lucy had dressed Kit and put a nappy on him. Both children had clean hair, so hair-washing could wait until another night when they felt more at ease.

We hadn't found any toothbrushes in their case, so I was using some from my spares. I always kept a supply of new children's toothbrushes, face flannels, pants and so on. Kit opened his mouth to allow Lucy to brush his teeth – he had his front teeth, top and bottom, and some molars coming through at the back. Clearly from the way he cooperated he was used to having his teeth brushed – a sign that the children had received some good parenting. Once Lucy had finished brushing Kit's teeth, I put a little toothpaste on Molly's toothbrush and passed her the brush.

'Can you give your teeth a little brush?' I asked her.

She took the brush and made a small attempt to clean her teeth, then burst into tears. 'I want my mummy!' she cried. 'Mummy, Mummy, where are you? I want you.'

It was heart-breaking and I felt my own eyes fill.

'Oh, love,' I said, taking the toothbrush and putting it to one side. 'You'll see Mummy soon.' I held her.

'I want my mummy,' she wept inconsolably. 'Where is she?'

'She's at home, love.'

'I want to go home.'

I wasn't surprised she was distraught now. She'd been bottling it up since she'd arrived and, now she was tired, it was all coming out. Kit, seeing his sister in tears, began to cry too. Lucy cuddled him as I cuddled Molly. We sat on the bathroom floor, gently rocking them and telling them it would be OK and trying to console them. Not for the first time since I'd begun fostering, I wished I had a magic wand I could wave that would undo the past and make everything bad that had happened go away.

Eventually the children's crying eased. 'Come on, let's get you both into bed,' I said, and stood. 'You'll feel better after a night's sleep.' It was a reassurance in which I had little faith. It would take many nights before they began to feel better. Lucy held Kit's hand and I held Molly's and we went round the landing to their bedroom.

As soon as we entered the room Molly became upset again. 'I want my mummy,' she cried, her tears flowing.

'I know you do, love,' I said. 'You'll see Mummy soon.' I helped her into bed, wiped her face, and then sat on the edge of the bed.

'I want Mummy now,' she said again and again, grief-stricken.

'Mummy, Mummy,' Kit said from his cot as Lucy tried to settle him.

'Would you like a bedtime story?' I asked Molly, trying to distract her. She shook her head and just sat in bed, tears rolling down her cheeks. 'Come on, love, lie down and try to get some sleep.' I wiped her cheeks again.

She laid her head on the pillow, Kit lay down too, then, as Molly pressed her face into her cuddly toy, Kit did the same. His cot was adjacent to Molly's bed – against the opposite wall – so he could see her through the slats. 'Does your cuddly have a name?' I asked her.

'I want Mummy.'

'Mummy,' Kit repeated.

I began stroking Molly's forehead, trying to soothe her off to sleep. Lucy was leaning over the cot and gently rubbing Kit's back.

'Lucy, you go, love, if you want to,' I told her after a few minutes. 'I'll stay with them.' I was mindful that she had come in straight from work and hadn't had a minute to herself.

'It's OK, Mum. I'll stay until they're asleep.'

'Thanks, love, I am grateful.'

For the next half an hour Lucy and I stayed with the children, Lucy by Kit's cot and me with Molly, soothing them, until eventually, exhausted, their eyes gradually closed. We waited another few minutes to check they were asleep and then crept from the room. With older children I usually ask them on their first night how they like to sleep – the curtains open or closed, the light on or off, the bedroom door open or shut, as it's little details like this that help a child settle in a strange room. But for now we left the curtains slightly parted, the light on low and the door open so I could hear them if they woke.

I thanked Lucy again for her help and she went to her bedroom. I cleared up the bathroom and took Kit's nappy downstairs to dispose of it. Adrian was in the kitchen, making himself a drink. 'Kirsty has gone home as we both have to be up for work in the morning,' he said. The kitchen was spotless.

'Thanks for your help,' I said. 'I'm sorry I didn't get a chance to talk to Kirsty.'

'She understands. She said to say good luck.'

'I think I'm going to need it.'

Adrian made me a cup of tea and I took it with a couple of biscuits into the living room to write up my log notes, while he went up to shower. All foster carers in the UK are required to keep a daily record of the child or children they are looking after. It includes appointments, the child's health and wellbeing, education, significant events and any disclosures the child may make about their past. As well as charting the child's progress, it can act as an aide-mémoire. When the child leaves this record is placed on file at the social services. Opening my folder, I took a fresh sheet of paper and headed it with the date. I wrote a short objective account of Molly and Kit's arrival and their evening with us. I was just finishing when I heard a bang come from Molly and Kit's room. I shot upstairs. Paula had heard it too and had come out of her room and was on the landing. 'Whatever was that?' she asked, concerned.

We went into the children's bedroom. By the dimmed light we could see they were both still asleep and nothing seemed out of place, but I noticed that Kit had turned over.

'I think it might have been his plaster cast banging against the cot slats,' I whispered to Paula. I couldn't see any other explanation.

We stood for a moment, looking at them. 'They're such sweet kids,' Paula whispered. I nodded. They were indeed, and generally appeared to have been well looked after, apart from the injuries to Kit's face and arm. They hadn't arrived filthy, in rags and with their hair full of nits. Yet all those visits to the doctor and hospital told a very different story, one that I hoped would become clearer in time.

By 10.30 p.m. we were all in our bedrooms either getting ready for bed or in bed (none of us stays up late during the working week). When I said goodnight to Adrian, Lucy and Paula, I told them that if they heard the children in the night to turn over and go back to sleep, as I would settle them. I was expecting a broken night, and I wasn't disappointed. Just as I was dropping off to sleep, around 11 p.m., Molly woke and began to cry out hysterically, 'Mummy, Mummy, where are you? Mummy!'

I was straight out of bed and, throwing on my dressing gown, I hurried round the landing, hoping her cries hadn't woken Kit.

'Ssh, quiet, love,' I said as I went into their room. She was standing by her bed. 'Do you want the toilet?' I asked her quietly. She shook her head.

'I want my mummy!' she cried.

'I know, love. You're safe. Let's get you into bed.' I persuaded her in and had just got her to lie down when Kit woke with a start behind me and, crying, stood up in his cot.

'Mummy!' he sobbed.

Leaving Molly, I turned to him.

'Come on, love, lie down. It's OK.' I laid him on his side. It was awkward with the plaster cast. As I settled him, Molly started crying again.

'I want my mummy,' she wept, sitting up in bed.

'Ssh, love. It's OK,' I said, going to her. Kit immediately stood up and sobbed loudly.

Lucy appeared in her pyjamas. 'I'm sorry you've been woken,' I said.

'I wasn't asleep.'

She went to Kit and began talking to him gently, laying him down each time he stood and rubbing his back as I soothed Molly. It was so much easier with two and after about fifteen minutes the children were asleep again and we crept out. I thanked Lucy and we returned to our bedrooms. About an hour later I heard Molly crying again. I wasn't asleep and managed to get to her before she woke Kit or anyone else. I stayed with her until she was asleep again and then returned to my own bed. I didn't immediately go back to sleep but lay in the dark, listening out for them. I heard Kit's plaster cast bang on the side of the cot as he turned over, then I must have dropped off, for I woke with a start at 2 a.m. Kit and Molly were both crying.

Light-headed from lack of sleep and getting out of bed too quickly, I rushed round the landing and into their bedroom. Molly was standing in the middle of the room. 'I need a wee-wee,' she wept.

'This way, love,' I said, and quickly guided her to the toilet. We got there just in time. Kit was still crying loudly and I heard Lucy's bedroom door open.

'I'm sorry,' I said to her as I steered Molly back to her bed. Lucy was kneeling beside Kit's cot with her hand between the slats, gently rubbing his back. She looked as shattered as I felt.

'It's OK, Mum,' she said, yawning. 'It's their first night. They're bound to be upset. I'm sure they'll be better tomorrow.' Which was the reassurance I needed and I was grateful.

It took about twenty minutes for us to settle the children again and then Lucy and I returned to our beds. The next time Molly woke I got to her in time (I don't think I was properly asleep) and managed to resettle her before she woke Kit. I was starting to wonder if having them together was a good idea or whether I should move Kit's cot into my bedroom. Foster carers are allowed to have babies and toddlers in their bedroom (but not their beds) up to the age of two. I'd find out from the children's parents tomorrow if they were used to sleeping together. It's information like this and the child's routine that is invaluable to foster carers when helping a child to settle.

Both children woke around 5 a.m. and I managed to settle them by myself. I think they were so tired they didn't put up much resistance. Ten minutes later I was in my bed again but I couldn't sleep. I lay in the dark with my thoughts buzzing and at 6 a.m. I showered and dressed so I was ready to meet the day. Adrian, Lucy and Paula took turns in the bathroom from seven o'clock, which was usual on a week day. When I asked Paula if she'd heard the children in the night, she said she had but, aware that Lucy was helping, she had turned over and gone back to sleep. 'We can take it in turns, Mum,' she offered. 'I'll get up tonight.'

'That's kind of you. I'm hoping they'll sleep a bit better tonight.'

'But if not, I can help.'

'Thanks, love.'

Incredibly, when I asked Adrian if he'd been woken by Molly and Kit, he hadn't, although he slept in the room next to theirs.

'Typical guy,' Lucy teased him. 'Only hears what he wants to.'

The children didn't wake again until just before 8 a.m. I heard Molly talking to Kit and went straight to their bedroom. 'Good morning,' I said brightly, smiling. Molly was standing by Kit's cot holding his hand through the slats. Although they weren't crying, they were clearly sad and confused.

'Where's my mummy?' Molly asked straight away, turning to me and dropping Kit's hand.

'She's at home, love. You'll see her before too long.' I couldn't give firm details until Tess told me the arrangements for contact.

'Can I go home now?' Molly asked imploringly. 'I promise to be good.' I could have wept.

'You are good, love,' I said, giving her a hug. 'That's not the reason you're staying with me. Your mummy and daddy need a bit of help, so I'm looking after you for a while.'

She stared at me wide-eyed and uncomprehending. I thought it best to keep her occupied and concentrated on something else. 'Can you show me what a big girl you are and dress yourself while I see to your brother?' I asked her. 'Here are your clothes.' I pointed to them on the bed and then lifted Kit out of his cot.

'I need to do a wee-wee,' she said.

'Good girl for telling me.'

I took Kit with us as I helped Molly in the toilet and then we returned to their bedroom. With a bit of encouragement, Molly began to dress herself and I dressed Kit. Paula, Lucy and Adrian either looked in to say goodbye or called from the hall as they left.

Many toddlers of Kit's age are like wriggly worms when you try to change their nappies and dress them, seeing it as a game. Kit just lay there on the changing mat, unresponsive and staring at me, clearly wondering where his mummy and daddy were, what he was doing here and who the hell I was. I smiled at him and spoke gently as I worked, so hopefully he could see I was friendly and would do him no harm. At his age it would be impossible to give him any understanding of the situation. Molly would have some understanding and might start talking about the abuse in time, but Kit was unlikely to ever be able to verbalize what he'd seen and heard. Babies and toddlers intuit, feeling rather than reasoning – sensations, impressions and random images that might fade with time. Neither child spoke or made any noise as Molly dressed herself and I dressed Kit. I found their silence as upsetting as their crying.

Once they were ready, I took hold of their hands and we went carefully downstairs. Included in the equipment I'd brought down from the loft was a stair gate and I'd put it in place once Kit started exploring. There was no sign of him doing that yet. He was staying close and clinging to either Molly or me.

In the kitchen-diner I asked Molly what she and Kit usually had for breakfast and she said yoghurt.

'What about some cereal and toast as well?' I asked. I opened the cupboard door where the packets of cereals were kept to show her and she pointed to the hot oat cereal – a smooth porridge.

'Good girl.' I took it out. 'Does Kit have this too?' She nodded. 'What about toast?' She shook her head. 'What would you like to drink?'

'Juice,' she replied. 'Where's my mummy?'

'At home, love. I expect she's having her breakfast too.'

Kit was standing where I'd put him by my leg and I now lifted him up and carried him to the table where I strapped him into the booster seat, then gave him his trainer cup. Molly slipped into the chair beside him. 'Good girl. Can you watch your brother while I make your porridge?' I said, although I could see them both from the kitchen.

I warmed the porridge in the microwave, took the yoghurt from the fridge and joined them at the table. I'd had my breakfast earlier. Molly fed herself and I fed Kit. He tried to pick up his spoon, but the plaster cast clunked heavily against the bowl, making it impossible to dip in the spoon. They ate most of the porridge and a little yoghurt, and drank their juice, so I was happy with that and praised them.

'We've got a busy day,' I said, lifting Kit out of the seat. 'First, we'll go into the living room where the toys are and you can play while I make a phone call.' I needed to speak to Edith.

I took them by the hand and they came with me into the living room, silent and obedient, where I settled them with some toys on the floor. It was now just after 9 a.m. and I was hoping Edith would be at her desk. Taking the handset from the corner unit, I keyed in her number and she answered.

'Hello. How are you?' she asked.

'OK. Molly and Kit were placed yesterday late afternoon.'

'Yes, Preeta left a message.'

'I need some cover. Tess has arranged a meeting at one o'clock with the children's parents, but I haven't got anyone to look after the children.'

'Who are your nominated support carers?' she asked.

'Lucy and Paula, but they are at work and college and it's too short notice for them to take half a day off.'

'Don't the children go to nursery?' she asked.

'Not as far as I know.'

'I don't think we have anyone free. Can't you take them with you?'

'No.' I kept my patience. 'Can I suggest you try another foster carer – Maggie Taylor? We've helped each other out in the past.'

'I can try, but if she can't do it, can you change the day of the meeting?'

'I doubt it. You'd have to ask Tess.'

'I'll see what I can do,' she said with a small sigh. She clearly didn't need this first thing on a Friday morning and neither did I, but part of her role was to support foster carers.

I then had a nail-biting wait. Foster carers are expected to provide their own support, and usually I did, but sometimes we need help and we shouldn't have to jump through hoops or be made to feel guilty for asking. I'd found before that Edith wasn't the most proactive of supervising social workers compared to Jill, who'd been my supervising social worker at Homefinders, the independent agency I used to foster for. She was a gem, but when their local office had closed and Jill had left, I'd transferred to the local authority. It didn't make any difference to the children I fostered, but it was at times like this I missed the high level of support and understanding the agency gave its carers twenty-four hours a day, every day of the year.

Thankfully when Edith returned my call an hour later she said Maggie could help and she'd phone me to arrange the details. I breathed a sigh of relief.

CHAPTER FOUR

GOOD MOTHER

Maggie telephoned ten minutes after Edith, bright and bubbly, and very willing to help. 'I hear you've got two little ones. That'll make a nice change,' she said.

'Yes, although they're missing their parents dreadfully and we've been up all night.'

'Join the club. Anyway, happy to help. As the children have only just been placed with you, I suggest I come to you to look after them, rather than you bringing them here, so they don't have another change of house.'

'Yes, please. That would be perfect.' I had thought similar myself.

'I'll have to bring Keelie with me,' Maggie said. 'She's been excluded from school again. But she's good with kids and can help me. What time do you want us?'

'The meeting is at one o'clock so twelve-thirty would be good.'

'Fine. We'll see you then.'

'Thank you so much.'

'You're welcome.'

I knew Keelie. She was thirteen and Maggie and her husband had been fostering her for four years. She'd always shown some challenging behaviour, as it's called, but since she'd hit puberty it had got a lot worse – staying out at night, drinking, smoking and generally getting into trouble at home, school and with the police. I guessed she was the reason Maggie had been up all night. Thankfully she and her husband were highly experienced foster carers and were taking it in their stride. Keelie was with them long term so was a permanent member of their family.

I explained to Molly and Kit what was going to happen – that my friend, Maggie, and a 'big girl' called Keelie were coming to look after them while I went to a meeting, and I would come back later. I didn't tell them I was going to meet their parents, as it would have been confusing and upsetting for them. Both children just looked at me. I didn't expect Kit to understand, but Molly should have some understanding of what I'd said.

The morning disappeared. I stayed in the living room for most of it, trying to engage the children in play. I had some success, although I wouldn't call it playing. They looked at and held the toys, games and puzzles as I showed them, but didn't actually play. Sammy came to investigate and to begin with was as nervous of them as they were of him. I showed them how to stroke his fur smoothly – running their hands down from his head to his tail. Neither of the children had shown any signs of a fur allergy, and coupled with their father telling Tess he didn't think they had any allergies I was reasonably confident they weren't allergic to cat fur at least.

At twelve noon I made us a sandwich lunch, followed by fruit, which they ate. Some children won't eat fruit and vege-tables when they first come into care, as these foods have never been part of their diet. But Molly and Kit ate the sliced banana, tangerine segments and halved grapes I arranged in little pots. Because the fruit could be eaten using fingers, Kit fed himself. They ate slowly and unenthusiastically, but at least they ate. I smiled and praised them. 'Do you have food like this at home?' I asked without thinking, and I could have kicked myself.

'I want to go home,' Molly said, rubbing her eyes as if about to cry at the reminder of home. 'I want my mummy.'

'Mummy, Mummy,' Kit said, his bottom lip trembling.

'It's OK. You'll see her soon.' I gave them a hug and took out some more toys to distract them.

Maggie and Keelie arrived just before 12.30 and the children came with me to the front door.

'Hello, baby!' Keelie squealed excitedly as soon as she saw Kit. She rushed in and picked him up.

'Steady,' Maggie warned her. 'He's already got one broken arm, he doesn't want another one.'

I smiled while Keelie scowled at her, and Kit just looked bemused.

'How are you, Keelie?' I asked her as we went through to the living room. I hadn't seen her for a few months.

'Excluded,' she said as if this was her sole purpose in life and her claim to fame. 'Suits me. I don't like school and I get a lie-in.'

Maggie threw me a knowing look. Many schools have stopped the practice of excluding pupils for bad behaviour for this reason. It's counter-productive. Why should a young person who's got into trouble be rewarded with time off while their hard-working classmates are busy at school? Also having them unoccupied for large periods of time is likely to lead to more trouble.

'She's going back to school on Monday,' Maggie said. Keelie was exploring the toy box with more enthusiasm than the children.

'In your dreams,' she retorted. But I knew she would be in school on Monday. Maggie and her husband would make sure of it, just as they had all the other times she'd been excluded. They knew when to be firm.

'Help yourself to whatever you want,' I told Maggie. 'You know where the tea, coffee and biscuits are. Clean nappies and wipes are in their bedroom if you need them. I should be back around two-thirty. I've tried to explain to Molly and Kit what is happening,' I said, glancing at then, 'but not who I'm meeting.'

She nodded. 'I understand. Don't worry. They'll be fine.'

'Do they talk?' Keelie asked. The children were standing in silence, watching her as she continued to explore the toys and games.

'Molly does a little,' I said. 'It's likely Kit will have some language at his age. But they only arrived yesterday, so they are both shy.'

'Was I shy?' Keelie asked Maggie, glancing up at her.

'No, love, shyness wasn't really your thing. You showed your upset in other ways.'

'I bet I was a right pain in the arse.' Keelie grinned.

'Not as much as you are now,' Maggie replied affectionately, and they both laughed. Despite their banter, I knew how close they were and that Maggie and her husband had worked wonders with Keelie and loved her, as I was sure Keelie loved them.

I said goodbye and drove to the council offices, where I parked in a side road. It was a bright, sunny day and the early-September sun still had some strength in it. I signed in at the reception desk, completing the boxes that asked the reason for my visit and my time of arrival.

'Which room is the meeting in?' I asked the receptionist as I hung the security pass around my neck.

'Room six on the second floor.'

I thanked her and began up the staircase. I'd been here before. Most of the social services meetings were in rooms on the second floor. I was anxious at meeting the children's parents, Aneta and Filip, for the first time, but I reassured myself I'd met countless parents during my fostering career, and that they were likely to be as anxious as me. When I'd fostered for Homefinders Jill had accompanied me to most meetings, but Edith didn't. It wasn't part of the supervising social worker's role at the local authority. I thought it probably should be, especially for new carers who must find some of these meetings quite daunting.

I was a few minutes early as I arrived outside room six, knocked on the door and went in. A man and a woman I took to be Molly and Kit's parents sat at the table with their backs to me. At right angles to them and at the end of the table was Tess. Preeta sat opposite the couple. As I entered they fell silent and everyone looked at me. The faces of the parents were the epitome of grief and worry.

'Hello, I'm Cathy,' I said as I sat opposite them and next to Preeta. 'I hope I'm not late.'

'No. We were early,' Tess said. Then to the parents, 'Cathy is the foster carer.'

I threw them a small smile. Aneta just stared at me a bit like the children did, while her husband gave a short nod and looked away. I knew him to be older than his wife, but clearly the worry had aged them both. They had dark circles around their eyes, their foreheads were furrowed in permanent lines, and Aneta had a tissue pressed to her cheek from where she'd been crying. I could see the familial likeness, especially in Filip. Kit was the image of him. Both parents were dressed smart casual, in jeans and jerseys.

'OK, let's begin,' Tess said, drawing herself upright in her chair. 'This is a short informal meeting so you can all meet. I won't be taking minutes, but Preeta will make a few notes.' Aneta sniffed and I could see she wasn't far from tears. 'I appreciate this is a very emotional time for you,' Tess said, looking at the parents, 'so we'll keep this meeting short, then you can see Molly and Kit.'

'When can I see them?' Aneta asked. I took my pen and notepad from my bag.

'I've arranged contact at the Family Centre for four o'clock this afternoon,' Tess said. Then to me, 'That will give you time to go home, collect the children, and take them there.'

'Yes,' I said as I wrote: *4 p.m., Family Centre*.

'After today we can probably make contact earlier when the Family Centre is less busy, but I'll let you know. Cathy, can you tell us how Molly and Kit are settling in, please?'

I looked at the parents. It was heart-breaking to see their anguish. Aneta was wiping away fresh tears. How parents cope with losing their children I'll never know. Whatever had happened, they didn't set out to lose their children.

'Molly and Kit are lovely children,' I began. 'They are a credit to you. They're obviously missing you, but they're eating well and –'

'What have you given them to eat?' Aneta interrupted anxiously.

I thought back. 'For dinner last night we had cottage pie,' I said. 'For breakfast they had hot oat cereal, which Molly chose, and then some yoghurt. For lunch today they had a cheese sandwich and some fruit.'

Filip nodded, but Aneta was looking even more worried and I wondered if there was something wrong in what I'd said. 'Will the person looking after them now give them anything to eat?' she asked, so I guessed Tess or Preeta had told them of the child-minding arrangements.

'Possibly a drink and a biscuit,' I replied. 'Why? Is there a problem?'

'You have to be very careful what you give them to eat and drink,' Aneta said intensely. 'My children have a lot of allergies and can easily fall sick.'

'Can you tell me what the allergies are?' I asked, my pen ready. 'So I know which foods to avoid. I understood they didn't have any allergies.' Preeta was ready to write too.

'Lots of things make them sick,' Aneta said defensively. 'I can't tell you them all, and they change. I'm always at the doctor's or hospital with my children. Not even the doctors can find out what's wrong with them.'

'I see,' I said. Of course, Tess had told me the doctor's view was that they didn't have any allergies. 'Can you narrow down the allergy to a group of foods? For example, is it dairy produce?'

'Can you narrow it down at all?' Tess asked, and I thought she looked sceptical.

Aneta shook her head. 'No, and it's not always food,' she said vehemently. 'Sometimes it can be the stuff I wash clothes in, or they brush past something or it's in the air. You mustn't use bubble bath.'

'No, I don't anyway. Young skin is delicate so I keep bathing simple – just a bit of baby shampoo for their hair.'

'That can cause an allergic reaction too,' she said with anxious satisfaction. I noticed she was becoming more agitated as she spoke, while Filip sat with his eyes down, concentrating on the table, apparently completely out of his depth.

'How do these allergic reactions manifest themselves?' Preeta asked. I'd written *allergies* on my notepad ready to list them, but so far I'd just put *bubble bath*, which I didn't use anyway.

'My children get a temperature and start vomiting,' Aneta said animatedly. 'I have to get an emergency appointment at the doctor's or call an ambulance. But it stops as suddenly as it starts.'

'Do they have a rash?' I asked.

'Sometimes, but usually they vomit.' Her face crumpled and her tears fell again. 'You should never have taken my children away,' she said to Tess. 'I haven't done anything wrong. I'm innocent. I love my children and they need me. I'm the only one who can look after them.'

Filip placed a reassuring hand on his wife's arm but didn't look at her or speak. I thought he was barely coping too.

'I love my children,' Aneta wept. 'I'm a good mother. My only crime was to take them to the doctor's if they were ill, or if they fell and hurt themselves. They bruise easily. I'm being punished for looking after them properly. It's not right.' So upset and sincere, it again flashed across my mind that I hoped the social services had got it right in bringing the children into care.

'So to be clear,' Tess said. 'There is nothing specific you can tell Cathy about which foods trigger an allergic reaction in either of your children?'

'No,' Aneta said, wiping her eyes.

'Have you ever kept a food diary?' Tess asked. 'It's often recommended by doctors as a way of finding out what a child is allergic to. You keep a record of what they have eaten and any symptoms they have experienced.'

'No,' Aneta said, 'because it's not just food. It's lots of things, not even the doctors know.'

'Cathy,' Tess said, turning to me, 'can you start a food diary, please? Note everything the children eat and drink, and obviously seek medical help if necessary.'

'Yes, of course,' I said, and wrote *food diary* on my notepad. 'I assume a peanut allergy has been ruled out?' I asked. 'The children have never suffered from anaphylactic shock and have auto-injectors?' I thought something as serious as this would have been mentioned by now, but the children had been placed with me so quickly I decided it was best to ask.

'No, they don't,' Aneta said.

There was a short silence and I wondered if Tess was expecting me to continue talking about how the children had settled in, but instead she said, 'Cathy, is there anything else you want to ask Aneta and Filip that would help in the care of the children? I'm mindful of the time.'

'Knowing the children's routine would be useful,' I said. 'I'll keep to it as much as possible. Also, I'm assuming there is a follow-up appointment at the fracture clinic?'

'It's on Monday morning,' Aneta said, wiping her eyes. 'I've got an appointment card at home, and a fact sheet about the care of the plaster cast the nurse gave to me.'

'Could you bring them to contact today, please?' I asked.

'I'll bring the sheet, but you won't need the appointment card. I'll take Kit to the hospital,' Aneta said. 'They know me there.'

I left it to Tess to explain. 'While the children are in care, Cathy will take them to any medical appointments.'

'But I want to go!' Aneta exclaimed.

'That wouldn't be appropriate,' Tess said gently but firmly. 'You'll be seeing the children regularly at the Family Centre. It would be confusing and upsetting for them if you just appeared.'

'But they're my children. It's not right. You won't even tell me where they are staying. I should be with them when they're ill.' Aneta was crying again and I felt so sorry for her. Of course a mother would want to be with her children when they were poorly, but Molly and Kit were in care because of possible abuse, so she couldn't be alone with them at all. Contact at the Family Centre would be supervised.

'I'll take good care of them, I promise you,' I said to her.

'But it's not right. I always go with them to the hospital,' Aneta persisted. 'I know the staff and they know me.'

Filip now spoke for the first time. 'Leave it, Aneta,' he said firmly. 'We have to do what they say now.' There was an edge of recrimination in his voice and I assumed he was blaming Aneta for the children being taken into care.

'Can you tell Cathy something about the children's routine?' Tess prompted.

Aneta shook her head. 'I don't know what you mean.'

'What time they go to bed. What they like doing during the day. When they have their meals. That sort of thing,' Tess said.

'I can't remember, I can't think straight,' Aneta said. 'I'm too upset.'

'It's OK,' I said, my heart going out to her. 'It's not essential.'

'Do you know the children's routine?' Tess asked Filip.

'No, I'm at work. I don't know what they do all day. Aneta gets them up after I've left in the morning and they're in bed by the time I get home. I work a lot of overtime to make ends meet.'

'Weekends?' Tess asked.

'I work most weekends too,' he said. So it appeared he had very little input in his children's lives.

'What sort of things do the children like to do?' I asked.

Aneta shrugged.

'Do they go to nursery or a pre-school play group?' Preeta asked.

'No,' Aneta said. 'I took Molly once when she was little, but she didn't like it. All those children. She got pushed over and hurt her knee. I had to take her to the hospital. I worry about germs. They get ill so easily.'

I nodded and made a note, then asked, 'Would it be possible for the children to have some more of their clothes and toys? I can buy new ones, but it's nicer for them if they have what is familiar.'

Aneta was in tears again, but Filip said, 'I'll see to it.'

'Thank you,' I said.

'Can you take them with you to contact tonight?' Tess asked Filip. He nodded. 'Is there anything either of you want to ask?'

Aneta didn't reply, but Filip said, 'How long will my children be in care?'

'We don't know at present,' Tess replied. 'If you stay behind at the end of this meeting we can have another chat.' I was sure she would have explained the procedure to them already, but doubtless with the worry of it all Filip had forgotten. 'Anything else?' Tess asked, glancing around the table. 'OK, in that case, I'll see you at contact at four o'clock.'

I stood to leave as the others remained seated, but as I did Aneta suddenly asked me, 'Do my children miss me?'

'Yes, of course,' I said.

A small smile crossed her face. 'Good. I wondered if they'd be pleased to be away from me.'

I was surprised by her comment but thought she was probably feeling sorry for herself and looking for some reassurance. Tess, however, said quite pointedly, 'Why would you think that, Aneta?'

She shrugged and looked away, and just for a moment I thought she looked guilty. I said goodbye and left.

CHAPTER FIVE

DISTRESSING

W hy would Aneta doubt her children's love for her and think they would be pleased to be away from her? I wondered as I drove home. Could it be guilt? It would make sense. If she had been abusing them then she had reason to believe they would be better off without her. The edge to Tess's voice when she'd asked her had suggested she thought so too. Yet Molly and Kit did miss their mother dreadfully, and she was clearly beside herself with grief at being parted from them. However, most parents are distraught if their children are taken into care whether they have been abusing them or not. In my experience, anger and grief are not indicators of the level of care children have been receiving at home. Aneta had been very upset but not angry. She appeared over-protective – not taking her children to pre-school for fear of accidents and germs. As for Filip, I wasn't sure what to make of him. He looked shattered and overwhelmed, but seemed to have had little contact with his children because of the hours he worked. Did he know what had been going on at home?

It was 2.30 when I arrived home. As I let myself in I could hear Keelie's highly excitable voice trilling from the living room. I think most of the street could hear her. 'Beep. Beep. Beep. Brumm-brumm. Nnneeaoowww!' she screeched.

'Chuff-chuff, choo-choo!' Then what sounded like her imitating the loud wail of a siren. Strewth! I thought. Whatever was she doing?

I went through to the living room. Maggie was sitting on the sofa, watching the children play. 'Everything OK?' I asked, my gaze sweeping the room, which was now covered with toys, games and puzzles.

'Nnneeaoowww!' Keelie cried again, bringing the toy aeroplane she was holding low over the scene below.

'Keelie found some more toy boxes in the cupboard,' Maggie said. 'Hope that was all right. She's been keeping Molly and Kit very well amused.'

'Yes, of course, thank you,' I said.

There wasn't space to move for the toys covering the floor, and Molly and Kit, while not actually playing, were clearly mesmerized by Keelie. The playmat that showed a busy street scene was in the centre of the room and crammed full of toy vehicles, farmyard and zoo animals, play people and buildings constructed from Lego. It wasn't so much a busy street scene as a giant metropolis, where police cars, fire engines, lorries, tankers, ambulances, boats and cars fought for space on the roads and pavements with dinosaurs, people and tower blocks. Every so often Kellie picked up a fighter jet, space rocket, flying saucer or pterodactyl and dropped miniature barrels of hay on those below. They landed with a loud 'Bang!' or 'Whoosh!' I thought how conservative and timid my play must have seemed to Molly and Kit compared with this.

'Very imaginative,' I said.

'Bang! Boom! Gotcha!' Keelie cried, as a brontosaurus landed on a boat on the duck pond. 'I wanted to put water in it, but Maggie wouldn't let me,' Keelie lamented, pulling a face.

'You can thank me later,' Maggie said, and I smiled.

While Molly and Kit weren't joining in, they were clearly enthralled and couldn't take their eyes off Keelie. As Maggie had said, she had clearly kept them very well amused.

'How did your meeting go?' Maggie asked.

'OK, thanks. We've got contact at four o'clock.'

'We'll be off then. Time to pack away,' she told Keelie.

'Oh, do I have to?' Keelie bemoaned like a young child might.

'Yes,' Maggie said. 'If you put away the toys nicely perhaps Cathy will invite you to another play date.'

Keelie stuck her tongue out good humouredly, and Maggie and I smiled.

'Don't worry, I'll do it later,' I said.

'No, you won't,' Maggie replied. 'We will *all* help.'

Maggie and I joined Keelie on the floor and began packing away as Molly and Kit continued to watch Keelie, probably having never seen a teenager playing so enthusiastically before.

'I've got to start a food diary to try to identify if the children are allergic to anything,' I told Maggie as we tidied away. 'Have Molly and Kit had anything to eat and drink this afternoon? I'll make a note.'

'Just apple juice. They didn't want a snack.'

'OK, thanks.'

Before long most of the toys were in their boxes, although I left some out for Molly and Kit to play with while I saw Maggie and Keelie out. I gave Maggie a box of chocolates as a thank-you gift.

'You shouldn't have done that,' she said.

'Yes, she should,' Keelie said, taking them from her. 'If you don't want them, I'll have them – I did all the work.'

'You can have a couple and we'll save the rest for later,' Maggie told her, and Keelie pulled a face. Opening the front door, she began down the path eating the chocolates as she went. Maggie turned to me thoughtfully. 'Molly and Kit were fine, they didn't cry, but there's something about them, isn't there?'

'What do you mean?' I asked.

'I know they've just come into care so they're bound to be quiet, but they wouldn't talk, not even to Keelie, and there's a haunted look in their eyes. I'm sure they've got secrets. Anyway, let me know if you need any help again.'

'Yes, I will, thank you.'

I watched her go and then slowly closed the door. A haunted look … yes, that summed up Molly and Kit perfectly, I thought. Even when they weren't upset there was something in their eyes, a burden they carried, which at their age they found impossible to understand or communicate. If they couldn't verbalize their suffering, it might come out in play, but not yet. They were where I'd left them in the living room, sitting on the floor by the toy box, and Molly had her arm around Kit.

'Did you have a nice time with Keelie?' I asked.

Both children stared at me, and then Molly managed a small nod.

'Good. You're going to see your mummy and daddy soon, so let's get you ready.'

'Mummy?' Molly asked.

'Yes, we are going in my car so you can see Mummy and Daddy at what's called a Family Centre.'

Holding a hand each, I took the children upstairs where I washed their hands and faces and then changed Kit's top and nappy. Molly's clothes were still clean. I always liked the

51

children I cared for to look smart for contact, as it helped to reassure the parents and gave their meeting a sense of occasion, although of course Molly and Kit were too young to appreciate that.

'Mummy?' Molly asked again as we returned downstairs.

'Yes, you're going to see Mummy and Daddy very soon.'

'At my home?'

'No, love, at the Family Centre. It's like a home, with toys, books, games and chairs to sit on. You will see them for an hour or so and then I'll bring you back here.' I wasn't sure how long contact would be, as Tess hadn't told me, but it's usually an hour and a half, sometimes two.

Before I left the house, I sent a message to Paula, Lucy and Adrian on our WhatsApp group to let them know I was taking Molly and Kit to contact and wasn't sure what time I'd be back.

I was glad I'd already fixed the car seats in place the day before, because I'd forgotten how long it took to leave the house with two little ones. I'd also packed a bag with nappies, wipes and a drink of water for both children. The clothes the children were wearing were suitable for early September, but if no warmer clothes arrived from home then I'd buy winter clothes soon before the weather turned cold.

'Where's Mummy?' Molly asked from the back seat as I drove.

'At the Family Centre. You're going to see Mummy and Daddy there soon.' The children only ever asked for Mummy, not Daddy, which made more sense now I knew Filip worked very long hours. Aneta had been the children's main caregiver, so it was natural that they would ask for her.

* * *

I'd taken many children I'd fostered in the past to the Family Centre to see their parents, and I knew that to begin with it could be difficult for everyone. Feelings run high, the children are upset, and the parents are angry that their children are in care and the only way they can see them is in supervised contact at the Family Centre for a few hours a week. Children usually adapt more quickly than their parents. The Family Centre has six contact rooms, which are attractively decorated and furnished to look like living rooms, all well stocked with games and toys. There's a communal kitchen, bathroom and separate WCs, but the parents are continually observed with their children by a contact supervisor who also takes notes. The parents are aware that their report will go to the social worker who will incorporate it into their report to the judge, so ultimately what the contact supervisor writes will form part of the judge's decision on whether the child is allowed home. The supervisor's report includes comments on the parents' relationship with their child – positive and negative. I think it's an awful position for a parent to be in, but there is little alternative if contact needs to be supervised.

'Is Mummy here?' Molly asked as I parked outside the Family Centre.

'Yes, Mummy and Daddy should be waiting inside,' I replied. Molly was looking out of her side window at the building, while Kit was cautiously watching me. I met his gaze and smiled. The poor child looked scared and confused. I hoped that seeing their parents would reassure the children.

I undid their harnesses and helped them out of their car seats. Taking them by the hand, I walked with them slowly up the path to the security-locked main door where I pressed the buzzer. The closed-circuit television camera above us was monitored in the office, and a few moments later the door clicked open and we went in. Tess was waiting in reception. 'Hello,' she said brightly to us all.

Sometimes the social worker is present at the first contact, then after that they observe contact every few months, although they are sent the supervisor's reports after each session. The parents would have been shown around the building and had the house rules explained to them. They would also have signed a written agreement that outlined the arrangements and expectations for contact.

'The parents are in Blue Room,' Tess said. Each of the rooms is known by the colour it is decorated. 'I'll take the children through. Filip has brought in some more of the children's belongings.' She nodded to a suitcase standing to one side. 'He said he's put the appointment card for the fracture clinic in there with the notes they were given on the care of the plaster.'

'Thank you.'

'Also, I've arranged a medical for the children on Monday afternoon,' Tess continued as the children stood quietly beside me. 'I've emailed the details to you.'

'OK, thanks. I haven't had a chance to check my emails yet. I'll have a look this evening. What time is contact finishing today?'

'Five-thirty, when the centre closes. The details of future contacts are in the email.'

'All right.'

'Come on, then, let's see Mummy and Daddy,' Tess said to the children.

'Have a good time,' I said, but the children just looked at me with sad, wary eyes.

Tess took them by the hand and, with a few words of reassurance, led them down the corridor in the direction of Blue

Room. I picked up the suitcase, smiled at the receptionist, who I knew a little from my previous visits, and left.

There was just enough time to make it worth my while going home. I wanted to unpack the case so the children had their own belongings in their bedroom. I doubted there'd be much time when we got back. The drive from the Family Centre to my house is usually between fifteen and thirty minutes, depending on the traffic, and I arrived home just before four-thirty. I was the only one in, apart from Sammy, and he watched me heave the case upstairs and into Molly and Kit's bedroom. I opened it and found the hospital appointment card and the printout on plaster-cast care at the top. I put them to one side and quickly unpacked the rest of the case. There were no toys, which was a pity, but I appreciated how difficult it was for parents to send their children's belongings to the foster carer. Although it helps the children to settle, parents can feel as though they are collaborating in sending their children away. Still, I had plenty of toys, and Molly and Kit now had more of their own clothes, and the soft toys they'd arrived with.

With the case empty, I took it and their other bag downstairs to return them to the parents at contact. It was five o'clock now and I had to leave to collect the children. I put the appointment card and printout with some other paperwork to one side to deal with later and opened the front door. Paula was just coming in, having returned from college. We exchanged a few words and I said we'd catch up later.

When children first come into care the end of contact is often distressing for all the family. In the past I'd had to carry a child screaming and crying from the room, as there'd been no other way. Gradually the parents and children adapt to the arrangements and it becomes less fraught, although saying goodbye at the end is always very emotional. I was therefore expecting Kit and Molly to be upset when they had to say goodbye, but nothing could have prepared me for what actually happened.

I parked outside the Family Centre, took the empty cases from the car and went up to the door, where I buzzed to be let in. It's usual procedure for foster carers to collect the child or children from the room at the end of contact. 'It's five-thirty, so go down,' the receptionist told me.

I signed the Visitors' Book and continued to Blue Room. The centre closed shortly, so other families were saying goodbye and leaving. I passed a young lad aged about eight leaving with a man I knew to be his foster carer and we said hello.

The door to Blue Room was closed. Painted royal blue, it's imaginatively decorated with pictures of blue objects – cars, flowers, butterflies, a hat, the sky, the sea, blueberries and so on. Indeed, the whole centre is decorated appealingly to make it child-friendly. I knocked on the door, pushed it open and took a few steps in. I was immediately struck by how quiet and tidy the room was. Usually when I collect a child at the end of contact – even the first one – they are still playing, so there is a last-minute scramble to clear up, as the room has to be left clean and tidy.

'Hello,' I said quietly. 'I've brought these back.' I placed the cases to one side, out of the way.

Aneta and Filip were sitting on the sofa with the children between them. They had some picture books open on their laps, but I didn't get the impression they'd been reading to the children, perhaps just looking at the pictures. The contact supervisor was still sitting at the table making notes on a large pad. Everyone looked at me, Aneta hostile, Filip and the children bewildered. I knew my arrival was unwelcome, as it signalled the end of contact. Tess wasn't there, so I assumed she'd gone.

Eventually Filip realized why I was there. 'It's time for you to go,' he said in a deadpan voice, putting the books to one side. He was a big man with broad shoulders, now slumped under the crushing weight of losing his children.

'No. I'm not letting them go again!' Aneta suddenly shrieked, and clasped both children to her. She took Kit on her lap and had her other arm tightly around Molly. Indeed, she was holding them so tightly I thought they must be uncomfortable, but they didn't squirm or try to pull away. 'I'm not letting them go!' Aneta cried again, her face contorted in panic and fear. She clung desperately to her children. It was pitiful and I knew it would be upsetting for Molly and Kit. The sooner we left the better, but it wasn't for me to take the initiative. I looked at the supervisor.

'It's after five-thirty,' she said, glancing up from writing. Perhaps she was inexperienced – some of them are – for I would have thought her priority ought to have been to end contact as positively as possible, and then finish writing her notes after.

'Go away! You're not having my children!' Aneta shrieked hysterically, jerking the children closer. They both began to cry.

'I think they have to go,' Filip said ineffectually.

'No, never! You'll have to tear them off me.' I'm sure Aneta didn't appreciate that her behaviour was upsetting the children. Most parents don't want to say goodbye at the end of contact, but they put on a brave face for the sake of their children. Sometimes I've looked back as I've left contact and seen parents crying, having waited until their children couldn't see them. But Aneta appeared to be so wound up in her own grief that she was blind to the effect it was having on Molly and Kit, who were now sobbing uncontrollably.

'Tell her to go away!' she cried, meaning me. I could see my presence was antagonizing her.

'Shall I wait outside?' I asked the contact supervisor.

She just looked at me, not sure what to do for the best. 'It's the end of contact,' she said to Aneta and Filip.

'Don't care!' Aneta cried. 'She's not having my children!'

'I'll wait outside,' I said, and, going out, I closed the door behind me. I could hear Aneta shouting and crying and the children sobbing – so could others in the building. It was very disturbing.

A few minutes later the door opened and the contact supervisor came out, flustered. 'I'm going to get the manager,' she said, and closed the door behind her, effectively leaving the children with their parents unsupervised.

As I waited, other children leaving with their carers looked over, worried and able to identify with this family's distress. It was upsetting for everyone. Aneta's hysterical shouting and crying continued, but I couldn't hear Filip say anything. Presently the contact supervisor returned with the manager. Both looked anxious and disappeared into the room without comment, closing the door behind them.

I waited. I could hear the low tone of the manger's voice as she talked steadily and calmly to Aneta. The centre emptied and gradually Aneta's hysteria eased. The children stopped crying too. Fifteen minutes or so later the door opened and the contact supervisor appeared with Molly and Kit. 'Take them now and leave,' she said, urgency in her voice. I could see past her to where Aneta was sitting on the sofa, Filip on one side and the manager on the other, leaning into her.

'This is for you,' the contact supervisor said, handing me a carrier bag. 'It's the children's medicines. In case they're ill. There's a lot.'

'Oh,' I said, surprised. 'Does anything have to be taken now?' It hadn't been mentioned.

'I don't think so. Aneta said to follow the instructions on the packet.'

I hung the bag over my arm and took the children by the hand. At that moment Aneta seemed to realize what was happening and with a shriek of sheer distress like a wounded animal she made a dash for the door. Filip shot after her and grabbed her. The last image the children had of their parents was of their mother, her face twisted in anguish, being restrained by their father. It was an image that would stay with them for a very long time.

CHAPTER SIX

I WANT MUMMY

I hurried out of the Family Centre with the children and to the car, the carrier bag of medicines weighing heavily on my arm. 'I feel sick,' Molly said, and, leaning forward, she vomited onto the pavement.

'It's OK, love,' I soothed gently. 'Don't worry. You're just upset.' I assumed that was the reason, and smoothed her hair back as she vomited again. 'Take a few deep breaths,' I told her. She did, and then slowly straightened. 'Do you feel a bit better?'

She nodded. 'Good girl.' I took a wipe from the bag and cleaned her face and hands. I had one eye on the door to the Family Centre, hoping the parents wouldn't leave until the children were safely in the car. Kit was looking very anxious too.

'It's all right, love,' I reassured him. 'Molly's better now.'

'I am better,' she told him.

'Big girl,' I praised her. She was being so brave; most children her age would panic if they were sick, but she seemed to be coping very well.

'Can I have some water?' she asked.

'Yes, of course.' I took the water bottle from the bag and handed it to her.

She took a few sips and passed it back. 'Mummy gives me water when I'm sick.'

'Do you feel well enough to get in the car now?' I asked.

'Yes,' came her small reply.

I helped them both into their seats and fastened their harnesses. 'OK?' I asked her again.

'Yes.' She managed a small smile. It was the first time I'd seen her smile and I kissed her cheek.

'It's like being at home,' she said. I guessed she meant my kiss.

'Does Mummy kiss your cheek?'

'Yes. After I've been sick she gives me lots of kisses.'

'To make you feel better.' I smiled. 'Are you often sick?'

She nodded. 'Lots.'

'Don't worry. We're going to try to find out what's making you sick and stop it.' I kissed them both and then closed their car door and got into the driver's seat. Just in time, for as I pulled away Filip and Aneta came out of the Family Centre, heads down and looking dejected. I felt sorry for them, I really did, but if they were all going to enjoy contact Aneta would need to make a big effort to contain her emotions – as Filip had done – for the sake of their children. Making a child leave contact so distraught that she had vomited was unkind and couldn't be repeated. It was of course possible that it wasn't distress that had caused Molly to be sick, but at that point it seemed the most likely cause. She wasn't showing any signs of an allergic reaction and the sickness had passed quickly. She'd wet herself twice yesterday from distress and now she'd been sick. Young children can't verbalize or deal with their distress in the same way adults can, so it comes out in physical ways or through challenging behaviour. When I got home I'd enter everything I'd given the children to eat and drink in the food diary, although I was pretty sure that Molly vomiting now was from upset.

As I drove, I kept glancing at the children in the rear-view mirror. The colour had returned to Molly's face and, while not laughing, they had both calmed down. They were pale-skinned anyway, but Molly had gone as white as a sheet earlier when she'd been sick. About five minutes from home they both fell sleep – exhausted from a disturbed night and the distress at contact. I felt bad waking them, but they needed dinner before they went to bed, so, once parked on the drive, I gently woke them, then helped them out of the car. I let us in to the welcoming smell of spaghetti bolognese. Lucy and Paula appeared in the hall. 'Dinner's ready,' Paula said.

'Thank you so much.'

Both girls took over and I was so pleased to have their help. They slipped off the children's jackets and shoes and carried them to their chairs at the dining table. Five minutes later we were all eating. A large plate of spag bol was in front of me, topped with parmesan and garnished with salad, together with a mug of tea. I was truly grateful.

'Thank you so much,' I said again.

When we fostered older children or teenagers there was a limit to how much help my children could give, but now, with two little ones, they came into their own. Lucy fed Kit and Paula helped Molly, who seemed none the worse for her ordeal and ate.

'This is delicious,' I said, and made a mental note to include the ingredients in the children's food diary.

'I'm collecting a car tomorrow,' Adrian announced as we ate.

'Are you?' I knew he'd been saving for a car for a while, but I didn't know he'd been looking for one. The old banger he'd had at university had given up some time ago.

'It belongs to a guy at work,' he said. 'It was his elderly mother's, but she died and he wants to get rid of it quickly. It's only done a few miles. It's a bargain.'

'Sounds good,' I said.

'As long as her ghost doesn't haunt it,' Lucy put in.

Adrian paused from eating to look at her. 'How does a ghost stay safe in a car?' he asked. I'd heard this joke before but couldn't remember the punchline. Neither apparently could Lucy or Paula.

'Go on, tell us,' Lucy said.

'Puts on its sheet belt!' Adrian said. We all laughed.

'What's a ghost's favourite dessert?' Paula asked.

'I scream,' Adrian replied. 'What kind of roads do ghosts haunt?'

There was silence as we thought. 'Dead ends,' he said, and we groaned.

'What did the polite ghost say to her child?' Lucy asked.

I knew this one. 'Don't spook until your spooken to!' I said. We laughed again and little Kit chuckled. He obviously didn't know what he was laughing at as he was too young to understand the jokes, but it was lovely to hear him chuckle and see his little face light up. However, when I looked at Molly I saw she was anxious. 'Are you all right, love?' I asked, wondering if she was feeling ill again.

'We're not allowed to laugh when we eat,' she said seriously. 'Mummy says it makes us sick.'

'That's sensible,' I said. Although it seemed a bit harsh to me – never laughing at the meal table. I guessed Aneta worried more than the average mother about her children because they'd been ill so often. When I'd fostered a child with severe asthma, I was very watchful and overprotective. It was only natural as a parent or carer.

The children looked exhausted, so once we'd finished eating I said it was time for their bath and bed. Lucy and Paula were keen to help and came upstairs with me, while Adrian said he'd see to the dishes and was going out later. In the bathroom it soon became clear that I was superfluous, as Lucy and Paula took over. I hung around as they bathed the children, dressed them in their pyjamas and brushed their teeth. Once in their bedroom, Paula sat on Molly's bed to read her a story while Lucy settled Kit in his cot.

'You go down and get on with what you need to do,' Lucy said. 'We're OK here.'

'Yes, go on, Mum,' Paula encouraged. 'We can manage. We'll call you if we need you.'

'OK, thanks.' I kissed Molly and Kit goodnight and came out, leaving their bedroom door open. I had a long list of things I needed to do so was grateful for the opportunity.

Downstairs, Adrian was in the hall about to go out and I thanked him for his help.

'See you tomorrow,' he said, kissing my cheek. 'I expect you'll be in bed before I'm back.' It was Friday and he and Kirsty usually went out somewhere.

I wished him a good evening and told him to say hi to Kirsty for me, and then I went into the kitchen. First, I wanted to sort through the bag of medicines I'd been given for Molly and Kit. The contact supervisor had said she didn't think any of it was needed now, so I'd put the bag on a top shelf in a kitchen cupboard while we'd had dinner. I now took it down and began to go through the contents, taking them out one at a time, reading the labels and placing them on the work surface. It soon looked like a mini pharmacy with all the bottles, screw-top jars, packets and so on. There was antihistamine syrup to control allergic reactions, antihistamine cream in a tube, medicine to control sickness, Calpol for reducing fevers and high temperature, cough syrup, vitamin drops, eye drops, ear drops, nasal spray, laxatives, antiseptic cream, medicine for colic, stomach upsets, diarrhoea, sachets to rehydrate after sickness or diarrhoea, and so on. There was also an inhaler for asthma, although asthma hadn't been mentioned. I counted forty-five items.

All the medicine was relatively recent and in date, some had been used while other bottles and packets remained unopened. A few items had been prescribed by a doctor or the hospital, but most of it had been bought over the counter. There was also a syringe for giving liquid medicine to very young children. None of it was needed now; they were used to treat symptoms as and when they appeared. There was nothing wrong with Molly and Kit as far as I knew – Molly was over her sickness and hadn't developed any other symptoms – so they didn't need them. I couldn't fit all these items in my lockable medicine cabinet, and I thought they should all be kept together in one place, so, repacking the bag, I labelled it *Molly and Kit's medicine* and returned it to the top shelf of the cupboard. Was this amount of medicine excessive? Yes, I thought so, although the children had been ill an awful lot, so I guessed Aneta liked to be prepared.

On my list of things to do was to start a food diary. I opened an exercise book, divided the page into two, then wrote Molly's and Kit's names at the top of each column and listed everything they'd had to eat and drink since they'd arrived yesterday. I also noted beside Molly's entry that after contact she'd been sick and wrote, *Due to upset?* I would also note this in my log when I wrote it up later, and mention it to Tess when I spoke to her. Having brought the food diary up to date with this evening's meal I left it in the kitchen where it could be seen as a reminder to fill it in.

I went into the front room and switched on the computer to read my emails. I prefer the large screen of the desktop computer to my phone and it was where I stored important files. As it sprung to life Paula and Lucy crept downstairs and into the front room. 'They're both fast asleep,' Lucy whispered. 'They were exhausted.'

'Thank you so much. Was Molly all right? She's not feeling sick again?' I asked.

'No, she seems fine,' Paula said. 'She said she missed her mummy, but I told her she'd see her soon.'

'Thank you both,' I said again. 'Now you can chill.' It was their Friday evening and they disappeared into the living room to stream a film, as I concentrated on the computer screen.

Tess's email came through with the Essential Information Form attached. The social services, like many organizations, were trying to go paperless and I now had a folder on my computer for files relating to the children I was fostering as well as a physical folder. I was still keeping my log notes in a book; most foster carers were, simply because it's easier to pick up to add to during the day, although many forms were now completed and stored online.

I read Tess's email first. She'd arranged a medical for Kit and Molly for 1 p.m. on Monday and contact for 3–5 p.m. that afternoon. Then contact would be every Monday, Wednesday and Friday. Fetching my diary, I entered all of this and then picked up the appointment card for the fracture clinic. It was for 10 a.m. on Monday. With the hospital appointment, the medical and contact, Monday was full. I now read the print-out from the hospital on the care of a plaster cast. The main points were that the cast should be kept dry, the patient's fingers exercised by wriggling, and to contact A&E if extreme pain or numbness were experienced or if the fingers became blue, swollen or began to discharge. I'd keep an eye on Kit's hand, but so far it looked good. I now opened the Essential Information Form that Tess had sent, which should give me some background information on the children to help me care for them.

It was a standard form and began with the children's and parents' full names, home address and dates of birth. In the box about other family members it showed that Aneta had a mother and sister living abroad but they weren't in contact. Filip had no close family members. Ethnicity was given as British, language as English and beside religion it said none. The children's legal status was an interim care order, and beside school or nursery was written none. Next was the contact arrangements – which I'd already taken from the email – followed by special health concerns: *The mother claims that both children suffer from multiple and undiagnosed allergies, which can result in vomiting, diarrhoea, rashes, bruising, difficulty in breathing* (so I guessed that was why an inhaler was in their bag of medicines) *and seizures* – that hadn't been mentioned before either. I paused, very concerned. I'd need to ask Tess for more details about the seizures, how often they occurred and how long they lasted. I'd also have to let the rest of the family know and check they knew what to do if Kit or Molly did fit. I had a first-aid certificate – all foster carers do – and Lucy had one because she worked in a nursery. However, I knew from experience how frightening it can be to see someone fit, so I needed to have a chat with my family to make sure Paula and Adrian knew what to do too.

I returned to the form and the entry about the children's health: *Kit sustained a broken arm and has bruising and swelling to his face* – which I obviously knew. The next point and those following were more relevant to older children: Behaviour problems? Did the young person drink, smoke or take drugs? *No* had been entered by each one. Apart from the section on health, the Essential Information Form hadn't really told me much more than I already knew, largely, I thought, because the social services hadn't been involved with the family until the start of the week.

My gaze returned to the comments in respect of the children's health, particularly about the undiagnosed allergies. These applied to both children. Aneta wouldn't make all this up, so I wondered if the children could be suffering from a rare genetic condition that hadn't yet been identified. I knew nothing about the testing that had been done to try to establish what triggered the reactions, only that the cause was 'undiagnosed'. I then did what many of us do now and consulted to Dr Google. I typed *allergic reaction resulting in vomiting, diarrhoea, rashes, bruising, seizures, difficulty in breathing* into the search engine. Pages of websites came up. I began reading and soon discovered that there were over eighty allergic reactions that could produce symptoms of fever, nausea, vomiting and skin rashes – indeed, these were the most common reactions to allergens. But I also found that a purple-blue rash like a bruise could appear in a few bad allergic reactions and they were genetic. However, these severe rashes lasted four to six weeks, which wasn't what Aneta had described at all. She'd said the symptoms came and went quickly. I was about to continue my research when I heard Kit's plaster cast bang against the cot side, followed by his startled cry. I went straight upstairs. Kit was standing up in his cot, his little face puckered into tears.

'It's all right, love,' I said, picking him up and holding him close. 'There, there,' I soothed. Molly slept on in her bed close by. It occurred to me that cot bumpers would have cushioned the blow when Kit's plaster hit the sides, but they were now deemed unsafe as some infants had tragically become entangled in them and suffocated.

Eventually Kit began to relax against me and his eyes grew heavy and closed. I lay him on his side in the cot and gently rubbed his back. I also had a closer look at his arm in the plaster cast. I could see by the dimmed light that his hand and fingers were a healthy colour and weren't swollen so I didn't think it was causing him a problem, apart from being uncomfortable and hitting the cot when he turned over. After about ten minutes of rubbing his back, he appeared to be fully asleep and I crept from the room. I'd just got outside when I heard his startled cry again and went straight back. Not quickly enough. He'd woken Molly. 'I want my mummy!' she cried, sitting bolt upright in bed.

'It's OK, love, you'll see her soon,' I said. 'Lie down and go back to sleep.'

Molly lay down but didn't go back to sleep. 'I want my mummy!' she cried over and over again.

I picked up Kit and held him on my lap as I sat on the edge of Molly's bed and calmed her too. If a child who has been with me for some time wakes at night I go into their room, resettle them and come out, and repeat until they're asleep. But this was only Kit and Molly's second night in a strange room and Molly had been sick earlier, so I stayed with them. 'Do you feel all right?' I asked her.

'No, I want my mummy,' she said plaintively.

'I know you do, love, and you'll see Mummy and Daddy soon. But now I want you to get some sleep.' I tucked her soft toy in beside her and stayed sitting on the bed, soothing Molly and gently rocking Kit back to sleep.

Time passed and eventually they both appeared to be asleep. I carefully stood and returned Kit to his cot. He licked his lips, murmured something and turned over but didn't wake. I waited a few more minutes to make sure neither of them woke, and then crept out. It was now 10.30 p.m.

Downstairs, I shut down the computer, then stayed in the front room and wrote up my log notes. Ten minutes later Lucy and Paula finished watching their film and came into the front room on their way upstairs to bed. I reminded them to be quiet as Molly and Kit's bedroom door was open. Telling me I should wake them if I needed help in the night, they kissed me goodnight and went up. I finished writing my log notes, put Sammy to bed, then went upstairs too. I checked on Molly and Kit and they were both fast asleep. I then lay in my bed listening out for them. Around midnight I heard Adrian quietly let himself in and then nothing more until 2 a.m., when Molly and Kit woke. I managed to settle them reasonably quickly without waking the rest of the house and they then slept until 7 a.m. – a huge improvement on the night before. However, as soon as Molly woke she was in tears. 'I want my mummy,' she sobbed. 'When can I see Mummy? I want to go home.' Seeing his sister so upset made Kit cry. 'Mummy, Mummy,' he wailed. So at 7 a.m. on a Saturday morning I had two children on my lap, crying their hearts out for their mother. I felt like a wicked witch.

When I foster older children, I find it is easier to explain to them why they are in care and when they will see their parents, but at three and a half years of age and eighteen months it was virtually impossible, and I knew from experience it would take time for them to adjust. 'You'll see Mummy and Daddy again after two sleeps,' I said.

'I want to go home,' Molly cried, tears rolling down her cheeks.

'I know, love. But Tess, your social worker, one of the ladies who brought you here, wants you and Kit to stay here for now.'

'Why?'

'Because she feels it's better for you. Mummy and Daddy need some help.' Which was all I could offer.

Despite my best efforts to pacify them, their crying woke the others and it wasn't long before Lucy and Paula appeared in their pyjamas, yawning and their hair all over the place. 'What's all this noise?' Lucy asked, managing a smile.

Both children stopped crying and looked at the girls, as well they might. Usually well turned out, they looked like they'd been dragged through a hedge backwards, to use my mother's expression.

'Shall we play?' Paula asked Molly as Lucy picked up Kit.

'You are treasures,' I said. 'If you could just keep them amused while I shower and dress, that would be fantastic.'

CHAPTER SEVEN

SICK

It wasn't an easy weekend. I knew Molly and Kit would be unsettled. Regardless of whatever had happened at home, they missed their parents, especially their mother, who'd been their main care-giver. I was unusually anxious over the weekend, thinking they might suddenly fall ill and fit, so I watched them like a hawk for any symptoms. So too did Adrian, Paula and Lucy once I'd explained the children's health concerns on Saturday morning – we were all up early. I went through what they should do if Molly and Kit did fit: don't panic, call me, place the child on their side to prevent choking and make them as comfortable as possible. Don't put anything in their mouth during a convulsion. Wipe away saliva from their lips, and note how long the seizure lasts and call an ambulance. I wasn't planning on leaving the children in their care, but it was important everyone knew what to do. I might be in the bathroom, for example, when it happened.

Adrian collected his car on Saturday morning and when he returned we all went out the front to admire it, then he drove off to see Kirsty. It was a fine day, so after lunch the girls and I decided to take the children to the park. It was so much easier leaving the house with their help. Lucy got Kit into his shoes and jacket and then pushed him in the stroller, while Paula held Molly's hand as we walked to our local park. I think there was a novelty for my family in having two little ones living with us, and I hoped it didn't wear off.

The park has a children's play area with swings, slides, rockers, climbing frames and so on. Part of the area is railed off for toddlers and that's where Molly wanted to go. Even so, she was very cautious and reluctant to have a go on anything, although Kit was willing to try. Lucy helped him onto one of the sprung rockers – it was shaped and painted like a tiger. There were six sprung rockers in the shape of different animals and birds. Molly stood between Paula and me, holding our hands and watching.

'Would you like a go?' I asked her. She shook her head.

'Let's try the slide,' Paula encouraged. It wasn't steep and children younger than Molly were clambering up and sliding down, but she shook her head again.

'Maybe in a minute,' I said.

We continued to watch the other children play and Lucy now helped Kit onto the mini roundabout. He chuckled as she slowly turned it and was enjoying himself, but Molly continued to stand beside us. 'Are you OK?' I asked her.

'Mummy wouldn't like it,' she said. Paula and I looked at her. 'It's got germs.'

'What has?' I asked.

'Those things.' She pointed to the play equipment and I exchanged a questioning look with Paula. I'd never brought a child to the park before and had them tell me it had germs!

'I guess they have,' I said. 'But a few germs won't hurt you.' Or would they? I wondered. With so many undiagnosed allergies, perhaps there was something in the park that could trigger a reaction. Aneta had said it could be something in the air. I immediately grew concerned.

'Did your mother never take you to the park?' I asked Molly.

'Yes, but Mummy wipes them,' she said.

'Wipes what?' Paula asked before I could.

'The bit you hold.'

'OK, I can do that,' I said, and took a packet of antibacterial wipes from my bag.

'You have to wipe our hands after as well,' Molly said.

'I will. Now, what would you like to go on first?'

She pointed to the sprung rocker in the shape of an elephant and we went over. She waited while I wiped the handlebars and then she clambered on. 'You have to wipe Kit too,' she said.

'Don't worry. I'll wipe his hands when he's finished,' I said. He was up and down the slide and on and off the equipment, so it was unrealistic to wipe everything he was about to touch and I was sure his mother hadn't.

Molly finally started rocking, not enthusiastically, but at least she was occupied and not fretting. We then persuaded her to have a go on the slide and swings. We stayed in the playground for about half an hour and when the children had had enough I wiped their hands with the antibacterial wipes, at the same time checking Kit's fingers in the plaster cast, which looked all right.

'It's dirty,' Molly said, watching me. The white plaster was a bit grubby, which was only to be expected.

'Don't worry. It'll be fine,' I reassured her.

Now Molly was talking to me more I wondered what she could tell me, if anything, about how Kit sustained his injuries. As we walked slowly home I lightly asked her, 'How did Kit hurt his arm and face? Do you know?'

'He fell downstairs,' she said.

'Did you see him fall?'

'Don't know.'

'OK, I was just wondering.' I was therefore none the wiser. Had she seen him fall downstairs or was it something her mother had told her to say? So many of the children I'd fostered who'd been neglected and abused had been warned by their parents not to talk about it to their foster carer or social worker. I can understand why, as what they say could incriminate them further, but it meant the child carried a burden of lies they struggled with on top of everything else they had to cope with.

Once home, Lucy changed Kit's nappy and then the girls kept Molly and Kit amused in the living room while I did some housework, and then later made dinner. With their food diary to hand I noted everything they ate and drank as we went along. I also continued my watchful vigil for any signs of an allergic reaction. It was very worrying to be looking after two children who could fall seriously ill at any moment. I was half expecting to have to visit A&E over the weekend. Aneta had said they could become ill very quickly. They suffered no bad reaction after being in the park, and as each hour and meal passed and the children remained symptom-free I breathed a small sigh of relief.

After dinner Paula and Lucy read to Molly and Kit while I cleared up. Adrian wasn't due back until much later. Around 6.30 p.m. we took the children up for their bath and I felt we were starting to establish a routine, which always helps. We covered Kit's plaster and both girls helped me bathe the children. We put them in the bath together – Molly said that was what her mummy did at home – and I reminded her not to splash Kit's arm. The bruises and swelling to his face were going down and didn't look so angry. The only word Kit had said so far was 'Mummy', but as we bathed him he said 'bath' and 'water'. The average eighteen-month-old can say around fifty words and doubtless Kit would say more as he felt happier and more relaxed being with us. As we washed the children I checked their skin for any rashes or hives, but they were both clear. Lucy and Paula offered to put the children to bed, so I went downstairs and wrote up my log notes, which included our visit to the park. Then I heard Molly, probably over-tired, begin to cry, so I went up.

'I want my mummy,' she said. 'I feel sick.' I was immediately concerned. Was this due to upset or something I'd given her? 'Have you got a tummy ache?' I asked her, checking her skin for a rash – it was clear.

'No, I want my mummy. I feel sick.'

'Shall I get a bucket, Mum?' Paula asked.

'Yes, please, and a drink of water.'

'You'll see Mummy and Daddy on Monday,' I told Molly as Lucy pacified Kit. 'That's the day after tomorrow.'

'I want Mummy. I'm sick.'

Paula appeared with the plastic bucket and a beaker of water. 'Would you like a drink of water?'

She nodded. 'Mummy gives me water when I'm sick.' Did this sound like an abusive mother, tending to her sick child? I thought not.

She had a few sips of water, said she felt a bit better and then lay down, snuggling up to her soft toy. 'When I think about Mummy it makes me feel sick,' she said.

'I think that's because you're getting upset. There is nothing for you to worry about. Mummy and Daddy are fine and you'll see them on Monday.' I sat on the edge of her bed with the bucket within reach and gently stroked her forehead.

Kit dropped off to sleep in his cot and Lucy crept from the room. I told Paula to go and I'd see to Molly. I sat on her bed and stroked her forehead until she finally fell asleep. Relieved, I crept out, returned the bucket downstairs, and then telephoned my mother for a chat as I often did, and always at the weekend if we weren't seeing each other. I told her a little about how the children were settling in, that Adrian had a car and I was hoping to see her the following weekend with the children. She told me what she'd been doing. Dad had died the year before and although my mother obviously missed him, as we all did, she had a positive outlook and knew Dad would have wanted her to enjoy the rest of her life and not sit at home and mope. She loved it when we visited and welcomed all the children we fostered into her home and heart.

That night Molly woke twice, but Kit, exhausted from playing in the park, managed to stay asleep. The first time I resettled Molly without too much trouble, but the second time she said she felt sick and then began to dry retch. I quickly took her from the bedroom to the toilet and held her while she tried to be sick, though nothing came up. As we stood there, I checked her skin for any sign of a rash or hives, but it remained clear.

'It's because I thought of Mummy,' she said, straightening.

'Is it, love?'

I fetched her water, and she had a few sips.

'You are a brave girl,' I praised her.

'That's what Mummy says.'

I smiled and, confident she wasn't going to be sick, I returned her to bed where I waited until she was asleep again.

The following morning Molly didn't wake up crying as she had the day before, but she was anxious at not being in her own bedroom.

'It's not like my room at home,' she said, worried and sad. It would have helped if the parents had sent some of the children's toys – I could have left some in their bedroom – but I didn't say that.

'What can I do to make it more like your room at home?' I asked her. Kit was sitting in his cot, looking at one of the picture books I'd given him.

'I want my room. I want to go home,' Molly said.

'I know, love.' I changed my approach. 'We could put some more pictures on the walls. What do you like?' There were already some posters of animals, and a brightly coloured ABC and number chart.

'I don't want pictures. I want to go home,' Molly said.

Best keep them occupied, I thought, so I got both of them up and took them downstairs for breakfast. Lucy and Paula joined us and Molly wasn't so gloomy. Kit made a good attempt at feeding himself, although there was porridge everywhere by the time he'd finished. The weather forecast was showers all day and it was already raining, so after breakfast I covered the table with a plastic cloth, set out the Play-Doh and we all sat at the table modelling it. I think Lucy, Paula and I enjoyed it as much as the children. We hadn't had an excuse to use it for a while. Once Molly and Kit had tired of the Play-Doh, we cleared it away and got out paints. Lucy helped Kit to paint, and Paula and I encouraged Molly. Now she was occupied she wasn't thinking of home the whole time, but she worried about Kit's plaster getting paint on it and I reassured her it wouldn't matter. Both children produced great swirls of colour. 'What's your picture?' Lucy asked Kit, who was now trying to taste the yellow paint on the end of his paintbrush.

Molly looked across the table at Kit's painting. 'It looks like when I'm sick,' she said.

'Oh gross!' Lucy exclaimed. Paula grimaced. I felt the poor child spent too much time thinking about being sick – probably because she had been sick so much.

'Or it could be a duck pond,' I suggested. I leant over and painted what was supposed to be a duck on Kit's paper, and Paula and Lucy laughed at my attempt.

Adrian decided on the spur of the moment to drive to Nana's and take her for a ride in his new car. She lived about an hour's drive away and I knew she'd be delighted to see him. He phoned first to make sure it was convenient. Kirsty didn't go with him; she was at home preparing lessons for the following week. I was planning that the rest of us would see Mum the following weekend.

Sunday afternoon was worrying as Molly kept asking if she was going to be sick, and I told her she wouldn't be, although of course I didn't really know. She'd been sick after contact and had felt sick in the night – on top of all the times she'd been unwell at home – so of course it was playing on her mind. She also asked me if we were going to the hospital today and I said I hoped not. I assumed this was because of all the visits she'd made with her mother and brother. Then it changed slightly and she asked, 'Can we go to the hospital?' as a child might ask to go to the seaside or fairground.

'No, love. We only go if one of us is very ill. I'm hoping that won't happen,' I told her.

'I like the hospital. Mummy likes it too,' Molly replied.

'That's because they made you and Kit better,' I said. I could imagine Aneta's (and Molly's) relief at arriving at the hospital and having the doctors take over, look after them and make them better. It must have been a huge relief – bordering on delight – so I could see why Molly and her mother liked the hospital.

As Sunday drew to a close, I was grateful that another day had passed without either child being ill, and I noted it in my log. However, given their previous record for falling ill – when they'd gone to their doctor's or the hospital every week – I felt the law of probability meant that it was bound to happen again before long. On a positive note, as I kissed Molly and Kit goodnight, I was able to say they would be seeing their mummy and daddy the following day – Monday. Kit said, 'Mummy and Daddy,' and smiled, so I guessed he had some understanding that he would be seeing them soon. At his age, children understand a lot more than they can verbalize.

'Am I seeing Mummy at home?' Molly asked.

'No, the Family Centre, where you saw them before.'

'I hope I'm not sick again.'

'You won't be,' I said, although my positive reply belied what I really felt.

Both Molly and Kit had a restless night, perhaps because we hadn't been out during the day. One time when I heard Kit cry out it took me a minute to shake off the sleep and go to answer his call. When I arrived in their bedroom, I found Molly out of bed and with her arms through the slats of the cot, trying to soothe him, I assumed.

'Good girl, you can go back to bed now,' I said. 'I'll see to Kit.'

Paula's bedroom door opened and she came to help. It was 1.30 a.m. She put Molly back into bed and sat with her as I resettled Kit. By 2 a.m. the children were asleep and Paula and I were in our own beds again, but I didn't sleep. I was wide awake now and thinking I needed to go to sleep as we had a very busy day tomorrow – the fracture clinic, the medical and then contact. Then I heard Molly get out of bed and I went straight round. She was on the landing, clutching her soft toy. 'I'm worried I might be sick,' she said, rubbing her eyes.

I looked at her. She wasn't pale and she had no symptoms to suggest she was going to be ill. 'I don't think you will be sick,' I said. 'But you will be tired tomorrow if you don't sleep. You don't want to be tired when you see Mummy and Daddy, do you?' She shook her head. 'Come on, then, good girl, back to bed.' I steered her to her bed and then sat with her until she was asleep.

She slept until 7 a.m., and her first words when I went into her room were, 'I wasn't sick.'

'No, and you won't be,' I said. However, I was soon to be proved wrong.

CHAPTER EIGHT

NEED TO KNOW?

The fracture clinic at the hospital on Monday morning was very busy with adults and children waiting to be seen. Many had a limb in plaster, others were heavily bandaged with their arms in splints and slings. Those with leg and ankle injuries were using crutches. I gave Kit's name and hospital number to the receptionist and also told her of his change of address. She updated his file on the computer and then told us to take a seat and wait to be called. I'd packed books and small toys to keep the children amused, as well as drinks. I sat Kit on my lap and we looked at a book while Molly sat beside me and stared at those around us as children her age do. Gradually patients were called in to see a doctor and others arrived. As we waited, the woman sitting next to me struck up a conversation. I guessed her son was a similar age to Molly and he had a broken arm. She told me he'd broken it by falling from the top bunk bed, where he wasn't supposed to be. He was the younger of two boys and slept in the bottom bunk bed, while his older brother had the top. She said she and her husband had told him repeatedly he wasn't to climb up to the top, as he could fall and hurt himself, and that's what had happened. 'But that's kids for you,' she said. 'Accidents do happen.' And I wondered how many accidents a child could have before suspicions were raised. 'How did your little boy break his arm?' she asked.

'He fell downstairs,' Molly said before I could.

'It's impossible to keep your kids safe all the time,' she said. 'But I do feel guilty.'

I agreed and we continued chatting until she was called in to see a doctor. I don't usually tell passing acquaintances that I am fostering the children. We were called in next and a healthcare assistant showed us into a consulting room, where a young doctor sat behind a desk, reading from a computer screen. He glanced up as we entered, said hello and told us to take a seat. I lifted Kit onto my lap as Molly sat on the chair beside me. The doctor read for a moment, then looked up and said, 'How is Kit's arm? No swelling or numbness?'

'No, it seems fine as far as I can see.'

'How is he coping with having a plaster cast?' he asked.

'He's managing, although it is cumbersome. It stops him from doing some things and I think it's uncomfortable for him at night when he turns over in his cot.'

'Yes, it would be,' he said. He read some more and looked at me again. 'I'm not the doctor who treated him before. Are you his mother?'

'No, his foster carer. The children were placed with me last Thursday.' He obviously had to know.

He nodded, typed and then said, 'I'll have a look at Kit's arm and then we'll see about taking off the plaster cast, as it's causing him a problem.'

'Really?' I asked, surprised. 'It's only been on a week. Will the bone have healed?' Far be it from me to question a doctor, but I felt sure this couldn't be right and perhaps he'd made a mistake with the dates.

'It won't completely heal for a few weeks,' he said. 'But it's a straightforward buckle fracture, the most common type of fracture in young children. It's caused when they put their hands out to save themselves. We used to plaster this type of fracture, but now we usually use a splint. They heal just as well, and in young children it's far more comfortable. It has to be worn at night, but it can be removed for showering and washing.'

'I see. So why was a plaster cast put on?' I asked, puzzled.

'Because the child's mother insisted,' the doctor said. 'Apparently she was very anxious and wanted a plaster cast, so we obliged – to reassure her.'

'I see.' He stood and came round to where Kit was sitting on my lap and, smiling at him, gently lifted his arm. He examined his hand and told him to wiggle his fingers, wiggling his own fingers to demonstrate. Kit obliged. The doctor then compared both Kit's hands. 'I have no concerns,' he said, and returned to his desk where he typed some more notes. 'If you think Kit would be more comfortable with a splint instead of a cast, I will arrange to have it replaced.'

This was a little difficult. 'If he was my son I would say yes straight away, but he's in care. What would be your advice?'

'To use a splint.'

'Then please arrange it and I'll tell his social worker.'

He nodded, made another note, then said, 'If you would like to wait outside again, I'll see if we can remove the cast today, otherwise we'll make an appointment for tomorrow.'

'Thank you,' I said. We left the room and returned to sit in the waiting area, which was slowly emptying. I would need to update Tess as soon as possible, for I could see that if Kit arrived at contact with a splint instead of the plaster Aneta had insisted on, she was likely to be upset and angry. It wasn't appropriate to phone her now from the hospital waiting area with Molly and Kit with me, so I'd phone her as soon as we returned home.

'Doesn't Kit need a plaster?' Molly asked, clearly having understood much of the conversation I'd had with the doctor.

'No. Apparently not,' I said.

'Why?'

'Because his arm will heal just as well without it.'

She looked thoughtful but didn't comment and the three of us then looked at a book. After about ten minutes a health-care assistant came over to us with a new appointment card. 'Sorry to keep you waiting,' she said. 'Monday is always busy, so I've booked in Kit for ten o'clock tomorrow to have the plaster removed and a splint fitted.'

'Thank you very much,' I said.

As I drove home I wondered why Aneta had gone against medical advice and insisted on a plaster cast when a splint would have done. The doctor had said she was anxious, which I'd already seen in her, especially in connection with her children's health. I supposed she thought it was better for Kit; a cast was certainly more robust, but I trusted the doctor's judgement and a splint would be far more comfortable for Kit.

It was 11.30 a.m. when we arrived home and, mindful that Kit and Molly had a medical booked for 1 p.m. and I needed to speak to Tess before contact, I made them an early lunch. As they ate I used the phone in the kitchen to call Tess so I could keep an eye on them but they wouldn't be able to hear every word. It's so much easier to hold a private conversation when I'm fostering an older child. They're at school during the week and if I have to make or receive a private call when they're home they can be left watching television or playing while I'm on the phone.

Tess was at her desk and had been about to phone me. 'I've just finished talking to Aneta,' she said. 'How are Kit and Molly? What sort of weekend did they have?'

'They are settling in slowly,' I said. 'Molly is talking more but misses her mother. We're keeping her occupied, but at night she's very tearful. Kit seems to be coping a bit better. I've just come from his hospital appointment at the fracture clinic.' I then told her what the doctor had said.

'I understand,' she said, as though Aneta's behaviour at the hospital wasn't a complete surprise. 'I'll inform the parents that Kit's plaster cast is being removed tomorrow and he will be fitted with a splint. I'll need a copy of the doctor's report,' she added, thinking aloud. 'I'll request it.'

I had a number of matters I needed to discuss with Tess. 'The Essential Information Form –' I began, but before I got any further, she said:

'Kit and Molly share a bedroom, don't they?'

'Yes.' I'd shown her the room when she'd first placed the children.

'They'll need to be separated. Aneta is saying that Molly was responsible for Kit's injuries.'

'What?' I gasped.

'She said Molly pushed Kit downstairs and has hurt him before. Aneta is saying she took the blame to protect Molly, but she is innocent and Molly is responsible. Can you move Kit's cot out before tonight, please?'

'Yes. It will have to go in my bedroom, though,' I said, shocked from what I'd heard.

'That will be all right. He's only eighteen months. He can go in your bedroom for now. Our policy is that an infant can sleep in the foster carer's room until they're two and a half, but not their bed.' Which I knew. 'From what I remember, you have space in your bedroom to accommodate his cot?'

'Yes, I do.'

'Have you witnessed any incidents of Molly hurting Kit?'

'No. Not at all. She seems very close to him and protective. Last night when he woke she got out of bed to comfort him. At least, I assume that's what she was doing. She had her hands between the slats of the cot. I'm sure she wouldn't intentionally harm him.'

'Monitor them and let me know if you see her intentionally trying to hurt him. There may be some truth in what Aneta is saying, although I doubt the child is responsible for all their visits to hospital.'

I was so thrown by the suggestion that Molly had intentionally harmed her younger brother that it took me a few moments to recover my thoughts. I knew sibling rivalry did occur and that a child could go through a phase of being quite spiteful to a sibling, but with the parents' help they learn it is wrong and no real damage is done. I also knew that a child could unintentionally harm a sibling, not realizing the outcome their actions could have. But to suggest that Molly had intentionally pushed Kit downstairs and inflicted other injuries on him severe enough to require hospital treatment was rare and very worrying.

'You mentioned the Essential Information Form,' Tess prompted.

'Yes,' I said, reining in my thoughts. 'In the section on health it says the children have seizures. It wasn't mentioned when I met Aneta and Filip. Do they have epilepsy?'

'Not as far as we know. Aneta claims the children have fitted, but it's never been observed by a medic. The fit stopped before the ambulance arrived. I'm waiting to see their full medical records, but it's likely if one of them did have a fit it was a febrile convulsion brought on by a sharp rise in temperature.'

I was partly reassured. While a febrile convulsion is alarming to watch, I knew they were quite common in young children and they passed quickly, and were not usually harmful to the child. The main treatment is to bring down the child's temperature.

'But obviously keep an eye on their health and give them their medicine,' Tess said.

'Which medicine?' I asked, alarmed.

'You were given a bag at contact on Friday containing the children's medicines.'

'Yes, but there's nothing in there to be taken regularly. I checked. It contains things like antihistamine, Calpol, cough syrup, eye and ear drops, medicine for stomach upset. They are all medicines to be given if the child is ill. There's also an inhaler I was going to ask you about. I went through the bag carefully – there's a lot of medicine, but none of it is to be taken regularly.'

'You're sure?' Tess asked.

'Yes, positive. I'll look again, but all the instructions are to take when symptoms first appear or as and when required. I assumed the inhaler was to be given if one of them had difficulty breathing after an allergic reaction, as asthma hadn't been mentioned.'

'I'll check with Aneta and get back to you,' she said. 'Have the children been ill at all over the weekend?'

'Molly was sick when she came out of contact on Friday, but I put it down to upset. She soon recovered. It was quite traumatic when it was time for them to say goodbye.'

'In what way?' Tess asked. 'I haven't got the contact supervisor's report yet.'

'Aneta was very upset and couldn't bring herself to say goodbye, which of course upset Molly and Kit. Once we were outside Molly vomited but recovered after I comforted her and gave her some water. Then on Saturday night she said she felt sick and tried to be sick but wasn't. She was talking about her mother a lot. She didn't have any other symptoms, and again she quickly recovered after being reassured. I think she spends too much time worrying about being sick.'

'So does her mother,' Tess said bluntly. 'You're keeping a note of all of this and a food diary?'

'Yes.'

'Aneta should be calmer this afternoon at contact. Filip took her to the doctor and he's prescribed a light sedative.' I felt for Aneta. The poor woman was so distraught at her children going into care that she was now being sedated to get through it. Surely this wasn't the reaction of an abusive parent? For a split second I wondered if Molly could have been responsible for Kit falling downstairs.

'Tess,' I said, moving on, 'the allergic reactions the children have that result in vomiting, diarrhoea, rashes, bruising and difficulty in breathing, could it be an inherited condition? It's strange that both children have them.'

'It was mentioned, but nothing has been identified. Neither of the parents have these symptoms, although it's something the doctors may need to investigate further. I'll know more when I've seen the medical reports.'

While I accepted this, I had the feeling that Tess knew a little more than she was willing to say at present. Information-sharing with foster carers has improved tremendously since I first started fostering twenty-five years ago, but we are still told on a 'need-to-know' basis. Perhaps I didn't need to know this – if indeed Tess was holding something back at all.

I was watching the children eat their lunch as I talked to Tess. Kit was doing well feeding himself, although some of the sandwich had slid from his plate and onto the table. As Tess spoke I went over and put it back on his plate, smiling encouragingly at them both.

'Aneta has asked me to tell you', Tess continued, 'that because the children are sensitive to germs, she disinfects everything they come into contact with every day. That includes their toys, cutlery, plates, mugs, the dining table and the furniture in their bedroom. She also washes their clothes, bed linen and towels every day.'

My mouth dropped open in amazement as the children continued to eat at a table that, while clean, hadn't been washed with disinfectant. The same applied to their plates, cutlery, the chairs they sat on and the rest of the house. 'Are you asking me to do that?' I asked in dismay. There weren't enough hours in the day.

'It seems a bit excessive,' Tess conceded. 'So use common sense. Follow good hygiene practice and make a note of any reactions the children may have.' I breathed a sigh of relief. Clearly if something was identified I'd have to take more precautions, but for now I could continue as I had been. 'What are the children doing now?' Tess asked.

'Having their lunch. I've already entered what they're eating in the food diary.'

'Good. I'll phone Aneta now and get back to you about the medicines.'

'I'll be on my mobile after twelve-thirty as we have their medical at one o'clock and then contact at three. Tess, just something that's crossed my mind as we've been talking, do Kit and Molly share a bedroom at home?'

'Yes.'

'Why? If Aneta thinks that Molly has been hurting Kit?'

'They live in a two-bedroom flat and there isn't room for the cot in their bedroom.'

'But surely they would make space for his cot in another room – the living room, for example – if there's a possibility Molly could be harming Kit?'

'I agree,' Tess said, and that was all she said. And again, I had the feeling that there was more to it. It didn't make sense. If Aneta truly believed that Molly had been hurting Kit, she'd have found a way to separate them at night – presumably the only time they weren't being watched. Why risk it?

CHAPTER NINE

SICK AGAIN

While Molly and Kit ate their lunch – they had yoghurt and fruit for dessert – I went through their bag of medicines again, checking the labels on each item, especially the prescription medication. I was worried I might have misread the instructions and the children had been without their medicine. I'd fostered children before who'd had to take medicine daily and I was meticulous in making sure they had it exactly as prescribed. This was all very confusing, but thankfully by the time I'd finished checking I knew I hadn't made a mistake and all of Kit and Molly's medicine was to be given as and when required. I was very relieved and I'd let Tess know when she telephoned.

Once the children had finished lunch, I cleared away, wiped their hands and faces, changed Kit's nappy and jersey and then we set off for the Health Centre. I'd taken children there before for medicals; most children who come into care have one. I explained to Molly and Kit where we were going and what a medical was. Some children who've had little contact with doctors are anxious at the thought of a medical, but for Molly, who was very used to doctors, it was like a day out. Kit, too young to know, just went along with it.

'Did I go there with Mummy?' Molly asked as I drove.

'I don't know, love, you might have done.' The clinic was

run by the National Health Service and as Kit and Molly's home address was in the catchment area it was possible Aneta had taken them there.

'Mummy?' Kit asked from the back seat, having heard Molly talking about her.

'You'll see Mummy later,' I said, glancing at him in the rear-view mirror.

'I like doctors and nurses. They're kind,' Molly said after a moment.

'Yes, they are,' I agreed.

As I drove, Molly started talking about hospitals, doctors and nurses and how Mummy liked them as they made people better. Molly was at her most talkative when it was something medical. I guessed because she and Kit had been ill so often it had played a huge part in their lives. I also knew it could have the opposite effect and that a child who spent a lot of time in hospitals could become phobic and distressed at the thought of another visit, but not so Molly.

'Mummy says I'm a good girl when I go to the doctor's,' she continued as I pulled into the Health Centre's car park.

'Excellent.'

'She gives me hugs and sweets if I'm good.'

'I don't have any sweets, but I can give you a hug,' I said as we got out.

Molly didn't recognize the Health Centre, so I assumed she hadn't been to this one before. I held their hands and we went into reception, where I gave the children's names. The receptionist told us to take a seat in the waiting area and we would be called.

'Am I ill?' Molly asked me as we sat down.

'No, love.' I explained again that we'd come here for a medical and what it entailed.

'Will I be sick?' she asked as I put my mobile on silent.

'No. The doctor will listen to your heart, weigh you, and check your eyes and ears.' Which I'd said before. 'Come on, let's look at a book.' I took one of the picture books from the table, and with Molly sitting beside me and Kit on my lap I began to read the story, pointing to the brightly coloured illustrations as Molly turned the pages. There were about a dozen other people waiting, some with children. The Health Centre ran various clinics.

'We're not allowed these books,' Molly suddenly said, taking her hand from the page and sitting on it.

'Why not?'

'They have germs that can make you sick.'

'Is that what Mummy told you?'

She nodded.

'Well, in that case just listen to the story and look at the pictures, although I don't think germs on this book will make you sick.'

'Won't you get sick?' she asked, concerned.

'No, and I don't think you will either.' Of course, at this stage I really didn't know what could make Molly and Kit sick, but I thought it best to stay positive and not dwell on germs and sickness. I continued to read, with Kit looking at the pictures and Molly watching the other children, some of whom were playing with the toys provided.

'Are they ill?' she whispered after a while.

'I think most of them will be here like you to make sure they stay healthy,' I said, and thought again that Molly spent far too much time fixating on illness.

Five minutes later Kit and Molly's names and 'Consulting Room 5' flashed on the electronic display board. We stood, I returned the book to the table and, holding their hands, we went down the corridor to Room 5. A young female paediatrician greeted us with a welcoming smile. 'I'm Doctor Robinson. You must be Molly and Kit. Come and sit down.'

Beside her desk were two chairs and I took Kit onto my lap again as Molly sat beside me. There was silence for a few moments as Dr Robinson read from her computer screen. Until recently, the forms for medicals were sent in the post and had to be completed by hand, but now, in line with many other social services' forms, they were usually completed using a secure online portal. As the foster carer, I wouldn't normally have a copy of the social worker's request for a medical or the doctor's medical report.

'So you're the children's foster carer?' Dr Robinson said. 'Can I take your contact details?'

I told her.

'And Molly is three and a half, and Kit is eighteen months,' she confirmed. 'I have their date of births as ...'

'Yes, that's correct.' She would have been given the basic details about the children and relevant background information.

'How is Kit's face healing?' she asked, turning from the screen to look at him.

'The swelling and bruising is going down,' I said. 'He had an appointment at the fracture clinic this morning and they're going to replace the plaster cast with a splint tomorrow.'

She nodded and typed.

'How have they been since they came to you? Any sickness?'

'Molly was sick once after contact on Friday, and felt sick on Saturday night but wasn't. I'm keeping a food diary to try to identify any food allergies.'

'Good,' she said, and typed some more. 'So no severe allergic reactions so far?'

'No. Although Molly worries a lot about being sick and

about germs, as she has been ill so often in the past.'

'That's understandable,' Dr Robinson said. She finished typing and turned to Molly. 'How are you feeling now?'

Molly shrugged.

'You look well enough to me,' she said. 'I'll examine you first and then your brother.'

Molly looked as though she'd just been given first prize in a competition and proudly took a step forward. Dr Robinson smiled and, taking an otoscope from the top drawer of her desk, checked Molly's ears, then she removed a tongue depressor from a sealed packet and checked her throat and mouth. She asked her to read from a chart on the wall to check her eyesight and then weighed and measured her.

'That's fine,' she said, returning to the computer to input the information. 'She's average weight and height.'

She then took a stethoscope from her desk and, lifting up Molly's top, listened to her chest and back. 'That all sounds healthy,' she said.

Finally, she asked Molly to lie on the couch so she could examine her tummy. Molly was happy to oblige. 'You are a good girl,' the doctor praised her.

'That's what Mummy says.'

The examination complete, Dr Robinson helped Molly from the couch, returned to her desk and typed up her findings, then asked me about Molly's self-care skills, and if she went to the toilet regularly. She finished completing the form for Molly and then began the same examination for Kit as he sat on my lap.

'Does he have any other bruising or swelling apart from on his face?' she asked me.

'There are some bruises on his legs,' I said, and eased up his joggers to show her. She made a note.

'And it's his left arm that has the fracture,' she said, glancing at him as she typed. 'I'm assuming the social worker will have the hospital report.'

'I believe so.'

Kit was as good as gold as she examined him. He was too young to read from the wall chart to check his eyesight, so she asked him to point to a dog and then a house on a picture board, which he was able to do. 'Do you have any concerns about his hearing or eyesight?' she asked me.

'No.'

Once she'd finished she gave both children a sticker with a picture of a smiling face. I thanked her and we left.

'Is it finished?' Molly asked as we left the clinic, sounding almost disappointed.

'Yes, that's it. All done.'

'It's not like at the hospital.'

'No. It's a Health Centre.'

It was now 2.20 p.m. and we had contact at 3.00. We returned to the car, but I didn't drive away. I gave the children the drink and snack I'd packed, and checked my mobile, switching on the volume again. There were some WhatsApp messages from my children, a text from a friend, but nothing from their social worker, Tess. Once Kit and Molly had finished eating and drinking, I wiped their hands and faces and then drove to the Family Centre.

'Mummy, Daddy,' Kit said as I parked outside, clearly remembering the building from Friday.

'Yes, that's right. Good boy. You're seeing Mummy and Daddy in there.'

Molly had fallen quiet and was looking worried. 'I hope I'm not sick again,' she said.

'No, you won't be,' I said positively.

Tess had said that Aneta had been prescribed a sedative by her doctor, so I was expecting her to be calmer and better able to deal with having to say goodbye to her children at the end of contact, although it was never going to be easy.

I took their hands and we went up the path to the main entrance, where I pressed the security buzzer. Inside, the receptionist recognized the children from Friday and smiled at them. 'Their parents are here in Blue Room,' she said to me. 'You can take them in.' The centre tried to give the families the same room for each contact so it became familiar, but families weren't allowed to leave belongings in the room between visits, as it was used by others.

I signed in the Visitors' Book and, taking the children by the hand again, headed down the corridor towards Blue Room. It's usual for the foster carer to take the children into the room at the start of contact and then collect them from there at the end.

The door to Blue Room was partially open. I knocked, and we went in. The contact supervisor was at the table, notepad open, and Filip and Aneta were sitting on the sofa. It was Filip who rushed to greet the children. 'Hello!' he cried and, scooping them into his arms, hugged them tightly. They clung to him, Kit's little fists clutching his father's shirt, and Molly covering his face in kisses. 'I've missed you,' he said, burying his face in their hair. His voice was thick with emotion.

'I've missed you, Daddy,' Molly said.

Aneta was sitting on the sofa watching them and I threw her a small smile, but she looked away, blanking me. I didn't take it personally. I was used to parents ignoring me or being rude and aggressive. Sometimes our relationship improved with time, but not always. It helps the children if they can see their parents working with the foster carer.

Having seen the children into the room, it was time for me to leave. This was the family's time together and if the parents had anything to discuss with me they usually did so at the end.

'See you later then,' I said. 'Have a nice time.'

'Thank you,' Filip said, while Aneta ignored me.

I came out, closing the door behind me, and returned to reception where I signed out of the Visitors' Book. There was enough time to make it worth my while going home, but as I started the engine my mobile rang. It was Tess, so I switched off the engine.

'Are the children with their parents now?' she asked.

'Yes. I've just seen them into the Family Centre.'

'Sorry it's taken me a while to get back to you. I've spent most of the day on the phone trying to sort this out. Aneta didn't want Kit's plaster cast to be removed. She felt a splint would give him less protection if he fell again. She says he's very accident prone. I've now spoken to the doctor you saw and I am satisfied it's in Kit's best interest to have the plaster cast replaced with a splint. He said it should heal just as well and will be more comfortable. The cast wouldn't have been put on at all had it not been for Aneta's insistence, so go ahead with the appointment tomorrow, but try not to let him have any more accidents,' she added semi-jokingly.

'He's quite steady on his feet,' I said. 'He doesn't seem to fall over any more than other children his age.'

'That's not what Aneta says. Obviously make a note of any accidents he has.'

'Yes, I will.' Foster carers have to log all accidents, illnesses and injuries just as schools, nurseries and child-minders do, whether medical assistance is sought or not.

'Now, about the bag of medicines,' Tess continued. 'Aneta has confirmed they are to be taken as and when required, but she says they are needed most days as the children are ill so often. You'll have to use common sense.'

'OK, and the inhaler?' I asked.

'Sometimes when the children suffer an allergic reaction they get short of breath and that's when the inhaler is needed. It was prescribed for Molly, but Aneta has been giving it to Kit too, which I told her she shouldn't have done. Children should never share medicines, neither should adults. If you have any concerns, consult a doctor.'

'Yes, of course. The children haven't needed any medicine yet,' I said. 'They've had their medicals, and they went well.'

'Good. I'll have a look at the reports when they come through. I've now seen the contact supervisor's report for Friday. Hopefully it will be better today.'

'Yes, that reminds me. Could the contact supervisor make a note of everything the children eat and drink while they're at contact so I can enter it in the food diary?'

'Good point,' Tess said. 'I'll tell her.'

'Thank you.' We said goodbye.

When I returned to collect the children, parting was easier. I waited just inside the door while Aneta kissed them goodbye, then Filip brought them to me. As he handed them over he thanked me for looking after them, which was thoughtful. He also said he'd taken compassionate leave from work and was seeing more of his children now than he ever had.

However, while parting had been calmer, halfway home in the car both children were violently sick.

CHAPTER TEN

BONDING

I pulled into a side road where I cleaned up Molly and Kit as best I could with wipes, reassured them, and then continued to drive home with the windows down. Paula was already home and, while not overjoyed at the prospect of dealing with sick, helped me strip the children and bath them. Once they were clean and we'd washed their hair, we dressed them in their pyjamas and took them downstairs to play. They were able to play more now, which was a good sign and showed they were starting to accept their new surroundings. Lucy returned home from work. 'Mum, do you know you've left the windows down on your car?' she called, coming into the living room.

'Yes, love, there's a reason for that,' I said, and told her the children had been sick in the car. I left her with Paula to entertain Kit and Molly while I filled a bucket with hot water and disinfectant and went out to clean up the car.

As anyone who has ever had to clean vomit from a car knows, it goes everywhere – into the material, door pockets, seams and crevices – and the smell is overpowering and lingers for weeks. It had happened to me a couple of times before and eventually I'd paid to have the car valeted to get rid of the smell, and might do so again. But more worrying was what had made Kit and Molly so sick. They appeared to have no other symptoms, although I'd be keeping a close eye on them. Their sickness had been violent and sudden. Later, when I had the chance, I'd go through the food diary looking for a possible culprit. I felt dreadful that something I'd given them might have caused them both to be sick. Yet at the same time it could help identify what had caused the reaction. I wondered why Aneta hadn't kept a food diary if it was going to help identify their allergies.

After half an hour of scrubbing, the back of the car was clean but now reeked of disinfectant – marginally preferable to vomit. I closed the car doors but left all the windows down a little, and returned indoors. The children were still being entertained by Paula and Lucy in the living room and, having checked on them, I set about preparing dinner, although I didn't have much of an appetite after cleaning the car. I thought the children should probably have something plain, so I made a pasta bake and added a side of chicken pieces for those who wanted it.

Adrian arrived home as I was cooking and, coming into the kitchen, said helpfully, 'Mum, you've forgotten to close your car windows. If you give me your keys, I'll close them.'

'It's OK, love, I didn't forget.' I told him that Molly and Kit had been sick in the car and I was airing it.

'Glad I've got my own car,' he quipped.

'Yes, and I might be using it if I can't get rid of the smell,' I returned, and then asked him if he could help me move Kit's cot into my bedroom, and explained why.

'You really think Molly is capable of harming her brother?' he asked, astounded.

'No, I don't, but their social worker wants them separated, although they share a bedroom at home.'

He shrugged non-committally, then came with me upstairs to help me move the cot while the dinner cooked in the oven. 'Adrian, if you do see Molly hurting her brother in any way, you'd let me know, wouldn't you? I'll mention it to Lucy and Paula too.'

'Yes.' But I could see from his expression he doubted Molly would harm her brother.

It was 6.45 by the time we all sat down to dinner. Molly and Kit were still not showing any signs of an allergic reaction and, having recovered from being sick, ate a reasonable amount, but they were tired. By the end of the meal they were both yawning. I had yet to tell Molly of the change in sleeping arrangements.

'Time for bed,' I said. 'Now you're a big girl you can have a bedroom all to yourself. Kit will sleep in his cot in my room.' I told Paula and Lucy I'd explain the reason to them later.

It had occurred to me that having Kit and Molly sleeping in different rooms also meant that they were unlikely to wake each other and I could put them to bed at different times. I usually take the youngest up first. 'So now you're a big girl,' I continued positively, 'you can stay up a bit later and play for longer, while I put Kit to bed.'

She liked this. I picked up Kit and everyone kissed him goodnight. He giggled. Lucy and Paula took Molly into the living room to play and read her some stories, while I put Kit to bed. Adrian went to his room as he had some work to do on his laptop. I brushed Kit's teeth and then settled him in his cot in my room. To begin with he kept standing up and looking around, intrigued. Clearly it was another change for him, but eventually he stayed lying down and, with me stroking his forehead, he drifted off to sleep. I crept out, reminding myself that I'd have to be careful not to disturb him when I came to bed. No more listening to the radio or reading by the light of the lamp.

It was now Molly's bedtime. Lucy and Paula kissed her goodnight and I took her up to the bathroom and helped her brush her teeth. It was only when we went into her bedroom that she fully appreciated Kit wasn't there.

'Where's Kit?' she asked anxiously.

'He's sleeping in my bedroom. Remember, I told you downstairs?'

'Why?'

'Because your social worker feels it's better for you both. As you're a big girl you can have your own bedroom like Paula, Lucy and Adrian have.'

'I don't want my own bedroom. I want Kit.' Her face crumbled and she began to cry.

'Oh, love, don't upset yourself.' I put my arm around her, trying to comfort her. 'You'll see Kit in the morning.'

'I want to see him now,' she said. 'I want Kit. I want Mummy, I want to go home.'

Unsurprisingly the change in arrangements had unsettled her and she got very upset and then angry, demanding I bring Kit back. Adrian looked in to see what was the matter and I signalled to him that it was OK, so he left us to it. Eventually I asked Molly, 'Would you like to see where Kit is sleeping?' She nodded. I probably should have shown her before. 'OK, let's dry your tears and I'll show you. You'll have to be very quiet, we don't want to wake him.'

I wiped her face with a tissue and then, holding her hand, I led her round the landing to my room. I'd left the door slightly ajar so I could hear him if he woke. 'Very quietly,' I whispered, and put my finger to my lips to emphasize this. 'We mustn't wake him.'

I eased the door open and we crept across the room to Kit's cot. It was against the opposite wall so I could see him from my bed. He was fast asleep, lying flat on his back, mouth relaxed open, and his arms flung out, the picture of peacefulness and cherubic innocence. I was about to take Molly out again now she'd seen him, when she suddenly grabbed the side of the cot and shook it violently. 'Wake up!' she shouted at the top of her voice. Kit's eyes shot open and he began to cry.

'That was naughty,' I told Molly as I picked up Kit.

'I don't want him in here,' she cried angrily.

Taking Molly's hand, I took her back to her room. 'Stay there while I see to Kit,' I told her firmly. 'That was naughty to wake him after I asked you to be quiet.'

Bad as I felt for telling her off, she needed to learn, and I left her for a few minutes to reflect on what she'd done wrong, while I retuned Kit to his cot. I had no idea why she'd purposely woken him. Perhaps it was jealousy or simply a wish to have her own way. As I resettled Kit, I heard Adrian come out of his room and ask Molly, 'What's the matter?'

She stopped crying.

Then I heard Lucy go into Molly's room.

Five minutes later Kit was asleep again and I went to Molly. I thanked Adrian and Lucy for their help and they returned to their rooms. Molly was in bed and calm now – the incident had passed and we could move on. 'Off to sleep now, good girl. It's getting late.'

She closed her eyes and was soon asleep.

I went to Paula and Lucy and explained why Kit and Molly had to sleep apart. I asked them to tell me of any incidents they witnessed of Molly hurting Kit, as I would need to log them and tell their social worker. At some point the case would go back to court and if there was evidence that Molly was harming Kit it could support some of what Aneta was claiming and cast doubt on whether she was abusing her children. It was important I noted every incident accurately. Paula, like Adrian, doubted that Molly could intentionally hurt Kit, but Lucy, with childcare qualifications and working in a nursery, said, 'Children can be quite cruel to each other, even little ones. We have a boy at the nursery who is just three and he tries to harm others. He hits them, sometimes with objects, pinches them, pulls their hair and pushes them over. We have to watch him the whole time. His mother says it started when his younger sister was born, so she thinks it's jealousy.'

I nodded. It was plausible that Molly was harming Kit out of jealousy, but why had Aneta let them share a bedroom? If she believed Molly was capable of hurting Kit, surely she would have separated them? It still didn't make sense.

That evening I wrote up my log notes, and then carefully went through the food diary for the day. Virtually everything I'd given Kit and Molly to eat they'd had in some form before and it hadn't caused a reaction – milk, eggs, pasta, bread, fruit, yoghurt and so on. The only new item was the cream cheese I'd put in their sandwiches, which I'd given to them as a snack after their medical and they'd eaten in the car. I doubted that had made them sick, but I made a note and would leave it out of their diet for now, maybe try it again in a few weeks. Before I went to bed I emailed Tess so she would read it in the morning. I said contact seemed to end well but both children had been sick in the car on the way home. I wrote that they had no other symptoms and the only new food I'd introduced that day was cheese spread, which I wouldn't give them again. I reminded her to let me know what food they'd had at contact.

It was nearly midnight by the time I was ready for bed and crept into my bedroom, careful not to disturb Kit. I'm a light sleeper and am used to sleeping by myself, so I heard Kit's every movement that night: his snuffles, smacking his lips and of course his plaster cast banging against the side of the cot, which woke me but not him. I didn't mind. It was a long time since I'd had a little one in my bedroom and it brought back many happy memories of my own children and those I'd fostered. After a while you don't remember the sleepless nights and exhaustion of looking after little ones, just the good bits. However, shortly after 2 a.m. I got the shock of my life. I was half asleep, lying on my side, facing Kit's cot, when I heard my bedroom door open behind me. I turned and sat bolt upright, my heart pounding. There stood Molly, framed in the small light coming from the landing. 'I want Kit,' she said.

I was out of bed in a second. 'Sshh, love, quietly.' I took her hand and led her back to her room. 'You need to stay in your own bed. Kit's asleep and you'll see him in the morning.'

'I want him now,' she demanded.

'In the morning,' I said gently but firmly. I put her back to bed and tucked her in. The poor child had had so many changes to cope with, doubtless she'd taken comfort from having Kit in her room. I settled her with her soft toy, said goodnight, came out and returned to my bed. Kit was still asleep. Ten minutes later Molly reappeared at my door. 'I want Kit,' she said loudly.

Again, I was straight out of bed. 'You'll see him in the morning,' I said more firmly and took her back to bed.

I waited on the landing and in a few minutes she came out of her room again. I took her back, and she repeated this another four times, before eventually staying in bed and going back to sleep. She was persistent to say the least, as many children her age are, but it didn't mean she was capable of harming her brother, she just wanted to be near him.

The next time I woke it was after 6 a.m. and as I opened my eyes I saw Kit standing in his cot and looking at me, grinning. I smiled back, got straight out of bed and picked him up to give him a hug. He was such a dear little chap and was taking all the changes really well. His nappy needed changing and I realized the clean nappies and wipes were still in what was now Molly's room. I returned Kit to his cot, gave him his soft toy and went round to Molly's room. She was still asleep. I quietly collected together the items I needed, plus a few toys to keep Kit amused, and returned to my bedroom. He grinned at me as I changed him and then, pointing to me, said, 'Mummy.' My heart clenched.

'No, love, I'm Cathy. You'll see Mummy and Daddy again tomorrow.' But how confusing it must be for a child of his age.

I returned him to his cot with his toys so that I could quickly shower. I needed to be ready before the children were up, otherwise I wouldn't get another opportunity. Having showered, I dressed in my bedroom so I could keep an eye on Kit, who was still amusing himself. 'Good boy.'

I'd just finished dressing when I heard a sound outside my bedroom door. Opening it, I found Molly, clutching her soft toy and looking a bit sheepish.

'Good morning, love,' I said brightly. 'You can come in now and see Kit. Well done for staying in your bed.'

She went over and, reaching through the slats of the cot, hugged him. 'I love you, Kit,' she said. I could easily have said, 'So do I,' for I knew I was quickly bonding with both children and it was going to be agony if and when I eventually had to say goodbye.

We spent most of Tuesday morning at the hospital having Kit's plaster cast removed and the splint fitted. The nurse was lovely and gave Kit and Molly noise-reducing headphones to wear as she cut through the plaster with an electronic cutter. I could have done with a pair. The cutter made a high-pitched grating noise, which would be quite alarming to young children. After the plaster was cut off the nurse fitted the correct-size splint, showed me how tight it should be and then gave me an instruction sheet on the care of the splinted arm. We had an appointment in four weeks' time, but she said to go back earlier if I had any concerns. We left with Kit waving his arm in the air and chuckling. It must have felt so much lighter now the plaster cast was off. He was lighter to pick up too.

We returned home for lunch and I noted what I'd given the children to eat in the food diary. As we ate, Molly remarked with a child's honesty that she liked my juice better than her mummy's, so I thought at least I'd done something right! With no contact that afternoon and the sun out I took them to our local park – the same park we'd been to with Lucy and Paula. It was early September and the air was starting to chill, especially in the evenings, so we had to make the most of fine days. The park was relatively empty as the schools and nurseries had returned for the autumn term. It was usual for a child of Molly's age to be attending playgroup or nursery for at least a few half-days a week so they could learn to socialize. It was something I would raise with Tess. The children seemed to have led very insular lives, and once they were more settled I felt it would do them both good to play with their peers. Social interaction is important for young children as it develops their sense of self, what others expect from them and skills that will set them up for life. As Kit was still very young I could take him to a toddler group where the parent or carer stayed, as I had done with my own children and others I'd fostered at his age.

We spent an hour in the park and Kit and Molly enjoyed themselves. While they were occupied, they didn't dwell so much on missing their parents; it was in the evening when they were tired that Molly in particular became upset and wanted Mummy. When Paula, Lucy and Adrian came home they made a fuss of the children and admired Kit's splint. We all had dinner together at 6.30. Afterwards, when I bathed the children, I was able to remove Kit's splint and it was so much easier to wash him. I put the splint back on once I'd dried him. He didn't mind at all. Lucy then read Molly a bedtime story downstairs while I put Kit to bed. We didn't see much of Paula and Adrian that evening as they both had work to do – Paula for college and Adrian for the firm of accountants he worked for. He was five months into a trainee position and wanted to do well.

When I took Molly to bed she asked me, 'Am I seeing Mummy tomorrow?'

'Yes, love. You see Mummy and Daddy on Monday, Wednesday and Friday.' I pointed to the children's poster calendar I'd put on the wall. I didn't expect her to remember, but the calendar gave her a sense of the days and time passing. There was also a children's clock.

'I hope I'm not sick when I see Mummy,' she said as she climbed into bed.

'No, you won't be,' I replied, maintaining my positive attitude.

BONDING

Molly wasn't sick after contact on Wednesday, neither of them were. But on Friday, as we arrived home, they were both sick and Kit had a rash on his chest.

CHAPTER ELEVEN

EXASPERATED AND WORRIED

'It's only happening after contact,' I told Tess on the phone. Very worried, I'd telephoned her straight away, and thankfully she was still at her desk at 5.30 p.m. Lucy and Paula were taking care of Kit and Molly. 'Either the children are getting very upset at contact and they're reacting by being sick or it's something they're eating there. I can't think what else it can be.'

'They weren't ill on Wednesday, were they?' Tess pointed out.

'No. So what was different? I'll keep a close watch on Kit's rash and take him to the hospital if necessary. They haven't got any other symptoms and I've given them nothing new to eat. We're having lasagne for dinner, which they haven't had before, but we haven't had dinner yet.'

'How did they seem when they came out of contact?' Tess asked.

'Quiet, but not obviously upset.' Tess would know that most children took time to adjust to seeing their parents at contact, not because they didn't want to see them, but because they were anxious at being in care and only seeing them occasionally.

'I've read the contact supervisor's reports for Monday and Wednesday,' Tess said. 'Nothing stands out. I won't get today's report until Monday. I think I should observe contact on Monday. Will you tell Molly and Kit I'll be there, please?'

'Yes, and Tess, I'm still waiting for the details of any food they've had at contact.'

'I'll chase it up. Is it all right if I give the contact supervisor your email address and ask her to email you the details direct?'

'Yes, please,' I said. 'I find it difficult to believe it is anything they're eating there, as Aneta will be monitoring what they have closely, but I need to include it in the diary so we can eliminate it. Aneta sent some biscuits and juice home with them today, so I can cross those off.' Parents often take food and drink into contact for their children. If it's not consumed, they usually send it back with the children so it doesn't go to waste. The children love the food and snacks from their parents, they are very special and a tie with home. Sometimes parents prepare meals for the child to bring home and have at their carer's.

Having informed Tess that Kit and Molly had been ill again, there wasn't much else I could do but watch them closely. Neither of them was especially upset at being sick, I think because they'd been ill so often it had sadly become the norm for them. The rash on Kit's chest hadn't spread and both of them were breathing easily, although Molly did say she had a tummy ache. I told her I thought it would pass but to tell me if it didn't.

Paula, Lucy and I dressed the children in their pyjamas and we went downstairs. I served dinner around 6.30 p.m. Molly and Kit both ate a reasonable amount, so I didn't think it was a tummy bug they'd both picked up. After dinner we adopted our usual routine of Paula and Lucy looking after Molly while I took Kit up to bed. The children were more settled and didn't cry so often. The bruises and swelling on Kit's face were hardly visible now. As I settled him in his cot that night I checked the rash on his chest. It was fading fast. It appeared to be as Aneta had said – that the allergic reactions came and went very quickly. But what was causing them? I still hadn't a clue.

When I took Molly to bed she asked when she would be seeing Mummy and Daddy again. I explained it was the weekend and pointed to the calendar showing Saturday and Sunday, and then Monday when she next had contact. 'But on Sunday we are all going to see my mummy,' I said with a smile. 'She is Adrian, Lucy and Paula's nana.'

Molly looked a bit puzzled and I explained what a nana and grandpa were. As far as I knew she didn't have experience of grandparents. Filip's parents were dead and Aneta's mother lived abroad and they didn't see her. 'You'll like Nana,' I said. 'All the children I look after do.'

Molly snuggled down with her soft toy, I tucked her in and then sat with her for a while. After a few minutes I said, 'Goodnight, sleep tight, I'll see you in the morning.' I came out and left her to go to sleep. Now the children were more familiar with their surroundings, my family and me, it was reasonable they could go to sleep without one of us being there, though I would of course check on them, answer their cries and settle them as necessary. I waited on the landing for a few minutes, but Molly was soon asleep.

During the evening I checked Kit's rash a couple of times, tiptoeing to his cot and gently lifting his top. By the time I went to bed it had completely disappeared. I supposed that whatever had caused it was no longer in his system or he was no longer in contact with it. Aneta had said that it wasn't always food that caused a reaction, but it could be something in the air or that they brushed past, like pollen or germs or washing powder. It was a minefield and as far as I knew the tests done so far had failed to identify a cause.

That night both children slept through till morning and I praised them. Up until then one or other of them had woken and needed resettling. I felt on top of the world after seven hours sleep, and the children looked more refreshed too. Paula, Lucy and Adrian played with them first thing in the morning and then I took them supermarket shopping, which gave my family some time to themselves. Little ones are lovely, but they are full on and need to be watched and kept amused the whole time. In the supermarket I put Kit in the trolley seat and Molly walked beside me, helping to take the items we needed from the shelves. If she couldn't reach, I lifted her up. The shopping took twice as long as normal, but it kept the children amused. They were very well behaved. Kit sat contentedly in the trolley, watching everything going on around him, and Molly didn't demand sweets as some children do. I sensed that going to the supermarket was as much a novelty for them as it was for me shopping with two little ones. I loved it.

Once home, Adrian unpacked the car and helped put away the groceries, and then after lunch he went to see Kirsty. Lucy went out too later, and once Paula had finished her college work she came downstairs and joined me to play with Molly and Kit. I saw her looking at them a little sadly, clearly deep in thought.

'It must be awful for their parents at the weekend,' she said. 'Having all that time to fill without their children.'

'Yes,' I agreed. 'And for Aneta it's during the week too. Her husband worked long hours so for most of the day and evening there was just her and Molly and Kit.' I hardly dared think about it: to be a full-time mother, when your life revolved around your children – your reason for living – and then to suddenly have them taken away was the stuff of nightmares. Little wonder Aneta had needed a sedative.

'Do you think she did hurt them?' Paula presently asked. I'd told my family what they needed to know about the reasons the children were in care.

'I honestly don't know, but clearly the social services think so. Ultimately, the judge will decide.'

'I hope they get it right,' Paula said, worried.

'So do I.'

Usually, in respect of the children I fostered I felt the right decision had been made to bring them into care, but with Molly and Kit I harboured doubts. However, as the foster carer, I didn't have all the information the social services had, and my job was to look after the children, log anything relevant and basically do as I was told, not question decisions.

That night both children slept well again and I felt we had turned a corner, in their sleeping at least. Yes, they would have restless nights from time to time as all children do, but we had established a bedtime routine that was working. I think sleeping apart was helping too, as they didn't wake each other.

I took the food diary with us to my mother's on Sunday so I could add to it during the day. I'd booked a table at a pub restaurant not far from where she lived. We drove in convoy to her house, the children, Lucy and me in my car – the smell of disinfectant still lingering – and Adrian, Kirsty and Paula in his car. Mum lives about an hour's drive away and Lucy fed CDs of children's songs into the player to keep them amused.

Mum was overjoyed to see us all and completely taken by Molly and Kit, as I knew she would be. They took to her too. She's everybody's idea of what a grandmother should be: kind, caring, gentle, loving, attentive and with plenty of time for everyone. Molly was a little quiet to begin with but soon thawed out and from then on monopolized Mum. It wasn't long before Kit had scrambled onto her lap, where he stayed while she tried to talk to us.

I made us coffee and cold drinks for the children, and then just before one o'clock we drove to the restaurant. It was very popular for Sunday lunch and was buzzing with conversation. Adrian lifted Kit into the high chair provided and he and Kirsty sat either side of him. We sat Molly on a booster seat opposite Kit and between Lucy and Paula. I sat next to Mum so we could have a chat. On the floor by my chair was what had become known as The Bag. It contained Kit's nappies and changing paraphernalia, drinks and a change of clothes for both children, a few books and small toys to keep them amused, and of course the food diary. I explained to Mum about the food diary and that I noted everything they ate. They both had the children's Sunday roast, which contained plenty of food neither of them had eaten before with me – like stuffing and mashed parsnips. For dessert they had the children's trifle, which seemed to be mainly fruit set in orange jelly and topped with whipped cream. I noted it all down, and the blackcurrant drink that came with their meals.

We returned to Mum's for the afternoon and I watched both children carefully for any signs of illness. I tried to do it surreptitiously, as I didn't want to worry Mum, but certainly my family were aware it was possible that one or both children could fall ill at any time. It was very worrying. However, the afternoon passed without any sign of them being sick and when we said goodbye at six o'clock they were still well. By bedtime I was certain that all those new foods could be eliminated from causing their allergic reactions.

On Monday, when I took Molly and Kit to the Family Centre, Tess was already in Blue Room to observe contact. Filip, Aneta and the contact supervisor were there too, so I said a general hello and, having seen the children in, I left. When I returned at the end I sensed an atmosphere and as soon as Aneta saw me she grabbed the children and held them tightly to her. I knew we were going to have a scene and I immediately felt anxious. The contact supervisor was writing, and Tess was watching Aneta. Filip was tidying away the last of the toys.

'Time to go,' Tess said eventually, but Aneta clung tightly to Molly and Kit.

'They're mine,' she said to me. 'You can't have them. Go away and leave us alone.'

I remained where I was, just inside the door, unsure whether to wait or step outside. Then Tess said to me so everyone could hear, 'Aneta has been a bit upset because you've taken the children out. Molly has been talking about the park and going to Nana's. I've explained that while children are in care it is expected that the foster carer takes them on family outings.'

I was sorry that Aneta was upset, but what Tess had told her was true – while Molly and Kit were with me they were part of my family and would join in all family activities, including days out and holidays.

Aneta was still clinging to her children and it was clearly upsetting them. Molly began to cry. 'I don't want to go!' Which of course upset Kit.

'Perhaps you could take them to Cathy,' Tess said to Filip.

He went over to the sofa where Aneta was huddled with the children. 'Time to go,' he said firmly. 'We'll see you both on Wednesday.' Scooping them up, he brought them to me and set them down, more confident in his role as father now.

'Don't forget this,' the contact supervisor called, and brought over a small carrier bag containing their unfinished drinks and biscuits.

'Thank you.'

Filip kissed Molly and Kit goodbye. 'Love you both,' he said. Aneta stayed on the sofa, looking miserable and wiping her eyes. I felt sorry for her, but Molly and Kit had to go.

'See you Wednesday,' I said, and we left.

Molly began to cry loudly for her mother and I thought that if being upset was causing the children to be sick then it was going to happen now. Outside I calmed them both down before we got into the car, and then drove home, every so often glancing at them in the rear-view mirror. They weren't sick, and by the time we arrived home they were both happy to see Paula. However, the next day, Tuesday, when there was no contact, half an hour after lunch both children were sick. I had a feeling I knew what had caused it.

Once I'd cleaned them up, I looked at the food diary and, as I thought, the only new food they'd had for lunch was the shop-bought fish cakes. I took the packet from the freezer and examined the list of ingredients. In addition to the white fish, they were covered in a breadcrumb coating, which in this brand contained additives: flavour enhancers, food colouring and preservatives. I knew that some of these could trigger allergic reactions in some children. I noted them all down and in future would check on food labels for these. A very small number of children are allergic to a whole range of additives that have been passed by the Food Standards Agency and cause no problems for most of us. I didn't think that was so for Molly and Kit, and I felt it was only a matter of time before I identified which additives affected them.

My optimism was short-lived, for later that afternoon both children were sick again, and all they'd had was a drink of juice, which they'd had before. I supposed it could have been a continuation of their earlier sickness, but they'd been fine in between. Exasperated and worried, I updated the food diary, and then emailed Tess, adding that I thought the children should be tested further. Clearly they couldn't keep being sick, and whatever it was that was causing the problem needed to be identified quickly. While I was at my computer an email came through from the contact supervisor, listing what the children had had to eat and drink during contact. I added those to the food diary.

Molly and Kit weren't sick again that week and on Friday Aneta was less hostile towards me at contact. At the end, when I collected the children, she – not Filip – brought them to me and asked how they'd been. I said that overall they'd had a good week, although they had both been sick earlier in the week and I had no idea what could have caused it, but I was logging everything they'd had to eat and drink in the food diary as Tess had asked me to.

'Perhaps they'll believe me now,' she said, an edge to her voice. 'Either I'm innocent or you are as guilty as me.' She smiled humourlessly.

When children first come into care there is a lot of activity with meetings, medicals, phone calls, updates and so forth. Then it tends to settle down until the final court hearing approaches, when a decision will be made on where the children will live permanently and tension runs high. The final court hearing for Molly and Kit wouldn't be until the following year to allow time for enquiries to be made, assessments to be completed and reports filed. The next day Tess emailed with the date of the children's first review and said the booklets I needed to complete were in the post. All children in care have regular reviews. The children's parents, social worker, teacher (if they are of school age), foster carer, the foster carer's support social worker and any other professionals and adults closely connected with the children meet to ensure that everything is being done to help the child, and that the care plan (drawn up by the social services) is up to date. Very young children don't attend their reviews, while older children are expected to.

Molly and Kit's first review was the following Thursday at 2 p.m. at the council offices. Sometimes reviews are held at the foster carer's home, if the children have been placed in care voluntarily, the parents are cooperating and there are no safeguarding issues. Kit and Molly, however, were the subject of a court order and their parents hadn't been given my contact details. I emailed Edith, my supervising social worker, and asked if Maggie could babysit again while I attended the review. She replied by telephone and said she'd ask Maggie, and also that she needed to visit me, preferably the day after tomorrow at ten o'clock. As my supervising social worker, she visited every four to six weeks to check I was fostering to the required standard, give support and advice as necessary, discuss my training needs and sign off my log notes.

Just after her phone call the landline rang again and a woman introduced herself as Tamara Hastings, the Guardian ad Litem for Molly and Kit. The Guardian, as they are known for short, is appointed by the court in child-care proceedings for the duration of the case. He or she is a social worker but independent of the social services and has access to all the files. They see all parties involved in the case, including the children, their parents and social services, and report to the judge on what is in the best interest of the child. The judge usually follows their recommendation. I'd worked with many Guardians before and they are normally thorough and objective in their appraisal and report. I thought that if anyone could discover the truth of what had happened at Molly and Kit's home then she would.

CHAPTER TWELVE

PLAY NICELY

The review forms sent by Tess arrived – one for me as the foster carer to fill in and one for each child. Given that, at their ages, Molly and Kit couldn't read or write, I would complete their forms for them. They were standard review forms, brightly illustrated to encourage the children to give their views on being in care. At eighteen months old, Kit was more interested in playing than the form, but Molly looked at it as I pointed to the questions and read them out. The first question asked if they knew why they were in care. *Not really, only eighteen months old*, I wrote on Kit's. Molly said, 'Because we kept going to the hospital.' Which was interesting.

I wrote down exactly what she said but then reassured her that it wasn't wrong to go to the hospital and she was in care to help her mummy and daddy. The next question asked what the child liked about living with their foster carer and what they didn't like. On Kit's form I'd written: *Likes playing and going to the park, although he misses his mother. Unable to verbalize his feelings as only eighteen months old.* Molly said she liked playing with the big girls (Lucy and Paula) and didn't like not seeing her mummy. I wrote it down exactly. There were ten questions in all – some included emoji faces with various expressions, ranging from happy to sad to angry. I asked

Molly to point to the ones that showed how she was feeling and I circled them. On the back of the booklets was space where the child had to sign their name and I helped Molly write her name and she looked very pleased with herself. I put the biro into Kit's fist and helped him make a mark.

'Mine's better,' Molly said.

'Of course, you're older,' I smiled.

Beneath their 'signatures' was another space where the name of any person who had helped the child complete the form had to be entered and I wrote my name and role – foster carer. I would complete my form later when I had more time and then post them all to the reviewing officer in the envelope provided, so they arrived ahead of the review. The Independent Reviewing Officer (IRO) would run and chair the meeting.

Edith visited as planned and met Molly and Kit for the first time. She confirmed Maggie could babysit while I attended the review and that I should phone her to make the arrangements. We sat in the living room and as the children played she made notes on how the children were settling in – both from her observations and what I said. We discussed some of the issues that affected them, especially their illnesses. She read and signed my log notes and then produced a printed list of foster-carer training that was scheduled for the coming months. All foster carers are required to attend a minimum number of training sessions each year, and as an experienced carer I was expected to lead training too. So far this year I'd completed far more than the minimum, but I told Edith that while I'd fulfil my training obligations, I wouldn't be taking on extra as I'd have to find a babysitter each time for Molly and Kit, which she noted. When I'd worked for Homefinders, an independent fostering agency, they'd provided a crèche for carers who were looking after babies and pre-school children so the carer could attend training. The local authority didn't, and carers who foster infants sometimes struggle to meet their training requirements.

Edith concluded her visit by looking around my house and asking if there'd been any changes to my household, as she was obliged to do at each visit. All members of a fostering household are police-checked (DBS), even non-permanent members. So if, for example, Kirsty began staying at weekends, she'd have to be police-checked. It is intrusive and some might say unreasonable, but it's to protect the looked-after child and something foster carers have to accept. Satisfied all was well, Edith said she'd see me at the review and, saying goodbye to the children, she left.

Tamara Hastings, the Guardian ad Litem, was the next professional to visit. She arrived smartly dressed in grey trousers, jacket and blouse and was of average height and build. I guessed her to be in her fifties. She had a quiet, confident manner and was clearly used to talking to children. She accepted my offer of a coffee and drank it while sitting on the floor, playing with Molly and Kit and getting to know them. As she played she also talked to me, asking how they were settling in, what they liked to do, Molly's attitude to Kit and if they'd been ill at all. Clearly, she already had a good grasp of the issues that had brought the children into care. She said that if there was something we couldn't discuss in front of the children she'd phone me, and she'd also give me her number and email address before she left. She said she'd seen Molly and Kit's parents once and would be seeing them and the children again during the coming months. She then sat on the sofa to make some notes as the children played.

'When the children were ill did you seek medical help?' she asked after a moment.

'No, I didn't think it was necessary. Once they'd been sick they recovered quickly, and neither of them fitted or had difficulty breathing. Kit had a small rash on his stomach for a couple of hours, which I monitored, but it cleared up. I would seek medical help, even call an ambulance, if I thought it was necessary.'

'I am sure you would,' she said as she wrote. 'I am trying to gauge the seriousness of these mysterious illnesses that both children suffer from.' I thought the term 'mysterious illnesses' summed it up. 'Aneta appears to have become very anxious about her children's health. I am wondering if a less anxious parent might not have sought medical intervention as often as she did. Are you aware of the number of times she took them to the doctor and hospital?'

'I know it's a lot. I think she is anxious about them being ill and catching germs.' I told her what Molly had said in the park about germs and having to clean their hands and the play equipment with antibacterial wipes. She nodded as she wrote. 'But I understand the children were also taken to hospital with injuries,' I said. 'The last being Kit's broken arm.'

'Yes, that's correct,' she replied, but she didn't elaborate. 'How is his arm now? He seems to be using it without a problem.'

'It's far more comfortable now it's in a splint.' I explained what the doctor at the fracture clinic had said and gave her the date of the follow-up appointment.

'How would you say Kit and Molly get along?' she asked, glancing at the children as they played.

'Fine. They seem to be very close. They were sharing a bedroom, but Tess asked me to separate them. Kit's cot is in my room now.'

'How did that affect them?'

'The first night they were both unsettled and upset, but they've accepted the new arrangements now.'

'They share a bedroom at home,' Tamara said flatly.

'Yes, I know, which is why it seemed strange that I had to separate them here, although it's not a problem.'

'Aneta has a baby monitor in the children's bedroom at home,' Tamara said, 'so she can hear if Molly gets out of bed. She checks on them regularly and goes into their room if she hears anything suspicious.'

'I could have put a monitor in their room here,' I said. 'Then they could have stayed together.'

'Aneta didn't want that. She was concerned you wouldn't answer their calls or keep checking on them as she does, and that Molly would hurt Kit again.'

'Of course I would have checked on them,' I said, a little affronted. 'I am constantly checking on them, day and night.'

'I am sure you are, but it's appropriate for the social services to take into account the parents' wishes. It might be that the children are returned home. You're aware of the care plan?'

'Yes. Long-term foster care as far as I know.'

'That's correct, if the judge decides they can't return home, but we're a long way from that yet.' She made another note. From her remarks I assumed she had doubts as to whether the children would remain in care. The Guardian's recommendation to the judge on what is best for the children is based on their assessment. While the judge isn't bound to accept the Guardian's recommendations, they nearly always do, even if it goes against the social services' care plan.

Tamara asked about the children's routines, their likes and dislikes, if they were anxious and what they said about life at home. As we talked she kept glancing at the children, observing them as they played. She was with me nearly two hours, and although I didn't learn anything knew – that wasn't her role – she thanked me, said it had been helpful and she had a better understanding of the children, and added that she would see me at the review on Thursday.

I had told Tamara the children were close and appeared to get along well and I'd seen no incidents of Molly being unkind to Kit that could have resulted in him being injured. At that point, it was true. However, a day later when the children had been with us for three weeks and were perhaps more assured and relaxed in their surroundings, Molly started bullying Kit. It began with her snatching his toys, so whatever he picked up to play with she took from him, sometimes quite forcibly. That much younger and smaller, he didn't protest or try to take it back as an older child might. His little face crumpled and sometimes he cried. I told Molly it was unkind to snatch and kind to share. I gave the toy back to Kit and found her something else to play with. But as soon as I moved away or turned my back, she had snatched it back from him. I told her again it was not kind to snatch and returned the toy to Kit. This could be repeated a number of times and often Kit eventually gave her the toy, so I took it from her and put it away. I didn't want her thinking she could get her own way by bullying. Adrian, Paula and Lucy witnessed her behaviour too – she didn't hide it – and they approached it as I did by telling Molly it was kind to share and returning the toy to Kit.

Many siblings go through a phase of bullying and, thinking it might help, I emailed Tess and asked again if Molly and Kit could have some of their own toys from home. Tess replied that she had asked Aneta and Filip before and would do so again.

As well as taking Kit's toys, Molly began trying to scare him by jumping out and making a loud noise. He looked frightened and didn't know whether to laugh or cry. I told her not to and that she wouldn't like it if someone frightened her. If Kit fell asleep in his car seat, she screamed in his ear. He woke with such a start he was close to tears. I told her off and then moved her car seat so she wasn't next to him. She wasn't pleased, but she'd learn in the end. If Kit had a sleep during the day, which he did sometimes, I put him in his cot and then had to make sure Molly didn't creep upstairs and wake him. Going to nursery and socializing with other children helps teach children how to behave and what is acceptable. Molly and Kit appeared to have led isolated lives, and as far as Molly was concerned (that much older and bigger) she was top dog. Her behaviour towards Kit could have stemmed from jealousy or been just a phase she was going through, so while I always corrected it I wasn't unduly worried.

However, I then saw Molly intentionally push Kit over with a hefty shove. He didn't cry but was scared. I told her off and explained that she could have badly hurt him. Children of her age don't appreciate what harm they can do, which is why the age of criminal responsibility is set at ten – higher in some countries. Was she capable of pushing Kit downstairs, resulting in him breaking his arm as Aneta had claimed? Yes, I now thought she was, for she wouldn't know how dangerous it could be. I noted all this in my log and would update Tess.

* * *

I telephoned Maggie to arrange the time she should come to babysit for the review and she said she'd be bringing Keelie again.

'That's fine,' I said. 'Molly and Kit loved playing with her.'

'And she did them,' Maggie replied. 'She's a big kid herself, bless her. But I do need to find a school who can manage her behaviour.'

'I thought the last time I saw you she was returning to her present school?'

'She did for a day, but it didn't quite live up to expectations,' Maggie said dryly.

I had to smile although I sympathized with her. I'd fostered young people who'd been repeatedly excluded from school, and the longer they were out of full-time education, the more difficult it became to get them back into the school routine.

On Thursday morning I told Molly and Kit that Maggie and Keelie would be coming to look after them again for a little while that afternoon. Molly was pleased. 'I like that big girl,' she said happily. 'She is fun.'

'Yes, so you can all play nicely together,' I said. 'No pushing Kit or making him cry.' I'd mentioned the issues we were having with Molly to Maggie on the phone, so she'd keep an eye on them. I'd also said I'd leave the food diary out and asked that she or Keelie add anything the children had to eat or drink. She was slightly surprised the hospital weren't running more tests, as was I.

We had lunch and then I took the children with me upstairs so I could watch them while I changed into something smart for the review. I only let them out of my sight if Paula, Lucy or Adrian were with them or they were asleep. When the doorbell rang at 1.30 p.m. they both came with me to answer it. Molly was excited, nearly as much as Keelie!

'Hi, babies!' she cried. 'Look what I've brought!' She held up two carrier bags filled to bursting. 'Toys! For us to play with!'

'Wonderful,' I enthused. 'I'm still waiting for some of Molly's and Kit's to come from home.'

'Keelie spends most of her allowance on children's toys,' Maggie said, rolling her eyes indulgently. 'She didn't have any as a child, but she's made up for it since.' Which I found really touching.

'Good for you,' I said to Keelie. 'We all like toys.'

'Just make sure you share them with the children,' Maggie said as we went through to the living room. For a moment I thought she was serious, then Keelie laughed.

'Like I'm going to bring my toys and not let them play with them. Doh!'

Keelie sat on the floor with Molly and Kit and began taking out the toys. Many of them were pre-school, brightly coloured and still in their original boxes. Puzzles, cars, miniature play people and dolls. They were clearly treasured. It said a lot about Keelie's neglected childhood that at thirteen she spent most of her pocket money on toys. Molly and Kit were enthralled.

'Have you thought about a career working with children?' I asked Keelie. 'I am sure you'd be very good at it.'

'So am I,' Maggie agreed. 'But she'll need to get some qualifications first, and that relies on her staying in school for longer than a day.'

But it fell on deaf ears. Keelie was too engrossed in playing to think about going to school.

CHAPTER THIRTEEN

NOT RESPONSIBLE

I drove to the council offices, parked outside and went in the main door and to the reception desk, where I gave my name and the reason for my visit. The receptionist entered my details on his computer and gave me a visitor's ID to loop around my neck. A digital display board on the wall behind reception showed room numbers and meetings. 'Is that showing the correct room?' I asked. I knew from experience it didn't always.

'Should be,' he said, glancing up at it.

I thanked him and made my way upstairs to the room on the second floor where the meeting was to be held. I was five minutes early as I knocked on the door and went in. Tess, Filip and Aneta were already there. They fell silent as I entered. I said hello and sat next to Tess. She and Filip said hello, but Aneta kept her gaze down. I sensed an atmosphere. The door opened and Tamara, the Guardian, came in.

'We're just waiting for the IRO,' Tess said.

'And Edith, my supervising social worker,' I added.

Filip stood. 'I've brought some of Molly's and Kit's toys,' he said. He came round to my side of the table, carrying a large holdall, which he placed by my chair.

'Thank you. They'll love playing with those again.'

'Have you come by car?' Tamara asked, appreciating that I'd struggle on the bus with the holdall.

'Yes.'

'How were the children after contact yesterday?' Aneta asked.

'Fine,' I said, looking at her and Filip. 'There's always a period of adjustment straight after contact, but that's to be expected.'

'They weren't ill?' she asked.

'No, they haven't been ill this week at all.'

'Like I told the doctors, it comes and goes,' she said.

One of the matters I wanted to raise at the review was the need for further testing so we could try to establish what was causing the children's sickness. But it wasn't appropriate to discuss that or any other matter relating to the children until the reviewing officer was present, and the review had officially begun. At ten minutes past two, ten minutes after the review should have begun, the door opened and Edith came in with a woman I took to be the reviewing officer, both looking a little flustered.

'Sorry we're late,' Edith said. 'We were sent to the wrong room.'

'The display board playing up again?' Tess asked. It was notorious.

'I was here early and have been waiting in an empty room,' the IRO said, clearly not pleased. She sat at the end of the table where she could see us all and opened her laptop. 'Are we expecting anyone else?' she asked.

'No,' Tess said.

'Let's begin then. My name is Mary Bridges and I am the Independent Reviewing Officer for this review. I shall be chairing and minuting the meeting. This is the first review for Molly and Kit, and I'd like to start by introducing ourselves.' Introductions are standard at all social services meetings, even if there aren't many present and all parties know each other. Mary's manner was efficient and direct. We went round the table, stating our names and roles as she typed: 'Tess, social worker for Molly and Kit.' 'Edith, supervising social worker for Cathy,' and so on.

Once we'd finished, the IRO thanked us all for coming and, addressing Filip and Aneta, said: 'The purpose of this review is to make sure everything is being done as it should be to help your children while they are in care, and that the care plan is appropriate and up to date. You will have an opportunity to speak and ask questions and we will hear from the children's social worker, foster carer and Guardian ad Litem. This review can make recommendations and set targets, but it can't overturn the judge's decision.' Filip nodded, while Aneta concentrated on the table.

The first review can be emotional and fraught, but IROs are skilled at chairing and not letting any discussion get out of hand. As I was expecting, the IRO asked me to speak first and say how Kit and Molly were settling in. The foster carer is usually asked to go first, as generally they have the most up-to-date information on the child or children. With my notes on the table in front of me, I sat upright in my chair and began with the positives.

'Molly and Kit are settling in well,' I said. 'They take an interest in what is going on around them and are generally eating and sleeping well. They like to spend time playing with me and my adult children. Molly and Kit don't attend nursery, so I arrange activities at home, and I also take them out each day.'

'What sort of activities?' the IRO asked, glancing up from typing.

'Painting, crayoning, Play-Doh, playing with puzzles, building bricks, the farmyard set. We have a local park and I take them there on the days when they don't have contact.'

'Do the children play together nicely?' the IRO asked. She would have been given information on the case prior to the review, so would very likely know that Aneta was claiming Molly hurt Kit.

'Generally, yes,' I said. 'Although recently we've had a few instances of Molly being unkind to Kit by taking his toys, pushing him and trying to scare him. I think it could be a bit of sibling jealousy and obviously I'm dealing with it.' I saw Aneta smile to herself as though she had been proved right.

The IRO nodded for me to continue.

'The children were sleeping together, but now Molly has her own room, and Kit's cot is in my room. He had his plaster cast removed and replaced by a splint on –' I gave the date. 'His arm is healing well and we have another follow-up appointment next month. I am keeping a food diary, as Tess asked, and noting everything the children have to eat and drink. So far nothing obvious has come to light that could be responsible for the children's allergic reactions. I think they should be tested further to establish what is causing the problem.'

'It doesn't have to be food, it could be something in the air,' Aneta said. 'Like pollen, germs or car fumes. That's why I'm so careful and don't take them out.' She'd said similar before.

'I'll say more about the children's health when I give my report,' Tess said. 'I've seen their medical records now.'

The IRO nodded, typed and then asked me to continue.

'I took the children for their medicals and the paediatrician said they were in good health, apart from the allergic reactions of course. They are of average weight and height and their hearing and eyesight are fine. Aneta has given me a bag of their medicines to be used as and when necessary. But so far I haven't had to use any.'

'Why is that?' the IRO asked.

'They haven't needed it. They are sick once and get over it. It's short and violent. I give them water and reassure them. The sickness isn't prolonged. If it was, or if one of them fitted or had difficulty breathing, as I understand has happened when they were at home, I'd seek medical help straight away. I do think we need to try to find the cause of their sickness,' I said again. 'It's very worrying and upsetting for the children.'

'I agree,' the IRO said. Then looked at Tess. 'I assume you'll be covering this when you give your report?'

'Yes,' Tess said.

I glanced at my notes and continued. 'I know Aneta has concerns about the children going out in case they are ill, but I think they would benefit from mixing with other children their age. I could find a playgroup where I could stay so I could keep an eye on them.' Aneta was already shaking her head.

'Over my dead body,' she said.

'We'll come back to this in a moment,' the IRO said. 'How is contact going?'

'Well,' I said. 'The children see their parents on Monday, Wednesday and Friday at the Family Centre. I take and collect them. The children look forward to seeing their parents and have a nice time.'

'How are they after contact?' the IRO asked.

'It takes them a little while to settle, but that is only to be expected. They have been sick after contact, and to begin with I thought it might be emotional upset, but I'm not so sure now.'

'Why should seeing me make my children sick?' Aneta demanded.

'It's a very emotional time and children can react in different ways,' I said gently. 'Some children cry, some are naughty, while others show it in a physical way, for example, by wetting themselves. That's not to say they aren't pleased to see their parents, just that it can be difficult for them.'

'Are you receiving details of the food and drink consumed at contact from the supervisor?' Tess asked me.

'Yes. It usually arrives a day or so after and I enter it in the food diary.'

'I always show the contact supervisor what I'm giving Molly and Kit,' Aneta said more reasonably.

'Thank you,' Tess said.

The IRO finished typing and then asked, 'Has either child suffered any accident or injury while they've been in your care?' It's a standard question.

'Nothing serious,' I said. 'Just the occasional fall when they are running and playing. I've noted it all in my log.'

'They bruise easily,' Aneta said, which she'd claimed before.

'Thank you,' the IRO said. 'Is there anything else you want to tell this review, Cathy?'

I glanced at my notes. 'Only that I've started a Life Story Book for each child.'

'What's that?' Filip asked quietly.

Tess explained: 'We ask foster carers to keep a record of the children's time with the carer, which they take with them when they leave. It usually includes photographs and memorabilia with a short written narrative about what the children have been doing. It's to give the child something to look back on in the future and supplements their own memories. It's especially important for very young children who may not remember their time in care.'

Filip nodded. He seemed very subdued, while Aneta was more composed than I'd imagined she would be – not upset but angry. She had some handwritten notes in front of her.

'Thank you, Cathy,' the IRO said. 'We'll hear from Tess next, then the Guardian ad Litem, Aneta and Filip, and Cathy's supervising social worker.'

Edith sat beside me taking notes, as was the Guardian. All those present would have a copy of the minutes once they were circulated.

Tess began by stating when the children had come into care and gave the type of care order. There was no need for her to go into the background and the reasons for the children being brought into care, as everyone present would know what they needed to, and that wasn't the purpose of the review. 'My main concern at this point', Tess continued, 'is to try to establish why Molly and Kit are sick so often. Cathy keeps me regularly updated. I've now had a chance to look at the children's medical records. They've had many tests for a range of allergies and they've all come back negative. Some of those tests would have been very uncomfortable for the children – one involved a twenty-four-hour blood test with an overnight stay in hospital. It must have been distressing for the children to have been subjected to all these tests and I am reluctant to ask for more at present. Cathy is monitoring what the children eat and drink, so I'd like to see if the food diary reveals anything before further testing. Perhaps we can look at the situation again in a month's time.'

'Suits me,' Aneta said. 'But the food diary won't show anything.' She fiddled with the sheet of paper she had in front of her. Filip glanced at her but didn't say anything.

'So to be clear,' the IRO said, 'none of the tests on either of the children gave any indication as to what could be causing them to be ill?'

'That's right,' Tess said. 'Other than eliminating possible causes. They all came back clear, including tests for a number of genetic conditions. There are more tests that can be done, but I'd like to wait on that for now.'

The IRO nodded and typed. Once she'd finished, Tess continued.

'I think Molly and Kit would benefit from more contact with other children their age. It's usual for children of Kit's age to be attending a mother and toddler group, and at three and a half most children Molly's age are attending some form of playgroup or nursery. She will start school in a year and will be ill-prepared if she hasn't attended any pre-school group.' I saw Aneta's fingers tighten around the paper she was holding. 'However,' Tess continued, 'I know Aneta is anxious about the children being exposed to germs, so I would like to review this again in a month too, by which time I hope the food diary will have yielded some results. If we can establish what exactly is causing the children to be sick, Aneta needn't worry about them going outside or coming into contact with other children.' I thought Tess was relying rather heavily on the food diary. Was it really going to reveal what hospital tests had not? I doubted it.

'I'm reporting all this to my solicitor,' Aneta suddenly said icily, calm and controlled. 'We are seeing him next week. We're going back to court and my children will be returned to me. Then we'll sue the lot of you.' Parents of children in care are advised to seek legal advice. If they can't afford to fund it, they can apply for legal aid.

'Which part of what Tess has said has upset you?' the IRO asked in a conciliatory manner.

'All of it!' Aneta snapped. 'You have taken my children, and now you're going to make them more ill by sending them to nursery.'

'That isn't what Tess said,' the IRO pointed out. 'She said that she felt the children would benefit from mixing with their peers, as most children do. But she recognizes you have concerns and is suggesting we look at the situation again in a month, by which time hopefully we will have a better understanding of what is making the children sick.'

I expected Aneta to retaliate but she didn't. She sat back in her chair, folded her arms across her chest and glared at Tess as if challenging her. It was quite threatening and unsettling and not something I'd seen in her before. Filip had his eyes down, concentrating on the table, and kept quiet.

Tess ignored Aneta's condemnatory stare and continued by saying that contact was positive for the children and would continue on Monday, Wednesday and Friday, three till five o'clock, as it allowed Filip to work the early shift.

'That suits you?' the IRO asked him.

'Yes,' he said, glancing up.

The IRO asked Tess if there were any changes to the care plan – a standard question – and she replied that there weren't. So that meant the children would be staying in foster care long term, although I knew care plans could change. Tess confirmed that the children had settled in with me and that she had visited them in placement. Aneta was still staring at Tess intimidatingly. It was cold and threatening, but Tess seemed unfazed. I guessed that as a social worker she'd probably seen worse from angry parents.

Tamara, the Guardian, went next. She stated her role, said she had visited all parties and at this stage she was still gathering information.

The IRO thanked her for coming and looked at the parents. 'Would you like to speak next?'

Now that she'd been given the chance, I expected Aneta to vent her anger, but instead she lowered her arms and dissolved into tears. 'You keep blaming me,' she sobbed. 'My children were ill and I took them to the doctor's and the hospital and now I'm being punished. I don't deserve this. My life's not worth living any more.'

Filip went to put his arm around her to comfort her, but she threw it off, then suddenly pushed back her chair, stood and fled from the room.

'Sorry,' Filip said and went after her. The door closed behind him.

'Oh dear. She is upset,' the IRO said. We sat in uncomfortable silence, waiting for their return for about five minutes as the IRO typed – I assumed catching up with her note-taking. Then she said to Tess, 'Can you check they're OK?'

Tess left the room and the rest of us remained quiet. She returned a few minutes later and said Aneta and Filip were nowhere to be seen. She assumed they'd left the building.

'It's a pity they didn't feel they could stay,' the IRO said with a sigh. 'I'll minute that the parents left the review at two-fifty.'

'I'll phone them when we've finished here,' Tess said.

'Thank you,' the IRO said, and then looked at Edith. 'Would you like to add anything to the review? Then we'll wind up, as the parents aren't here to give their views.'

Edith said, 'My role is to supervise and monitor Cathy in all aspects of fostering. I visit her regularly and check her record-keeping is up to date and advise her on further training. I have observed Cathy with the children and am satisfied she is able to meet their needs.' Concise and to the point, it was pretty much what she said at all my reviews.

The IRO thanked her, then asked if anyone had anything else to say. No one did, so she asked if there were any complaints, which was another standard question. I thought if Aneta had stayed she would have something to say – her notes were still on the table. The IRO entered 'no complaints', then confirmed she'd received the children's and my review forms. She set the date for the next review in three months' time and, thanking us all for coming, closed the meeting.

I picked up the holdall containing the children's toys and left the room first. I made my way downstairs, deep in thought. Aneta had gone from being angry to distraught, which I supposed was understandable. Yet I didn't feel sorry for her as I had done when she'd been upset before. Perhaps I was being unkind, but her reaction seemed excessive and staged to me. Filip was the one I now felt sorry for. He seemed a decent, hard-working guy who was completely out of his depth and struggling to cope. His little gesture when he'd tried to comfort Aneta and she'd pushed him away had touched me. I was pretty sure, that whatever had happened at home to the children, he almost certainly wasn't responsible for and probably hadn't even been aware of it.

CHAPTER FOURTEEN

HOSPITAL

I drove home still deep in thought, now about all the tests Molly and Kit had been subjected to. It must have been very traumatic for them. I think parents and carers often suffer more than the child when they are poorly. I know I do. It's awful to watch a little one ill or in pain. You'd do anything to make them better. It must have been agonizing for Aneta and Filip to have to stand by and watch Molly and Kit undergo all those tests, some of which Tess had said had been very uncomfortable, and involved blood tests and a stay in hospital. While I'd initially asked for more tests to try to identify the cause of their allergies, I now felt Tess had made the right decision in not requesting them yet. She had seen their medical records, I hadn't, and I didn't want them to suffer another battery of tests if it wasn't completely necessary.

When I arrived home, I was greeted by Keelie's voice trilling from our kitchen-diner. 'Hi, Cathy! Welcome home. We're in here! Come and see what we've done!'

I steeled myself for what awaited me. 'Be with you in a moment,' I replied. 'Just taking off my coat and shoes. Can't wait to see!'

'I think you can,' Maggie called out dryly. I smiled to myself. Keelie was certainly a character, but there was no hidden side to her. What you saw was what you got.

Leaving the holdall containing the children's toys in the hall, I went into our kitchen-diner. They were all seated around the table modelling with Play-Doh. Keelie was in between Molly and Kit, and Maggie sat opposite.

'Wonderful,' I said. 'You have been busy!' The table was covered with different-sized lumps of dough, and cutters, rollers, piping equipment and so forth for producing shapes. I kept all the modelling kit in a large box in the toy cupboard together with a plastic tablecloth, and someone had had the good sense to put the cloth on the table. The children were clearly enjoying themselves. Even little Kit was making something.

'This is a dog Kit made,' Keelie said, picking up a lump of blue dough to show me.

'Very good,' I said, kissing his forehead. He chuckled.

'And this is a horse Molly made.' Keelie pointed to a larger lump of purple-and-yellow streaked dough.

'Excellent,' I said admiringly, and kissed Molly.

'And this is supposed to be me,' Maggie said, picking up a round lump of bright-green dough that could have been in the shape of a head. 'Keelie made it.' Flecked with orange it had holes for eyes, massive nose and ears, and hair that stuck out like gorgon snakes. I laughed out loud. 'She loves me really,' Maggie said.

'So everything was all right while I was out?' I asked.

'Yes,' Keelie said before Maggie could answer. 'Although I had to tell Molly off for being unkind to Kit.' I glanced at Maggie, who winked, signalling it wasn't anything too awful.

'What did I tell you?' Keelie now asked Molly.

'That I have to be kind to my little brother,' Molly said dutifully.

'That's right. And if you're not kind to him a dragon will eat you, won't it?'

Molly nodded. It wasn't a subtle approach to managing sibling rivalry and not one recommended in the foster carer's handbook, but it appeared to be working. Molly was now sharing everything she had with Kit, passing him lumps of dough and the shape cutters. 'Good girl,' I said.

'Time to pack away,' Maggie said. 'We need to be going.'

Keelie groaned.

'Don't worry about packing away,' I said. 'Molly and Kit can play with the dough for a bit longer. I'll put it away later.'

'Are you sure?' Maggie asked, aware of the amount of clearing up that needed to be done.

'Yes. Thank you so much for all your help.'

'Have you got us a box of chocolates?' Keelie asked.

'That's not very subtle,' Maggie chastised.

I went into the kitchen and took the box of chocolates I'd bought for them from the cupboard. 'I told you not to,' Maggie said as I placed them in her hand.

Keelie hugged both children goodbye and relieved Maggie of the chocolates. I saw them out. I returned to Molly and Kit and sat at the table with them to play, but now Keelie had gone the Play-Doh wasn't so much fun and presently they'd had enough. I helped Kit from the table and then fetched the holdall containing their toys from the hall. They were delighted to be reunited with them and played while I packed away the dough equipment and then began preparing dinner. It was only after playing for a while that Molly asked, 'Have you been to my house?'

'No, love. I had to go to a meeting and your mummy and daddy were there. They brought the toys with them.'

Molly thought about this for a moment and then asked, 'If I don't share my toys with Kit, will a dragon eat me?'

'No, love, but it's kind to share, isn't it?'

Another silence and then she asked, 'Will my mummy be eaten by a dragon if she does bad things?'

'No, there are no such things as dragons. What makes you say that?'

She shrugged. 'Don't know.' She continued playing and I thought no more about it.

At the review Aneta had said, as she had before, that the children's illnesses came and went quickly, which was what I was finding. Having had nearly a week illness-free, I was starting to think we might have turned a corner, although I didn't know why, but on Saturday afternoon Molly was suddenly violently sick. Without any warning, she threw up once and was then fine. I reassured her she was all right, cleaned her up, then carefully went through the food diary. I saw that the sausage casserole I'd made was the only dish they hadn't had before, so I underlined it in red. I thought about where we'd been that day, as Aneta had said it might not be food but something they came into contact with that they were allergic to, but nothing obvious showed up. We'd been to our local supermarket and then the park, but Molly had been to both places before and been fine. Had there been a new allergen present that hadn't been there before? It seemed unlikely, but I was running out of ideas. She was wearing a new dress I'd bought, but I'd washed it first, as I did all children's clothes before they wore them for the first time, and I'd already ruled out the washing powder.

As well as noting all this in the food diary, I entered a shorter version in my log, and once the children were in bed that night I emailed Tess an update. I also researched online again, this time *uncommon allergies*, and found that some people were allergic to citrus, spice and latex, as well as apples and bananas. It was very rare but a few people were allergic to nearly everything and hardly left the house. But that wasn't true of Molly and Kit. Their allergies seemed specific, and in between the attacks they were well. Tess must have read my email that evening at home because she replied half an hour later. *Can you double check everything Molly had to eat and drink today, including brand names? Different brands sometimes contain different ingredients. Also additives. Please list them all.*

It took me ages, but if it showed what was causing the problem it would be time well spent. Many of the products contained a gluten warning, but I'd already established Molly and Kit weren't gluten intolerant, as they'd had plenty of food containing gluten that had never caused either of them to be sick. The orange juice drink her mother had sent from contact on Friday, which Molly had finished off that afternoon, was a different brand to the one I bought, but it was the one her mother always used, so she'd had it plenty of times before without a problem. I always stored the opened drinks and food that came from contact in the fridge and threw them away if they weren't consumed within the time stated, so it couldn't be that. I listed all the ingredients in everything Molly had eaten that day, and then before I went to bed I emailed Tess saying I'd done as she'd asked and nothing had come to light so far, but I'd keep listing the ingredients. It was exhausting and worrying, and I lay in bed wondering if I'd missed something obvious, but what could it be?

On a positive note, both children were sleeping very well and I loved waking in the morning and seeing Kit in his cot. Sometimes he was awake before me and would be standing up and grinning at me. Occasionally he was upset and wanted his mummy, especially after contact, but that was only to be expected. Molly was sometimes fretful too after contact.

Seeing their parents was a reminder of home, but generally they'd both settled in.

September slipped into October and an autumnal chill could be felt in the air. Adrian and Paula saw their father on the first Sunday of the month. Now they were adults they made their own the arrangements to see him, and sometimes spoke on the phone in between. On average they saw him every six weeks. Lucy saw her birth mother about once a year.

Our routine continued and, wrapped up warm, I took Molly and Kit out each day if they didn't have contact, often to our local park. They loved watching the squirrels burying acorns for the winter. Kit chased them and was amazed at the speed with which they disappeared up the trees.

'I wish I could do that!' Molly said, peering into the branches overhead.

'So do I,' I laughed. 'You'd have a good view from up there.'

'I want to be a squirrel,' Molly said. She picked up an acorn and, holding it like a squirrel, pretended to nibble it. Kit copied her.

'So I'm looking after two squirrels instead of children,' I said. 'Acorn pie for dinner.'

Molly looked at me seriously for a moment before she realized I was joking and giggled.

As well as going to the park, I also began taking the children to a soft-play activity centre a short drive away that had a ball pond. They loved all the brightly coloured balls and apparatus and could play for hours alongside each other and other pre-school children. Generally, Molly treated Kit kindly, but sometimes she pushed him over or snatched something from him. Whether she'd ever intentionally caused him serious injury while at home, as Aneta was claiming, I'd no idea, but I doubted it. I was convinced it was sibling rivalry and if she had hurt Kit badly enough to warrant him going to hospital then it was because she'd had no idea of the outcome of her actions. Part of parenting is teaching children outcomes. When they were with other children, Molly was protective of Kit and looked out for him, and I praised her.

Aneta was hardly saying anything to me at the Family Centre. She asked at the start of contact if the children had been ill, but that was all. Filip talked to me more, and brought the children to me at the end, while Aneta busied herself by putting on her coat with her back to me. Filip always said they'd had a nice time and thanked me for what I was doing for the children, which was nice of him. Molly must have told him about the places we'd been to, because he said he wished he could join us, as he would love to see the children playing and having fun, but he appreciated that wasn't possible. I felt sorry for him. He clearly loved his children and I think he now regretted not spending more time with them in the past. He'd cut back and changed his working hours so he could attend every contact. He seemed to find it more difficult to say goodbye than Aneta did now. She said, 'Bye, Molly and Kit,' and, with no hug, reached for her coat. It was sad, but I thought it was probably her way of coping with the separation.

I was taking lots of photographs of Molly and Kit, as I did all the children I fostered. I put some in their Life Story Books and also gave a set to the parents at contact, so they could see what their children had been doing. It's considered good fostering practice. Filip was always grateful and looked at them straight away, but Aneta seemed to resent it and refused to look. I could understand why. While it was nice for her to have the photos, it was a harsh reminder that the children were doing these things without her and enjoying themselves. I started to give the photos to Filip in an envelope, so it was up to him if and when he shared them with his wife.

The second week in October, Kit had his follow-up appointment at the hospital to have his arm checked. It had all healed nicely and he no longer had to wear the splint. He was a bit upset at being parted from it, so once home I made a pretend splint and put it on one of the teddy bears. Molly then got out all the dolls and soft toys and began role playing doctors and nurses. She was very good at it, I guessed from all the visits she'd made to the hospital with her mother. She took the dolls' temperatures, looked in their ears, eyes and mouths, and felt their tummies. She asked them if they had a pain and to point to it and how often they were sick.

'Lots,' the doll told her.

'Good girl,' the mummy doll said.

'Do you like visiting the hospital?' the teddy bear asked.

'No, but Mummy does,' the child doll replied. 'She puts on her best clothes and lipstick.' Which of course must have been part of Molly's game, for if your child is sick enough to have to go to hospital as an emergency, you haven't got time to change or put on lipstick. You get there as soon as possible by car or ambulance.

The following week, Tess and Edith paid their scheduled visits, on Tuesday and Thursday when we didn't have contact. Naturally our main discussion centred around the children's health and the sporadic bouts of sickness, the cause of which I was no nearer to finding. I showed them the food diary, which had now grown to a ring-binder folder that I added to daily.

'I expect it's a food additive,' Edith said helpfully, perusing the pages and pages of ingredients I'd carefully written out.

'Yes, but which one?' I said. 'Some of them appear many times but only caused a problem once.'

'Perhaps it's a combination of additives,' she said. Which of course might be true.

When Tess visited, I asked if she was now considering getting the children tested some more. She'd said at the review she wanted to wait a month to see if the food diary revealed anything. Nearly a month had passed and it hadn't. I said I appreciated it was going to be uncomfortable for Molly and Kit to undergo further testing, but I'd be with them and I really didn't see an alternative. She agreed and said she'd speak to the parents and then the consultant.

I didn't hear anything further from Tess for nearly a week and when I next spoke to her she said Aneta wouldn't give her consent for the children to have further tests unless she was present at the hospital, which Tess didn't feel was appropriate. Tess said she was trying to speak to the consultant and once she'd spoken to him, she'd make a decision on further testing. I also asked her about taking the children to a playgroup. I'd found one locally that was on a Thursday morning for two hours where the parent or carer stayed. I'd previously emailed the details to her. She told me that Aneta remained strongly opposed to Molly and Kit mixing with other children until we knew what was causing them to be ill – to avoid unnecessary exposure to germs. This seemed reasonable on the surface until you considered she'd also said the children weren't to have any more tests unless she was present. So how were we supposed to progress? The food diary hadn't shown anything, and, from what I knew at this stage in the care proceedings, the social services would have to apply to court for permission to have the children tested if the parents withheld their permission.

I was at a complete loss as to what to do next and the strain was taking its toll on me, although I tried not to show it. Clearly Molly and Kit had to eat, but after each meal or snack I was on tenterhooks, watching and waiting for any sign they were going to be sick. I had a long list of suspect foods that I avoided, and more with question marks beside them that appeared to have caused one of the children to be sick at one time but not another time. Without further medical tests, I didn't see how we were ever going to identify what was causing them to be ill.

At the end of October both children were sick every day for a week and on the Friday evening Kit developed a blue rash and had difficulty breathing. I called an ambulance and while we waited for it to arrive, on the advice of the call handler, I gave him a puff of the inhaler. The ambulance took fifteen minutes to come, during which time Molly had recovered and Kit's breathing was easing. I explained the situation to the paramedics and that I was their foster carer as they examined both children in the living room. Molly was back to normal, but Kit still had a rash and the paramedics decided to take him into hospital. I went with him in the ambulance while Lucy and Paula stayed with Molly. Adrian was out. I was so stressed and worried that as I sat in the rear of the ambulance with Kit cradled in my arms I burst into tears. The paramedic was lovely.

'I can appreciate why you're upset,' she said, patting my arm. 'The children have been ill so much. Hopefully the doctors will be able to get to the bottom of it this time.'

I nodded dumbly.

On arrival, we were taken straight into a cubicle and Kit was checked by a nurse. She stayed with him while I went to the front desk to register him, where I was asked for his full name, date of birth and contact details. They had his previous address, so I gave mine and that of our doctor. I returned to Kit, and while we waited to see a doctor I telephoned the duty social worker, as foster carers are supposed to when a child is in hospital. I also phoned home, where Lucy and Paula were waiting anxiously for any news. I told them we were waiting to see a doctor and that I'd be in touch again when I knew more.

The young doctor we saw had access to Kit's medical records and he commented that Kit had had episodes like this before, which I knew. He examined Kit, and although Kit was fast recovering he decided to keep him in overnight for observation. We were taken to a side room in the children's ward and I spent the night in the chair by his cot, while a nurse checked him every hour. By 6 a.m. the rash had gone and he was jumping around and eager to be off.

We both had some breakfast and I then brought in some toys from the main children's ward while we waited for the doctor to discharge him. It was 10 a.m. before he arrived – the same doctor we'd seen the evening before – and, having examined Kit, he said he was well enough to go home. He also made a referral to the paediatric allergy clinic and would send a copy of the letter to our doctor. I asked for a copy to be sent to the social worker too, which is normal practice for looked-after children. I then telephoned home and Adrian said he'd come to collect us in his car. I reminded him to bring the children's car seats from my car. It was just after 11 a.m. when we arrived home and as we went in Paula came into the hall, holding Molly's hand.

'Thank you for all your help, I couldn't have managed without you,' I told Paula. It was true. But she was looking very worried. 'Is everything all right?' I asked her.

'No, Mum. Lucy's gone back to bed. She's been ever so sick.'

'Has she?' Adrian asked, surprised. 'She was fine when I left.'

'It came on all of a sudden. Just like Molly and Kit.'

CHAPTER FIFTEEN

A BREAKTHROUGH?

I left Paula and Adrian looking after Kit and Molly downstairs and hurried upstairs to Lucy's room. I couldn't remember the last time she'd been sick. She never was. Despite working with children, she didn't pick up the illnesses that seemed to go around the nursery, even in winter when many of them had coughs, colds and runny noses.

Lucy's bedroom door was ajar and I knocked and went in. She was lying on her bed, fully clothed, awake but very pale. A plastic bucket was beside her bed.

'You poor dear,' I said, going over and sitting on her bed. 'I wonder what brought that on. How do you feel now?' I stroked a loose strand of hair away from her forehead. She didn't feel hot, as though she had a temperature.

'I'm a bit better now,' she said. 'But it was horrible. I hate being sick.'

'I know, love. How many times were you sick?' The bucket was empty.

'Once, but it was very violent. I felt fine this morning. I had breakfast and then just after Adrian left to collect you and Kit I had a drink. About fifteen minutes later I felt very sick. I just made it to the loo in time.'

'What did you have for breakfast?' I asked, wondering if that was the cause.

'Scrambled eggs on toast.'

'Did Molly have them?'

'No. She had porridge. The eggs tasted fine, but I can't think what else it could be. Unless I've picked up something at work. One of the children was sick yesterday.'

'That'll be it, I'm sure. You'd have smelt it if the eggs were off. You can't miss it.'

'How's Kit?' she asked, propping herself up on the pillow.

'Back to normal. The doctor is making a referral to the allergy clinic. I'll discuss it with Tess. Do you want anything?'

'Just a glass of water, please. I'll be down soon, and can you take the bucket? I don't need it now. Paula put it there in case I was sick again.'

I kissed Lucy's cheek and, taking the bucket, I went downstairs and poured her a glass of water. Half an hour later she was up and about, the colour having returned to her cheeks, and feeling more or less back to normal, although she was worried in case she was sick again. Molly was worried too and kept watching her. 'You were sick like me,' she said.

'Everyone is sick sometimes,' Lucy said. 'Thankfully I'm not ill often.'

'I am,' Molly said.

'Yes, and I am trying to find out what is causing it so we can stop it happening,' I reassured her again.

It had crossed my mind for one horrible moment that possibly Molly and Kit had passed on a communicable disease to Lucy, but I couldn't think what it could be with these symptoms. Like all foster carers, we practised safer caring, as Lucy did at the nursery. So if a child was sick or soiled themselves, we put on rubber gloves to clear it up, thoroughly cleaned the area with hot water and disinfectant, and hot washed any clothes or bed linen. Likewise, when we changed Kit's nappy we did so using disposable gloves. I thought it was highly unlikely Lucy had caught something from Molly or Kit, but when I wrote up my log for the day I included that Lucy had been sick once in the morning but had recovered quickly. I also emailed Tess the same, adding that I felt it was essential we found out what was causing the children to be ill, not only for their sakes, but for that of anyone they came into contact with, as no one knew for certain they weren't carriers of a contagious disease.

Exhausted from no sleep the night before, I went to bed early on Saturday and slept like a log. I woke on Sunday morning to see Kit smiling happily at me from his cot. We were back to normal.

We all had breakfast together and then Adrian went out to spend the day with Kirsty. It was raining hard and forecast to continue for most of the day. Kit was full of energy, which needed to be burnt off, so I put on some music for him to dance to, as I'd done before. Most children like to dance and they seem to have a natural rhythm, but Kit's dancing was very enthusiastic and athletic. He jumped up and down on the spot with his hands in the air as if he was suspended on elastic. We laughed and clapped. I held his hands so he could jump even higher, while Lucy and Paula danced with Molly. It was great fun and we played the old favourites like 'Dancing Queen' by ABBA and 'One Love' by Bob Marley. Presently Lucy popped into the kitchen to get a drink and then re-joined us. We carried on dancing but she suddenly dropped Molly's hand and cried, 'I'm going to be sick, Mum!' And fled the room.

I left Paula to look after Molly and Kit and went after Lucy. She was in the kitchen bent over the sink and retching.

157

I held her hair away from her face until she was sick – a clear orange liquid. I reassured her and passed her a tissue. Straightening, she wiped her mouth.

'It was that juice, Mum,' she said. 'That's what I had just now.'

'The apple juice?' I asked, surprised.

'No, the orange juice.'

'I didn't think we had any.' It was on my list to buy. I turned to the fridge and opened the door. 'This one?' I asked, taking out the open litre packet of orange juice. She nodded. 'It's Molly and Kit's.'

'Sorry, I didn't know.'

'It doesn't matter,' I said.

Food and drink that was sent from contact I kept specifically for the children. It was important, as food is not just about eating but nurturing and love, and it's one of the ways parents can maintain a bond with their children while they're not living with them. It didn't really matter that Lucy had inadvertently drunk some of their juice on this occasion, apart from the fact that it had made her sick.

'I had some yesterday as well before I was sick,' she said, splashing cold water on her face.

'The same juice?'

'Yes. I thought it was ours.'

I looked at the packet for the use-by date and found it still had six months to go. I checked the ingredients. It was a different brand to the juice I usually bought, but it contained only water and *orange juice from concentrate*. That meant the oranges had been compressed to remove excess water before being packaged and transported, and had then had water added in the destination country before being sent to the shops. There were no additives listed.

'Perhaps it's been open a long time,' Lucy suggested, wiping her face and coming to stand beside me. She knew, as I did, that most products had to be consumed within a certain time after opening. Next to the use-by date were the words: *Store in a cool, dry place and consume within five days of opening.*

'I suppose it's possible it's been open a long time prior to Aneta taking it to contact,' I said. I wouldn't know, as most of the food and drink the children brought home from contact was open or half-eaten. 'Do you still feel sick?'

'No.'

I poured her a glass of water and she went to sit quietly for a while. I wasn't convinced the juice drink was responsible – it smelt fine to me – but to be on the safe side I tipped the last of it down the sink and threw the packet in the bin. I thought, as I had when Lucy had been sick the day before, that it was likely she had picked up a bug from work and it was still in her system. An hour later she was fully recovered and well enough to meet her friends and go to the cinema as she'd arranged.

On Monday our weekday routine began again and in the afternoon I took Kit and Molly to contact. I saw them into the room, said a general hello to Aneta, Filip and the contact supervisor, and left. Molly must have mentioned that Lucy had been ill, for when I collected the children at the end of contact Aneta called over, 'I hear your daughter was sick.'

'Yes, she was,' I said. 'But she seems fine now.' Aneta was busy buttoning up her coat.

'Do you know what caused it?' she asked, concentrating on her coat.

'No, not really.'

Then, as cold as ice, she looked up and said, 'Good, because now you know how I feel.'

I was taken aback and I saw the contact supervisor look at her. Aneta's comment was harsh and suggested I hadn't shown any empathy in respect of her children's illnesses, which I had. I was doing all I could to find out what was causing their sickness, and I had said on many occasions how worrying it was. Regardless of whether Aneta or Filip had intentionally harmed the children as the social services had suspected, I certainly appreciated how worried they must be in respect of their children's health.

I didn't reply. Aneta had turned away and Filip brought Molly and Kit to me with a carrier bag of snacks and drinks. 'I'm sorry your daughter was ill,' he said quietly. 'I hope she is fully recovered now.'

'Thank you,' I said.

I called goodbye and we left. Molly must have heard her mother's animosity towards me, for as I helped her and Kit into the car she threw her arms around me and said, 'I like you, even if Mummy doesn't. So does Kit.'

I was really touched and a lump rose in my throat. 'Thank you, love, that is kind. I like you and Kit too, lots and lots.'

I cooked fish, mashed potatoes and peas for dinner that evening, all of which Molly and Kit had had before. I made a parsley sauce to go with the fish but didn't give it to the children. I doubted they would like it anyway, but I was keeping their food simple until we knew what was causing them to be ill. We all ate together and Sammy, smelling the fish, sat beside Kit's chair, aware there could be bits dropping. Kit was good at feeding himself now and wanted to do it, but at his age he hadn't yet developed the hand–eye coordination that Molly had, so bits dropped off his spoon. If they fell into his bib, which had a scoop, he retrieved them, but if they fell to the floor I cleared them up after the meal and threw them away. However, if we had fish, Sammy always appeared. As we ate I saw Kit looking down at Sammy from his chair, fascinated, then he intentionally dropped some food for him.

'That's for you,' I said, 'not Sammy.'

He grinned mischievously and, when he thought I wasn't looking, dropped some more. Typical toddler doing as he wanted.

'That's your dinner, not Sammy's,' I said again. I could tell from Kit's expression he was going to do it again. Time for a little positive reinforcement, I thought – also known as a bribe. 'Eat your dinner and then you can help me give Sammy his dinner,' I told Kit. It worked. Apart from a few peas, which genuinely rolled off his spoon and onto the floor, he finished the lot.

Kit was generally a good eater. Molly tended to be fussy, as she worried about being sick, which was hardly surprising given the number of times she had been sick after eating or drinking something. I'd yet to speak to Tess about Kit's overnight stay in hospital last Friday and the referral to the allergy clinic. I'd updated her by email and I assumed she'd be in touch at some point when she had the chance.

For dessert we had homemade rice pudding, which we'd all had before. Adrian, Paula, Lucy and I had a blob of jam on it, but I didn't put any on Molly's and Kit's. Shop-bought jam was one of the suspect foods on my list and I hadn't yet worked out which ingredient could be causing the children a problem. Once we'd finished dinner, both Kit and Molly helped me feed Sammy, and then around 7.30 p.m. I began Kit's bath and bedtime routine while Paula looked after Molly downstairs, playing with her and reading her stories. I ran Kit's bath and he played in it for a while, then, once he was in his pyjamas, I sat on the edge of my bed and read him some stories, before laying him in his cot. Sometimes he didn't settle the first time and stood up, so I waited on the landing, ready to go in and resettle him if necessary. Once he was asleep, he usually slept through till morning. As I waited I could hear Paula's voice coming from the living room as she read Molly a story. Adrian was in his room working on his laptop, and Lucy was in her room talking on her phone. Suddenly the calm of the evening was shattered when Paula cried, 'Mum! Come quickly! Molly's been sick.'

I rushed downstairs and into the living room. Molly and Paula were on the sofa, a book between them and a puddle on the carpet in front of them.

'Sorry, I couldn't get the bucket in time,' Paula said, standing and grimacing.

'Don't worry. Just be careful you don't step in it,' I said to her, then to Molly, 'Are you going to be sick again?' She shook her head and I helped her from the sofa and around the mess on the carpet.

'Could you give her a drink of water while I clean the carpet, please?' I asked Paula.

'She isn't going to be sick again, is she?'

'No, I don't think so.'

I filled a bucket with hot water and disinfectant and set about cleaning the carpet, wondering what on earth had caused Molly to be sick this time. It had to be something I'd given her for dinner, but what? She and Kit had had it all before, and this time – to be on the safe side – I'd left out the vanilla extract and cinnamon I usually put in rice pudding. Kit had eaten exactly the same as Molly, but only she had been sick. It was ridiculous and very, very worrying, I thought, as I scrubbed the carpet. I just couldn't work it out. Again, I felt sorry for the parents who'd struggled with this for so long. I decided that first thing in the morning I would phone Tess and push the referral to the allergy clinic the doctor had mentioned, even it if meant going against the parents. This couldn't be allowed to continue.

Paula reappeared with Molly. 'Shall I take her up to bed now?'

'Yes, please, love. Can you run her bath and I'll be up as soon as I've finished here? Molly hasn't had anything to eat since dinner, has she?' I asked.

'No, only a drink. She wanted some of her chocolate milkshake.'

'OK, and that's all?'

'Yes.'

On their way upstairs I heard Paula reassuring Molly that she wouldn't be sick again and I continued to clean the carpet. The chocolate milkshake Molly had drunk had come from contact and I now began to wonder if that – like the juice – had been opened some time ago, been stored incorrectly and had gone off. Could it really be something that simple was causing the children to be sick? It was possible, I supposed. I knew Aneta and Filip were on a tight budget and perhaps they kept food and drink longer than was safe. Perhaps they didn't own a fridge or freezer? I didn't know, but it seemed incredible that they hadn't considered this possibility before when the children had been so ill at home, although sometimes the obvious is overlooked. However, at present, I just had the two drinks to go on and that wasn't enough. Before I raised this with Tess I'd have to have more evidence.

I fetched clean cloths and patted the carpet dry and then went upstairs to see to Molly. She was in the bath and I thanked Paula, who went off to do some college work.

Once I'd settled Molly in bed I returned downstairs and sat at the table in the kitchen-diner with the food diary. I began going through it, looking at all the times when Molly and/or Kit had been sick and what they'd had to eat or drink. I hadn't been noting where the food had come from – contact or if I'd bought it – as there'd been no reason to until now. If I was correct about the way the food and drink had been stored, then the children would only have been sick after consuming something from contact. Some of the instances where food had come from contact I remembered, but others I wasn't sure. Some were obvious because the food that had made them ill wasn't something I ever bought; for example, ready-made milkshakes and Pot Noodles. I could also include the times the children had been ill straight after contact – before I'd given them anything, and I knew from the contact supervisor what they'd had to eat and drink. As well as marking the examples in the food diary, I copied the details onto a separate sheet of paper, ready for when I told Tess.

It was time-consuming, but after an hour and a half I had twenty-two definites – instances of when the children's sickness was directly linked to something they'd either consumed at contact or had brought home and had. I set my pen down and allowed myself a small moment of congratulation. I was excited, there was no other word for it. At last we were getting somewhere and I'd phone Tess with what I'd discovered first thing in the morning. The children were being made ill from food and drink that was being stored incorrectly at home.

CHAPTER SIXTEEN

MY FAULT

I lay awake that night running through what I was going to say to Tess the following morning. I worried how Aneta would take the news. I thought she'd feel even more resentful towards me than she did already. No mother would thank you for suggesting she could be responsible – even inadvertently – for making her children ill. But if I was right (I was certain I was) and I'd identified the reason Molly and Kit were ill so often, then I assumed that once she and Filip had got over the shock they would be relieved and even grateful. Whether the children would be allowed to return home to live, I didn't know. There was still the outstanding matter of suspected non-accidental injuries, but that would be for the judge to decide based on the evidence presented at the final court hearing.

The following morning, once Adrian, Lucy and Paula had left, and the children were up and had had their breakfast, I settled them in the living room with lots of toys. I told Molly I had to make an important phone call and to play nicely with Kit. Taking the handset, I stood just outside the living-room door, where I could keep an eye on them but they couldn't easily overhear me. Molly, like most children her age, didn't miss much and I didn't want her hearing what I had to say to Tess. It was 9.15 a.m. and Tess was at her desk.

'I was going to phone you later,' she said apologetically. 'Sorry I haven't replied to your email. How is Kit?'

'All right now. He was kept in hospital overnight as a precaution, but he recovered quickly. I called an ambulance because he had difficulty breathing after being sick. The doctor has made a referral to the allergy clinic.'

'Yes, I saw that in your email. I'll have to talk to the parents again.'

'There's been a development since I sent that email,' I said, and felt my heart start to race as the adrenaline kicked in. 'Tess, I'm sure I've found what is causing Molly and Kit to be so sick.'

'Really? What?'

'I appreciate this is a bit sensitive, but I think it's the food and drink the parents are taking into contact that's gone off. I've been through the food diary and have found twenty-two instances where I can link food or drink consumed at contact to one or both of the children being sick.'

'Really?' she said again.

'Yes, they've either eaten it there or brought it back to finish here.' I then gave examples from the list I'd transcribed from the food diary and had copied onto a separate sheet. 'I became suspicious this weekend when my daughter, Lucy, twice had some of Kit and Molly's orange juice by mistake, and was violently sick soon both times. Then yesterday Molly was sick after finishing a milkshake that had come from contact. It's too much of a coincidence.'

There was a long silence before Tess asked, 'Have you kept any of the food and drink you think is responsible?'

'No. I threw it away. I didn't want to risk anyone having it.'

'Pity. We could have had it tested.'

'Sorry,' I said, 'I wasn't thinking.' I waited for something further to come from Tess, but when it didn't I added, 'I'm sure this is the answer, and if I'm right it would explain why it was happening at their home too before they came into care.'

'It could,' Tess said hesitantly. There was another pause, during which time I began to think she had doubts, as clearly she wasn't sharing my enthusiasm. 'The juice and milkshake were already open?' she asked at length.

'Yes. What they don't finish at contact Aneta sends back with them. They were in date, I checked, but I think they may have been open for too long prior to being taken to contact and perhaps not kept in a fridge. They didn't smell off, but that's not to say they weren't off. Presumably the contact supervisor will know if the packets and bottles were already open at the start of contact?'

'It's possible,' Tess said. 'But would food poisoning have caused Kit's breathing difficulty and a rash?'

'I don't know.'

Another pause and then Tess said, 'I'm going to have to discuss this with my line manager and get back to you.'

'OK.'

She said a quick goodbye, and I returned to the living room, my previous euphoria at having discovered the cause of the children's sickness largely gone. I could tell from Tess's voice that she had doubts and I felt a bit foolish. Perhaps I wasn't right. Yet there were issues that needed addressing quite quickly. The children had contact again tomorrow. Were they going to consume food and drink brought from home that could potentially make them ill again? Shouldn't Tess at least warn Aneta and Filip it could be a possibility? I would raise this with her when she telephoned back.

With no contact today we needed an outing, so I wrapped the children up warm, and with Kit in the stroller and Molly walking beside me we went to the High Street. I needed to buy groceries and also 5th November, Bonfire Night, was the day after tomorrow, and I wanted to buy some fireworks to left off in our garden. Molly and Kit were too young to be taken to a large organized display, they'd be frightened of the loud bangs and flashes of light, but a few pretty fireworks in our garden would be fine. We'd done this before; indeed, when my children had been younger we'd invited my parents, some friends and neighbours in for a little bonfire party with hotdogs and jacket potatoes. Now Lucy, Adrian and Paula tended to go to organized displays with their friends, usually on the following weekend.

As we walked towards the High Street I explained the significance of Bonfire Night to Molly and Kit. That over 400 years ago in 1605 a group of men led by Guy Fawkes planned to blow up the Houses of Parliament in London but were caught in time and we remembered the occasion with fireworks and bonfires. Molly nodded thoughtfully while Kit latched on to the word 'fireworks' and repeated it endlessly until Molly shouted at him. 'Yes, fireworks! You silly boy!'

'He's only little,' I reminded her. 'Children learn to talk by repeating words.'

The newsagent in the High Street stocked fireworks in the run-up to 5th November. They were in a locked glass display cabinet and Molly and Kit helped me choose some by pointing through the glass. Once home, I stored the bag of fireworks safely in the shed at the bottom of the garden. After lunch I showed Molly and Kit some YouTube videos of firework displays and then got out paper and crayons and encouraged them to draw and colour pictures of fireworks. Molly quickly became engaged in the project and produced page after page of colourful swirls, while Kit tried to eat the crayons and then scribbled on Molly's drawing, so she pushed him off his chair. I told her that was unkind and found him something else to do.

Tess didn't phone back until 4.30 p.m., and again I took the handset and moved out of earshot of the children. Her voice was calm and efficient. 'Thank you for what you did,' she began. 'I shall be observing contact tomorrow. Please take Molly and Kit as usual. There will be a temporary ban on all food and drink being brought into the Family Centre until we get to the bottom of this. I don't want Filip and Aneta singled out.'

'All right,' I said slowly, puzzled.

'I've spoken to the contact supervisor and the manager at the Family Centre. They can't be sure if any of the packets of food or drink were open when the parents brought them in. However, they are certain none of it was ever stored in the kitchen or fridge at the Family Centre.'

'Sorry, Tess, I must be missing something here,' I said, even more puzzled. 'Why should that matter?'

'It rules out the food and drink being contaminated in a communal area.'

'Oh, I see.'

'At this stage we can't be sure what is making Molly and Kit sick, only that it could come from food and drink the parents have taken in. I'll need to see your food diary. Can you bring it in to contact with you tomorrow?'

'Yes.' I thought I was starting to understand her reasoning now.

'I'll see you tomorrow, but don't say anything to Molly and Kit about this.'

'No, I won't.'

Tess said goodbye and I replaced the handset. 'Contaminated,' she'd said, whereas I'd used the term 'gone off'. I supposed it was the same in the end. It appeared Tess was now taking my concerns very seriously. Banning food and drink from being taken into the Family Centre was going to have an impact on all the families who used it, but I could see her logic. Also, she wanted my food diary, but I'd be lost without it. How would I know which foods to give the children and which to avoid? Then it dawned on me that if it was food that had gone off, resulting in a high level of bacteria that was causing the children to be sick, then they probably weren't allergic to anything. What a relief that would be! Not only for me, but for Aneta and Filip too. Although for the time being, until it was confirmed, I would err on the side of caution.

That evening when Molly and Kit were in bed and I had a moment, I looked online to see whether food poisoning could produce a rash and breathing difficulties. I found that in severe cases it could, although it was usually accompanied by a prolonged bout of vomiting. Molly, Kit and Lucy had only been sick once, but I supposed all cases were different. It seemed to strengthen my suggestion that it was food poisoning.

The following afternoon I put the food diary into my bag and we set off for the Family Centre, with Molly and Kit looking forward to seeing their parents again. Having been with me for two months, they were settled in the routine of seeing them every Monday, Wednesday and Friday. I was expecting this level of contact to remain the same until the final court hearing next year, when a decision would be made on where the children would live permanently. If it was decided they could return home then contact would be increased to every day with overnight stays in preparation for them returning. If it was decided they couldn't go home then contact would be drastically reduced, sometimes to only a few times a year, to allow the children to bond with their new family – whoever that would be.

As usual I parked outside the Family Centre five minutes early and we went in. A large handwritten notice fixed to an easel was positioned in reception where everyone could see it.

No food and drink to be brought
into contact until further notice.
Please hand food and drink you
have with you to the receptionist.
Sorry for the inconvenience.

A woman was remonstrating with the receptionist that she'd cooked a meal for her children and now they couldn't have it, and that the foster carer wouldn't have done them dinner as she knew they didn't need it on a Wednesday. The receptionist apologized and explained that some children had become ill after eating food on the premises and they were trying to find out what had caused it.

'My children aren't sick!' she said, annoyed.

I kept my head down and signed the Visitors' Book, feeling guilty that we were responsible for the upheaval. However, I knew that the foster carer concerned would give the children dinner if they hadn't eaten at contact. They wouldn't go hungry. As we went down the corridor towards Blue Room I heard the receptionist say that the centre would be providing a drink and a snack for all the children, and perhaps the dinner she'd cooked could be sent home with the children so it didn't go to waste.

'It's not the same,' the woman said emotionally. 'My kids have it with me. They look forward to it every Wednesday.' I felt sorry for her. She wasn't being awkward: very likely cooking her children dinner once a week and then eating it with them was the highlight of her week – a small occasion when she and her family were reunited around the meal table. It would be a huge disappointment for her and her children.

The door to Blue Room was open and Molly and Kit rushed in ahead of me. I sensed immediately the atmosphere was tense and I thought we should have waited outside until they'd finished talking. Aneta, Filip, Tess and the Family Centre manager were standing in the centre of the room, while the contact supervisor sat at the table, watching their heated discussion, clearly worried. I guessed what it was about before the manager said, 'I am sorry, but this does apply to everyone. I really can't let contact go ahead until you have given me the food and drink that is in your bag.'

Aneta's face was set in anger. She had the shopping bag she usually brought to contact held close to her side. 'You're not having it, but I promise I won't give it to the children,' she snapped.

'I'm afraid that won't do,' the manager said evenly.

Aneta stormed over to the sofa and plonked herself down while Filip remained standing with Tess and the manager. Molly and Kit had gone to their father, not their mother, and wrapped their arms around his legs.

'I will need to take the food and drink out of the room,' Tess said to Aneta. 'It should have been handed in at reception.' Aneta held on tightly to her bag. I assumed she and Filip had been told the same as everyone else: that some children had become sick after contact and until they could find out what was causing it, no food or drink was being allowed in.

There was a moment's impasse and then Filip, who was usually passive and said very little, said sharply, 'Aneta, will you just give it to them! I don't know why you're making all this fuss.'

Aneta must have realized she wasn't going to get her own way, for she suddenly jumped up from the sofa and, wrenching open her bag, took out a large carton of pineapple juice and a packet of biscuits and pushed them at the manager. 'There! Satisfied?' she snarled, and flounced angrily back to the sofa where she told Molly and Kit to come to her.

They were looking worried and stayed by their father. I wished I'd remained outside so the children hadn't had to witness this.

'Thank you,' the manager said calmly, and showed Tess the juice.

'It's open,' Tess said to Aneta. 'The seal is broken.'

'So? I was thirsty and had some coming here. Or is that not allowed either?'

'I'll take it outside,' the manager told Tess and came towards the door. I stepped aside to allow her to pass, then I went over to Tess and handed her the carrier bag containing the food diary. She glanced in and thanked me. I said goodbye to Molly and Kit, told them that I'd see them later, and left. The manager was nowhere to be seen. I wondered why Aneta had created such a fuss. Surely she realized it was for her children's good?

When I returned to collect Molly and Kit the manager was waiting in reception. 'You've come for Molly and Kit?' she asked. She wouldn't necessarily remember all the foster carers going in and out.

'Yes.'

'Their social worker wants to speak to the parents, so you can take the children now. It's nearly time.'

We went down the corridor to Blue Room where she gave a perfunctory knock on the door and we went in. It was quieter than usual for the end of contact when the children had been playing for two hours. The toys and games had already been packed away and Molly and Kit had their coats on. Tess and the contact supervisor were at the table, both writing. Aneta was sitting on the sofa and glared hostilely at me, which was nothing unusual. Filip was his usual affable self and told the children it was time to go. He took them over to their mother to kiss her goodbye, then brought them to me. I always waited just inside the door. I thanked him, said a general goodbye and left the room, holding the children's hands.

'Did you have a nice time?' I asked them as I always did as we made our way out.

Kit, who was going through a phase of saying yes to everything, said a resounding, 'Yes.' He was so cute.

Molly, that much older, with more advanced vocabulary, replied, 'Mummy said she couldn't give us juice and it was your fault.'

'I wonder why she said that,' I replied easily. I guessed Tess had told the parents my suspicions about the food and drink they were taking in.

'Don't know,' Molly said. And we left it at that.

By the time we were in the car it was forgotten and they were looking forward to playing with Paula, who would be home now.

CHAPTER SEVENTEEN

ACCUSED

The following day was Thursday, 5th November, Fireworks Night, so I made sure Sammy was indoors. Once everyone was home and it was dark outside, we put on our coats and went into the garden for our firework display. It was a clear, cold night with a crescent moon – perfect for letting off fireworks. Aware of keeping everyone safe, the girls and I stayed on the patio with the children while Adrian lit the fireworks at the end of the garden, using the light of a torch. Once he'd lit the touch paper of the first one, he walked swiftly away and joined us on the patio to watch it go off – there's always a few seconds' delay. We oohed and aahed and admired the various fountains of sparkling colours that shot from the firework and fell glittering to the ground, some sparks bouncing on the grass. Watching fireworks was a new experience for Molly and Kit and they were mesmerized, but also a little anxious, and stood very close to us. Adrian waited until the firework had completely extinguished before going down the garden to light the next one.

'Will Daddy be doing this?' Molly asked.

'I don't know, love. He might.'

'Whoosh!' said Kit, imitating a firework.

Neighbours began letting off much grander and louder fireworks in gardens around us. They exploded overhead in a volley of bangs, which frightened Kit. I picked him up and comforted him, but eventually I took him indoors and we watched the rest of our display through the patio windows where the sound was muted. Paula and Lucy stayed outside and looked after Molly, who was really enjoying it. Sammy was curled up behind the sofa with his paws over his ears.

Our display lasted about thirty minutes, which was long enough for the little ones. Once everyone was indoors, I served the hot dogs and jacket potatoes I'd left cooking in the oven. I thanked my family for helping, as this had been primarily for Molly and Kit's benefit, but they said they'd enjoyed it too. There were still plenty of fireworks going off when we took Molly and Kit up to bed at nine o'clock. It was past their bedtime and they were both tired. Lucy and Paula helped Molly get ready for bed while I saw to Kit. We skipped their baths for tonight and just gave them a good wash. The fireworks continued to explode and fizzle outside and it was some time before both children were asleep. It was midnight before all the fireworks stopped and the night was silent again, save for a lone dog barking in the distance.

I hadn't heard anything from Tess since I'd seen her on Wednesday, and I took the children to contact on Friday afternoon as usual. The notice about food and drink not being allowed in was still in reception. I signed the Visitors' Book and we went down the corridor and to the room. Only Filip and the contact supervisor were there, so I assumed Aneta was using the bathroom, until Filip said to the children, 'Mummy isn't coming today. She's not well.'

'Oh dear,' I said. 'Nothing serious, I hope.' Aneta hadn't missed a contact yet.

'No, she was feeling sick, so she's having a lie down.'

The children ran to him. He'd already set out some toys for them to play with.

'I hope she's better soon,' I said, and, saying goodbye, I left.

As I drove home it crossed my mind that if Aneta and Filip were storing food incorrectly or eating it beyond its use-by date then that could be the reason she was now ill. I assumed Tess would have talked to them about the importance of storing food correctly and food hygiene when she'd spoken to them on Wednesday.

When I returned to collect the children at the end of contact I could hear their whoops of joy from the corridor. I knocked on the door and went in. Filip was on his hands and knees, red in the face from giving the children a piggyback ride.

'Gee up, horsey!' Molly shouted, clinging to the back of his jumper to stay on. Kit was seated behind her with his arms wrapped tightly around her waist. They were having great fun and I laughed as the children clung to their father and he trotted horse-like around the room. Even the contact supervisor, who normally sat expressionless, was smiling. I remembered my father giving my brother and me rides like this when I was Molly's age.

'Final lap!' Filip cried, out of breath. 'Then it's time to go.'

He set off around the room one last time with the children shrieking with laughter, then drew to a halt by the sofa so they could dismount. He was a big-built man and the children must have felt they were riding very high while on his back. Once the children were off, he straightened and, kissing them both, lifted them from the sofa and onto the floor. Not for the first time I thought how far his relationship with his children had come since we'd first met. Back then he'd been working very long hours, seven days a week, and had hardly seen them. It was such a dreadful pity that it had taken the children coming into care to improve their relationship. I wondered how different their home life might have been if he'd spent more time there.

Molly and Kit were very hyped up and wanted to stay and play some more, so it took quite a bit of time and cajoling to get them to say goodbye.

'See you both on Monday,' Filip said, finally bringing them to me.

'Will Mummy be coming?' Molly asked him.

'Yes, I would think so,' Filip said.

I was expecting Molly to be pleased, but she looked disappointed. I put it down to the fun time they'd had playing with their father compared to the more controlled and subdued games and interaction that took place when their mother was there. I think it's probably true of many families that traditionally the father is allowed to play unreservedly and be a child again with his children, while the mother tends to remain in control and sound cautionary warnings about not getting overexcited and to play safely.

On Saturday I took Molly and Kit shopping, primarily for some more winter clothes for them and to have their feet measured for shoes. Molly liked the idea of new shoes, and in the shoe shop she stood still as the assistant measured her feet, and then cooperated as she brought various styles of shoes for her to try on. Kit was more interested in rearranging the displays of shoes on the many shelves that were within his reach, and brought the shoes over to show me. I kept returning them, but a few seconds later they would be thrust into my lap again as I tried to concentrate on Molly and what the assistant was saying. Then mischievously Kit took a shoe from an elderly woman who was about to try it on and ran off with it. She wasn't impressed! I caught up with him, gave the woman the shoe back, apologized and then strapped Kit in the stroller with a snack until I'd finished with Molly. An hour later we left the shop with a pair of shoes for each of the children, and I breathed a sigh of relief.

Some workmen were putting up Christmas lights in the shopping centre ready for 1st December when they would be turned on, another was erecting Santa's grotto, which we'd visit when it was open nearer Christmas. I stopped by the toy section in the department store so the children could have a look. The decorations were up, as were some of the Christmas displays of toys, and I bought a few stocking fillers for Molly and Kit. I felt a frisson of excitement at the thought of having two little ones with us for Christmas. But I also had great empathy for the parents who would wake on Christmas morning to face another day without their children – even more painful than usual. It's such a family time and I know many families who can't be together are pleased when it's all over. I assumed the family would swap presents at the last contact before Christmas. I'd buy some for Molly and Kit to give to their parents.

On Sunday we all went to see my mother, again in two cars, and Kirsty came. As before, we had lunch out and then returned to Mum's for a cup of tea and a slice of homemade cake. Although it was too much for her to cook meals for us all, she still liked to bake and make puddings, and we loved to eat them! We left with a box of cupcakes, beautifully decorated with icing and edible flowers.

Monday morning arrived and I realized a whole weekend had passed without either of the children being sick. Indeed, when I checked in my log I saw that a whole week had passed, and the last time Molly had become ill was after drinking the chocolate milkshake from contact the previous Monday. Since then, they hadn't had any more food and drink from their parents, which seemed to add weight to my suggestion it was food and drink the parents were giving them that was making them ill. I was expecting Tess to phone before long, and around mid-morning the house phone rang and it was her. I answered it in the kitchen-diner, upbeat and positive, but I sensed straight away something was wrong.

'How are you and the children?' Tess asked, her voice flat.

'Fine. We've had a nice weekend and no one has been sick for a whole week.'

'Good.' She paused and then said, 'I've just spoken to your supervising social worker, Edith. I'm afraid I'm going to have to remove Molly and Kit from your care.'

'What? What do you mean?' I gasped, thinking I'd misheard.

'We're going to have to find the children another place-ment. Somewhere else to live.'

'Why? Whatever for? They're settled here with me.' I felt my knees go weak, and I leant against the kitchen cabinet for support. Molly and Kit were at the dining table having a mid-morning snack. I thought I must have done something wrong, for why else would Tess be removing the children now? 'Why?' I asked again.

'We're having the food and drink the parents took into contact last Wednesday analysed to try to establish if it contains anything that could have caused the children to become ill. I explained this to the parents at the end of contact and your concerns about food poisoning. They seemed to accept it, but on Friday their solicitor phoned. Aneta is accusing you of making her children ill. She's saying if the tests come back positive then it's your fault, and it must be you who is keeping the food too long.'

'But that's ridiculous! I know about storing food and good food hygiene, and the children were ill a lot before they came into care.'

'I know. But Aneta isn't open to logic and is insisting that Molly and Kit are removed straight away. If we don't, their solicitor is threatening to apply to court to have the children returned home. At this stage they could win, as we don't have enough evidence. As their solicitor pointed out, the children have been ill just as much since they've been in foster care as before. You had to take Kit to the hospital just as Aneta did.'

'But they haven't been sick for a week – since I stopped giving them the food and drink from contact!' I cried. 'You've got the food diary too. It shows all those instances where their sickness can be linked directly to food and drink from contact.'

'But there is nothing to say that it didn't become contami nated   if the tests show it is contaminated – after it left contact. The children have never actually been sick at contact, it's always after, when they are with you. Your daughter was sick too, which Aneta is saying suggests the problem is with you. I'm not saying it is, but you can see their point.'

I couldn't believe what I was hearing. 'But that was the first time Lucy has been sick in years,' I retaliated sharply. 'And it was after she'd accidently drunk some of Molly and Kit's orange juice.'

'Aneta has told her solicitor that she didn't give the children orange juice that day but blackcurrant. The contact supervisor's report just refers to a packet of juice. So we don't know if it was hers or yours.'

'It was hers,' I said. Yet even as I said it I realized it was Aneta's word against mine. 'What has Filip said?'

'He can't remember what they had to drink, but just wants what's best for the children. Which of course is what we all want. Even if the test results come back positive,' Tess continued, 'we still have the issue of where the contamination occurred. We've only got one sample. Had you kept the other items we could have had those tested as well, but this is all we have at present.'

I was stunned. How easy it was to make someone look guilty if you set your mind to it, as Aneta clearly had.

'And what about the non-accidental injuries?' I asked. 'They were part of the reason the children were brought into care, weren't they?'

'We've got to prove those, and there's not enough evidence at present if it went back to court. I'm sorry, I know the children are settled with you and you've done a good job, but I can't risk losing a court case and having them returned home now.'

I was bitterly disappointed, but reluctantly I could see the logic in what Tess was saying, although it didn't make it any easier. I knew of other foster carers who'd had children removed after complaints from a parent. The allegations were unfounded, but the social services couldn't risk leaving the children with them. If a full care order was made at the final court hearing the social services would have more control, but until then it's often easier and cheaper to appease the parents than face another court case.

'When are you planning to remove them?' I asked, my voice trembling. I glanced at Molly and Kit, who were sitting innocently at the table just finishing their snacks.

'Edith is finding another carer now, hopefully one in the area who will be able to take them both, otherwise they will have to go out of the county.'

'Will it be today?' I asked.

'I don't know, but I suggest you start packing their things. Don't tell Molly and Kit yet until we know where they are going. Sorry,' Tess said again. Then, 'Don't forget they have contact this afternoon.'

'I won't.'

I put down the phone and looked at Molly and Kit with tears in my eyes. I couldn't help it. I was gutted, not only because we would be losing them at such short notice and in these circumstances, but because the move would be very upsetting and unsettling for them. Another family and another home to get used to when they were so settled with us. It was heart breaking, and at that moment I hated Aneta for what she was putting the children through. I didn't for one moment think she truly believed I was causing their sickness. She was angry – at having her children taken from her, and that I'd suggested it was food she was giving them that was making them ill. It was a pity Tess had told her. Aneta was now lashing out at me and wanting to get her own back, using Molly and Kit to do so. It was cruel, manipulative and selfish. Most parents of children in care eventually manage to put their children's welfare first, regardless of how angry they are.

One small mercy was that I didn't have to tell Molly and Kit they were moving yet – Tess has asked me to wait until she knew where they were going. I doubted I could have told them at present without bursting into tears. When the time came, I would act professionally and try to stay positive for their sakes. Now, I went over, kissed them, praised them for eating their snacks nicely, helped them down, and hugged and kissed them again.

I played with Molly and Kit for the rest of the morning, all the time dreading the moment when Edith would phone saying she'd found new foster carers for them. Tess had told me to start packing, and I would do so while the children were at contact. I made us lunch at one o'clock and we sat together at the table to eat. I thought I'd been hiding my feelings well, but Molly looked at me, worried, and said, 'Are you sad, Cathy?'

'A little. Why? Do I look sad?' I asked, trying to raise a smile.

'Yes. Like my daddy.'

'When does Daddy look sad?'

'When he has to say goodbye at contact,' Molly replied.

'Yes, that would make him sad,' I said, and, putting on a brave face, I changed the subject.

After lunch we played with some of their toys and then I got the children ready for contact. We left around 2.30 p.m. Edith still hadn't phoned, but that didn't mean the children wouldn't be moved that evening if she'd found somewhere suitable. I'd have to tell Paula, Lucy and Adrian when they came home and I knew they were going to be as heartbroken as I was.

I was dreading having to face Aneta again, although Molly and Kit were excited at the thought of seeing their parents – there was no reason for them not to be.

'I hope Daddy is a horse again,' Molly cried excitedly from the back seat as I drove. 'Gee up, horsey!'

'Gee up!' Kit said, copying his sister.

I smiled at them in the rear-view mirror, so naïve and trusting. How would they cope with the move, possibly right out of the area? Molly wanted the children's music on so I fed in a CD.

We arrived at the Family Centre five minutes early and I parked outside. Taking a hand each we went up the path to the front door where I buzzed to be let in. I guessed this would be my last visit to the centre with Molly and Kit, as they were sure to have been moved before the next contact.

The notice about not bringing in food and drink was still in reception. I said hello to the receptionist and signed the Visitors' Book. As we went down the corridor I felt my heart race as my anxiety levels rose at the prospect of having to see Aneta again. Perhaps she wouldn't be there, I thought. Perhaps it would just be Filip as it had been on Friday. But my hopes were soon dashed. Not only was Aneta there, but instead of sitting passively on the sofa as she often did, she was standing in the middle of the room facing the door, her expression triumphant. As soon as she saw the children, she flung her arms wide open theatrically and cried, 'Come to Mummy! You're safe now.'

Molly and Kit rushed to her while Filip, unable to look at me, said a quiet, 'Thank you.'

'Have a nice time,' I said to the children and turned to leave. As I did I heard Aneta telling the contact supervisor that she was innocent and I was to blame, and her children would be home again soon.

CHAPTER EIGHTEEN

LEAVING

I don't expect gratitude from the parents of children I foster, but Aneta telling Molly and Kit 'you're safe now' – suggesting they weren't safe with me – hurt. I wondered what exactly she'd told Tess. It was at times like this that I questioned why I continued to foster. I'd done my best for Molly and Kit and had been rewarded by being accused of harming them – the worst possible reason for ending a placement. Depending on the allegations Aneta had made, I could be suspended from fostering and even reported to the police while I was investigated. Edith would give me the details of what action they proposed to take; it was part of her role as my supervising social worker.

Once home, I poured myself a glass of water and, immersed in gloomy and depressing thoughts, I went upstairs to set about packing Kit's and Molly's belongings. Many of Kit's clothes were in my room so I began there. It was heart-rending folding and packing his little clothes that I'd carefully laundered and dressed him in each day. My only consolation was that the children weren't being returned home – it was one of the few times in twenty-five years of fostering that I'd felt that way. Although Tess had said she'd yet to prove their injuries were non-accidental, I now believed Aneta was capable of harming them. Using the children against me was the callous act of a vengeful woman. I thought she liked to be in control and if things didn't go her way or the children were playing up then she could hit out or push them, possibly causing the bruising and broken arm Kit had arrived with. What part Filip had played in the abuse I didn't know. However, given that he'd worked very long hours and his manner was much gentler than his wife's, my instinct was that he probably hadn't played any part at all. Although if he'd been aware of any abuse then he too would be culpable, as clearly he had a moral duty to protect his children.

Having finished packing Kit's clothes, I took the suitcase through to Molly's room and continued there. Both children's clothes were in there and also some of their toys. Many more toys and games were scattered throughout the house downstairs. Closer to when they were leaving, I'd have to gather them all together. As I worked I kept an eye on the time. I had to leave at 4.30 p.m. to collect the children from contact at five. Just after four the house phone rang and I felt my stomach churn. Leaving Molly's bedroom, I went round the landing and answered it on the extension in my bedroom. It was Edith.

'I've been told we have to move the children,' she said bluntly with no preamble. 'I've found carers who can take them both, but they are out of the area. I've spoken to Tess and she thinks it's best if the children stay with you tonight, then she will move them tomorrow, otherwise it's going to be very late when they arrive.'

'All right,' I said numbly. 'What time tomorrow?'

'I'm not sure yet. It will depend on when Tess is free. I'll phone you once I've heard.'

'OK, but I'll need some notice to pack the rest of their belongings. Do you know what Aneta has said about me?'

'Not the details yet, but that you are responsible for making the children ill, and also some bruises Kit has on his legs.'

'Those bruises were from falling over while playing,' I said, annoyed. 'I noted when and where they happened in my log. All children fall over while playing.'

'I'll need to look at your log when I come to see you. It needs to be soon. When are you free?'

'Any time after Tess has removed the children,' I said bitterly.

'I can't make tomorrow or Wednesday,' Edith said, presumably checking her diary. 'Thursday is looking full too. Let's make it Friday, eleven o'clock.'

'OK.'

'Either Tess or I will phone you tomorrow when she knows what time she is coming to collect the children. See you Friday.'

'Yes,' I said, and replaced the handset. Supervising social workers were supposed to offer support, I thought grimly.

Downstairs, I made a note of Edith's visit in my diary, not that I was likely to forget it. I had the children for another night, but that was bittersweet. In some ways it would have been less painful if they'd been taken today, as it seemed to prolong the agony. I'd have to start preparing them for leaving while not saying too much until tomorrow, otherwise they'd have all night to worry and fret. I returned to the packing, then at 4.30 I stopped, put the cases out of sight, and drove to the Family Centre.

Having signed in, I made my way along the corridor. As I approached the room, I heard Molly call out, 'Gee up, horsey!' So I thought their father was playing the same game he had on Friday. They'd loved that game and Molly had talked about it over the weekend.

However, when I opened the door, I saw it wasn't Filip on all fours pretending to be a horse but Aneta, with just Molly on her back. Filip was standing a short distance away, holding Kit. I could see straight away that the game wasn't working. Aneta was of a smaller build than Filip and could only manage a few faltering steps with the weight of Molly on her back. She was wearing a skirt that got caught in her knees as she tried to move forwards. To be honest, she looked ridiculous.

'Gee up!' Molly cried, and rocked backwards and forwards, trying to make her mother move.

I glanced at Filip and he nodded to me. Kit smiled.

'Faster! Like Daddy did!' Molly cried, and rocked harder.

'Ouch! That hurt!' Aneta suddenly shouted, any humour gone. Abruptly she stood, jettisoning Molly from her back so she landed heavily on the floor. Molly cried out and ran to her father. Aneta rubbed her back and glared at her daughter. I saw the contact supervisor making notes and I wondered what she was writing.

I waited in my usual spot by the door as Filip comforted Molly, and then told the children to say goodbye to their mother. As he brought them to me his face was expressionless. There was nothing to be read there. He kissed them, said goodbye to me and then added, 'I'm meeting the social worker tomorrow.'

I nodded, said goodbye and left. I had no idea why he'd told me he was seeing Tess the following day, and I assumed this was the last time I would see him or Aneta, as the children were moving tomorrow.

Molly and Kit were exceptionally quiet as we left the building and also in the car. 'Did you have a nice time?' I asked them as I drove us home.

'Yes,' Molly said without much enthusiasm.

'Yes,' Kit repeated.

'Mummy was angry,' Molly said after a moment.

I glanced at her in the rear-view mirror. 'Because of the horsey game?' I asked, assuming this was the reason. 'She'll be fine. She wasn't badly hurt.'

'No. Before you came. She was angry with Daddy,' Molly said.

'Why?'

'Don't know.'

I didn't pursue it. I had more important things on my mind, and I prepared myself to talk to them about them leaving. 'Sometimes when children are in foster care like you and Kit are, they have to change carers,' I began, concentrating on the road ahead. 'That means that their social worker comes to the house and moves them and all their belongings to a new home.'

'Why?' Molly asked.

'Because sometimes their social worker – yours is Tess – feels it's best.' I wasn't going to malign Aneta – she was their mother. 'Their foster carer is sad they are going, but she knows they will be fine.'

I glanced at them in the rear-view mirror. I didn't expect Kit to understand, but Molly was looking thoughtful. 'It's possible that could happen to you and Kit,' I said. 'If it does, we will have to say goodbye. It will feel strange to begin with in your new home, but you'll soon settle in and be happy as you have been with me.' I swallowed hard.

Molly didn't comment but asked for the children's songs. I left further talk about them leaving for now and fed in the CD. I'd planted the idea, so it would have time to grow and I'd return to the matter tomorrow when I had a definite time for them leaving and knew where they were going. It was going to be painful, but I'd have to stay positive for their sakes.

I told Lucy, Paula and Adrian what had happened one at a time as they arrived home, out of earshot of Molly and Kit, who'd suddenly become very clingy. Lucy was home first, having worked an early shift at the nursery. She was angry and, remembering some of her own negative experiences of being in care, said, 'Bloody social worker! She should know better!'

'I can see why Tess made the decision,' I said.

Paula was upset and her eyes filled. 'That's so sad,' she said. 'I'm going to miss Molly and Kit a lot. I was hoping they'd be here for Christmas. Will we be able to see them?'

'I'm not sure, but I'll ask Tess.'

When Adrian came home and I told him, he said, 'Is there nothing we can do? Accusing us of harming Molly and Kit is slanderous.'

'I know, but it doesn't work like that in fostering, does it?'

'I guess not, but it should. If I said things like that about a work colleague, I'd be answerable for them.'

And there lay a truth. A different set of rules seemed to apply in fostering so that allegations like this – and worse – could be made with impunity and the foster carer had no redress.

I decided not to tell my mother the children were having to move until after they'd gone, as all she could do was worry.

It's always sad when children you've looked after and grown close to leave, but usually there is some consolation as they are able to return home or go to live with a loving relative or adoptive parents. Now we didn't have those comforts. Molly and Kit were being moved because of Aneta's vicious allegations. I wondered what would happen if she made up things against the next carers. Would Tess move the children again? It does happen, and is dreadfully unsettling for the children. There is a saying that children are like plants and don't thrive if moved. It's true. Yet Aneta couldn't see that. Angry, she was thinking only of herself.

That evening, while I took Kit up for his bath, both Lucy and Paula stayed downstairs, playing with Molly and reading her stories. Usually they took it in turns, but this evening they both wanted to make the most of their last hours with her. Adrian said a prolonged goodnight to Kit and Molly before going to his room to do some work. He and the girls would say goodbye to the children in the morning before they left for work and college, as they would have gone by the time they returned.

Kit wouldn't settle in his cot and eventually I went to the top of the stairs and called down to the girls to bring Molly up to bed, as it was getting late. She heard Kit and wanted to come into my room to see him. He was still awake so with the light on low they all came in. Molly came to his cot and stood beside me as Lucy and Paula watched. Kit was sitting up, his face against the slats of the cot. Molly reached in and took his hand. 'It's going to be OK,' she soothed in a manner similar to mine. 'I'll be with you. Don't worry, little brother.' It was touching and my eyes filled. I guessed she was referring to the possibility of them moving and had instinctively recognized that this was why Kit wasn't settling. 'You have to go to sleep now,' she said, as I did sometimes.

'Yes,' he said cutely, and obligingly lay down.

I smiled at Lucy and Paula. Molly stayed by the cot, holding Kit's hand and talking to him gently. I would have to make the new carers aware that there had been issues about Molly hurting Kit, and what Aneta had claimed. Although I'd also make it clear that I'd only seen some sibling rivalry and the instances of those were decreasing. After a few minutes I told Molly to say goodnight to Kit, as it was her bedtime.

'Night, night, little Kit,' she said lovingly and, kissing his hand, came away.

'Good girl,' I said. After that, Kit settled.

Lucy, Paula and I got Molly ready for bed and took her to her bedroom. She loved all the attention, not realizing it was because this would be the last time we'd be putting her to bed. Tomorrow night she'd be in a strange house with new carers. We hugged and kissed her and said we'd see her in the morning. 'Sleep tight,' I said, giving her one last kiss. I felt my eyes fill again.

We came out and Paula and Lucy went to their rooms, while I went downstairs where I set about gathering together the children's toys. I packed most of them but left some in the living room for Molly and Kit to play with the following morning before Tess arrived. I assumed she would be moving them in the morning so they had the rest of the day to get used to their new home before bedtime. If children are moved it's usually done in the morning while they are fresh.

Kit was restless during the night and I had to settle him a number of times, then at around 3 a.m. Molly appeared at my bedroom door, giving me a shock. She hadn't done that since she'd first arrived. I took her back to bed and stayed with her until she was asleep again. In a way I was pleased she'd woken, as I felt I was being given extra time with her – the two of us together in the small light coming from the hall, as the rest of the house slept on.

The following morning everyone was subdued as we showered and dressed, and Adrian, Lucy and Paula prepared to say goodbye before they left. I asked them to keep their goodbyes short so that Molly and Kit wouldn't become upset. I still had to tell them they'd be going, which I would do when I was given a time for their move.

'Goodbye, little people,' Adrian said in the hall, and lifted them both up as Filip did. 'Be good and don't forget to text.'

Molly grinned. 'I haven't got a phone!'

'I'm sure you will have before long,' he joked.

'Yes,' Kit agreed, and we laughed.

Adrian set them down, kissed the tops of their heads and left.

Lucy had to leave next and she hugged Molly and Kit in turn. 'Love you loads,' she said, her voice unsteady.

'Love you,' Molly returned.

'Love-u,' Kit repeated as best he could and pursed his lips ready for a kiss. I could have cried. I saw Lucy tear up too.

When it was time for Paula to leave, both children were having breakfast. She kissed Kit goodbye first. 'You're a good boy, eating like that.'

'Yes,' he said in his cute way.

'Am I a good girl?' Molly asked.

'Of course.' Paula went round to where Molly was sitting and hugged and kissed her goodbye. 'I'll miss you both,' she said, her voice full of emotion.

'I'll miss you,' Molly said, while not appreciating they were going today.

Paula left very quickly, her eyes glistening, as mine were again.

After breakfast, I took Molly and Kit upstairs to brush their teeth. While we were in the bathroom Molly said, 'We're not sick any more.'

'No. You're not.'

'Why?' she asked.

'Why?' Kit repeated.

'Because I think I've found out what was causing you to be sick and you don't have it any more.'

'I'm happy I'm not sick,' Molly said, giving a little jump for joy.

'So am I,' I said.

'Will you tell Mummy?' she asked innocently.

'She knows,' I said.

Once we'd finished in the bathroom, I took the children downstairs and into the living room where I'd left out some of their toys. It was now 9.30 a.m. and I was expecting to hear from Edith or Tess at any moment. Once I had a definite time for them leaving, I'd explain what was happening to Molly and Kit and also enlist their help in packing the rest of their belongings so they were occupied. I hadn't had a chance to buy them a leaving gift as I normally did when children left us, so I'd put some money in a 'Good Luck' card, which I'd ask Tess to pass on to the carers to buy something for them. I put it with the information sheet I'd written for the new carers about the children's routine, likes and dislikes. It's usual for foster carers to do this, as it helps the children to settle.

The morning ticked by without any news and the waiting was agony. At 11 a.m. I made the children a snack, and after they'd finished I set out some activities on the table. Sammy came to investigate; indeed, it seemed he'd come to say good-bye as he put his front paw up on their chairs and meowed loudly. Kit tried to feed him some Play-Doh and Molly told him off. At noon when I still hadn't heard anything I tele-phoned Tess, moving away from the children and using the handset in the kitchen to make the call. It went through to voicemail, so I left a message asking if she knew yet what time she'd be arriving. I then telephoned Edith and asked her.

'Hasn't Tess been in touch?' she asked.

'No.'

'I'll see if I can find her. I saw her earlier, so she's definitely in.' Their office was open-plan, so they could see each other come and go.

An hour passed with no news from Tess or Edith and I gave the children lunch. Thank goodness I hadn't told them for certain they were leaving, I thought. They'd have had all this time to worry and fret as I had been doing. At two o'clock I phoned Edith again and she said Tess was in a meeting and she'd speak to her as soon as she was free.

'I've been waiting in all day,' I said, not bothering to hide my frustration. 'If I'd known it was going to be late afternoon I would have taken the children out this morning. I hope it's not going to be much later. They'll be tired.'

'I'll speak to Tess when she's free,' Edith said.

Not only was it unsettling, it was also highly unusual for the move to be left so late. At three o'clock when the phone rang again I snatched it up. It was Edith.

'I've spoken to Tess. She's only just come out of her meeting. She said to tell you that the children will be staying with you for another night and she'll speak to you tomorrow.'

'Really? Why?' I asked, taking the phone out of the room so Molly and Kit couldn't hear. 'Can't the new carers have them?'

'It's not that,' Edith said. 'They're still on standby to have them, but it won't be today. I understand it's to do with Filip. He's been in a meeting with Tess today, but I don't know the details.'

'Filip told me yesterday he was going to see Tess today, but he didn't give a reason.' It all seemed very strange, but I had to accept this, unnerving though it was.

'I'll phone you if I hear any more,' Edith said.

I returned to the children, who were still playing in the living room. 'You're both playing very nicely,' I said. 'Well done.'

I perched on the sofa and messaged our Glass WhatsApp group so Adrian, Lucy and Paula would all receive the same message.

> Molly and Kit staying another night.
> See you later. Love Mum.

I put my phone in my handbag and asked the children if they'd like to go to the park. Having been in all day, I felt the need for some fresh air and exercise.

'Yes!' Molly cried, jumping up and down. 'Can we feed the ducks?'

'Yes. Ducks!' Kit repeated, jumping up and down beside Molly.

'Molly, you know where the duck food is, can you be a big girl and fetch it, please, while I change Kit?'

Twenty minutes later the three of us were in our winter coats and shoes and going up the road to our local park. Kit was in the stroller and Molly was walking beside me, proudly carrying the bag of duck food pellets. It was invigorating to be outside in the fresh air, with a much-needed change of scenery, after being cooped up indoors all day. As we walked my mobile bleeped with an incoming text message. I took it from my bag. It was Lucy replying to my WhatsApp message: *WTF!*

For those who don't know what that means, I won't translate. Suffice it to say, Lucy was shocked. It was virtually unheard of to arrange to move a child and then, without any reason, suddenly decide to leave them for another night, especially when allegations had been made against the carer.

Paula's response came a minute later and was less explicit, but she was just as surprised and puzzled: *Good*.

Then Adrian's text came as we entered the park: *Why?*

No idea, I replied. *I hope someone will tell us tomorrow.*

CHAPTER NINETEEN

SHOCKING

Shortly after we arrived home from the park that afternoon, Molly began searching for the toys I'd packed away, so I got them out again. I'd have to repack in the morning once I knew what time Molly and Kit were leaving. Tomorrow was Wednesday and normally they had contact 3–5 p.m. I wondered if Tess had remembered, as she'd have to work the move around it. The children played as I prepared dinner and then as Paula, Lucy and Adrian returned home they ran to the door to greet them. Tonight, there were extra hugs all round. I told my family one at a time as they came in that I didn't know any more as to why the move hadn't taken place today. We obviously didn't discuss it in front of the children.

We all ate dinner together, then Adrian went out to see Kirsty while the girls helped me put Kit and Molly to bed. Once the children were asleep, Paula, Lucy and I talked a little about Tess's decision to leave the children with us another night and agreed it didn't make sense, especially as the other carers were still free to take them.

'They always moved me quickly,' Lucy said ruefully. 'Sometimes without any notice at all!' She'd had a very unsettled early life, both in and out of care, when she'd been passed around various relatives and had had to change foster carers before finally coming to live with me. She'd done very well to overcome her past and be able to move on with her life. I was proud of her, as of course I was of Adrian and Paula.

None of us could come up with a plausible explanation for Molly and Kit staying another night and the girls asked me to text them tomorrow as soon as I heard anything. During the evening and later when I tried to go to sleep, my thoughts kept returning to what might have happened. I imagined all sorts of scenarios, none of which made sense.

The children slept well, and the following morning Adrian, Paula and Lucy said goodbye to them again as if it would be the last time they'd see them, which I assumed it would be. I was anxious from the moment I got up, and watched the clock, waiting for 9 a.m. when the social services' offices would open. I'd decided that if I hadn't heard from Edith or Tess by ten o'clock I'd phone them to find out what the arrangements were for today and make sure Tess had remembered there was contact in the afternoon.

At 9.30 the house phone rang and I was relieved to hear Tess's voice. 'Sorry I couldn't get back to you yesterday,' she said. 'I ran out of time. Filip came to see me with some new information. I've discussed it with my manager and we're going to leave Molly and Kit with you until the end of the week, then we'll make a decision. I will have the lab results back by then.'

'I see,' I said slowly, trying to work this out. 'The results from the food and drink from contact?'

'Yes, and something Filip brought in yesterday. I can't say any more at present until we're certain. I'll phone you as soon as I have any more information. Sorry, I know it must be unsettling. How are Molly and Kit?'

'All right,' I said. 'I didn't tell them they were moving, I just touched on the subject. I started packing on Monday when I thought they were going.'

'Leave it for now. We'll make a decision on Friday. Thank you for your understanding.'

'Is contact going ahead this afternoon?' I asked.

'Yes, three till five as usual.'

We said goodbye and I replaced the handset, even more perplexed. The urgency to remove the children seemed to have vanished now. Based on what? Filip's meeting with Tess? I had no idea. I WhatsApped the Glass group again to let them know Molly and Kit would be staying with us until the end of the week but that I didn't know any more. I then cleared up the breakfast things and, only partially reassured, played with the children.

Mid-morning, Edith telephoned and she told me what I already knew. 'Tess is leaving the children with you for now. I've informed the other carers.'

'Yes, she phoned me. Do you know why?'

'She's waiting for some test results in respect of food contamination.' Which was more or less what Tess had said.

'Are you still coming to see me on Friday morning?' I asked.

'Yes.'

We said goodbye and, none the wiser, I returned to play with the children. As we had contact I didn't take Molly and Kit out, it would have been too much of a rush, so I arranged various activities indoors. I made us lunch around 12.30 and then got them ready for contact.

'Will Mummy and Daddy be there?' Molly asked as I drove.

'I think so.'

'I hope Daddy is the horse.'

I hoped so too, as Aneta's attempt hadn't ended well.

We arrived at the centre our usual five minutes early. I parked the car and helped the children from their seats. As I pressed the buzzer for us to be admitted, another family came out. The notice about not bringing food and drink in was still in place, now looking a bit dog-eared around the edges. I signed the Visitors' Book and the receptionist said that Molly and Kit's contact this afternoon was taking place in Yellow Room as Blue Room, one of the larger of the rooms, was needed for another family. This was reasonable, although I knew that Molly and Kit might find it a little unsettling. Children in care have so many changes that something relatively small like a change of contact room can make them anxious. 'Are both parents here?' I asked the receptionist.

'Yes, with the contact supervisor. You know where Yellow Room is?'

'I do, thank you.' I knew the layout of the building from having brought many children here in the past.

I took Molly and Kit by the hand and said positively, 'You're seeing Mummy and Daddy in a different room today – Yellow Room. It's got lots of toys just like Blue Room, but it's painted yellow. I wonder what pictures will be on the door? Can you guess?' I was trying to make it sound exciting so they wouldn't worry, and it worked. As we turned the corner and the door to Yellow Room came into view, Molly ran to it and began pointing and naming the yellow pictures on the door. 'A sunflower! A big yellow sun!' she cried, and so on.

'That's right,' I said. Kit began copying her, pointing to the pictures as his sister was and trying to repeat the words. Although this was fun and could have continued, I appreciated that this was supposed to be time with their parents.

'Come on, let's go in,' I said, my hand on the doorknob. 'Mummy and Daddy are waiting for you.'

I opened the door and the children ran in and then stopped. I could see there was a problem. Aneta was standing, hands on hips, beside the table where the contact supervisor was, clearly very angry. Her features were twisted, hard and unyielding.

'We're not staying here!' she said, now glaring at me. 'This room's too small! I've told them to find us a fucking bigger room.'

I was taken aback. The contact supervisor was in conversation on her mobile, I assumed with the manager. Filip was standing on the other side of the room, looking embarrassed. The children went to him. There was an awkward silence as the contact supervisor listened to what she was being told on the phone, while Aneta shook her head, suggesting she wouldn't accept any compromise – whatever it was.

I looked at Molly and Kit, who were now hiding behind their father's legs. I wondered how often their mother had lost her temper like this at home. It's frightening for children to see a parent angry, as it shows a loss of control, and children need to see that the adults responsible for them are in control. It feels safe.

The contact supervisor ended the call. 'We can use Red Room or stay here,' she said to Aneta. 'The manager is on her way to explain.'

'Is Red Room bigger?' Aneta demanded.

I knew the answer, it wasn't, but then none of the rooms were small and they were all well equipped and comfortable.

'The manager will explain,' the contact supervisor said evenly.

'There's no need to bother her,' Filip suddenly said, finally stepping up to the mark. 'This room is fine for us.'

'No, it's not!' Aneta retorted, eyes blazing.

'Aneta, please, not in front of the children,' Filip said wearily, as though he'd said it many times before.

'I'm not being given a fucking second-class room!' Aneta fired back. The children flinched. 'They can go and take a running jump. I'd rather go home.'

At that point the manager arrived and nodded for me to go. I'd never witnessed Aneta that angry before and I assumed it was probably due to stress. It was a complete over-reaction, but I'd seen parents of other children I'd fostered react disproportionately to quite minor issues and I appreciated why. Apart from the grief and worry of losing their child into care, they'd been stripped of most of the responsibility for their child and could only have a say in relatively minor matters. So, for example, they'd complain endlessly about the room being too hot or cold, or that it didn't have a television, or the way the foster carer had styled their child's hair, or the clothes and trainers they'd bought for them. It was the only control they had left, but the manager should be well equipped to deal with it.

When I returned to collect Molly and Kit, the receptionist told me they were still in Yellow Room. At exactly five o'clock I knocked on the door and went in. The four of them were sitting together on the sofa. Filip had Molly on his lap and was reading her a story. Kit was snuggled between him and Aneta. Filip looked up at me. 'Time to go,' he said gently and, closing the book, he eased Molly from his lap.

The children didn't want to leave, which was only to be expected. They loved their parents and they seemed to have had a nice time. But as before, Filip told them to kiss their mother goodbye and then brought them to me. Aneta stayed on the sofa looking grumpy – not overtly angry, but not happy either. I guessed she didn't like not getting her own way.

'See you Friday,' Filip said to me as he handed over the children.

'I hope so,' I replied. We said goodbye and left.

Filip seemed to have assumed the children would still be with me on Friday afternoon, but I wasn't so sure. Tess had said she would make a decision by the end of the week, but that decision could be to remove the children from me and send them to another carer as they'd planned. Unless, of course, Filip knew something I didn't – but what? It was a question I returned to repeatedly for the rest of the day.

On Thursday, with no contact, I took Molly and Kit out, this time to the soft-play centre I'd taken them to before. Molly was very excited, and Kit mirrored her enthusiasm while not really understanding where we were going until we arrived. As I watched them play, I checked my mobile regularly for any calls from Tess or Edith. With music playing throughout the centre, together with the excited shouts coming from the children, I wouldn't hear my phone ring. However, by the time we left in the late afternoon I'd had a missed call from a friend and a few text messages, but nothing from Tess or Edith. Tomorrow was Friday and the end of the week, when Tess had said she'd make her decision. It also marked the end of another week without Molly or Kit being sick. In that respect I was delighted.

I had gradually begun to reintroduce foods that I'd stopped giving the children as I'd thought they might cause an allergic reaction. Now they were having them without any ill effect, and were generally less anxious about their health and trying new foods. The colour had returned to their cheeks and they'd lost that sickly pallor. I also thought they were more active, so I told myself that even if they were taken from me the following day, at least I'd helped them in this. I'd identified what had been causing them to be sick, for I was more convinced than ever that it had been food from home that had been stored incorrectly and gone off.

That evening, as we all sat down to dinner, my family and I did so in the knowledge that it could be our last evening meal together. Had I known for certain Molly and Kit were leaving the next day, I'd have given them a little leaving party as I'd done with other children I'd fostered. I would have invited my mother and some friends with their children and made a special party tea. When school-age children left I usually invited their close friends and sometimes their teacher and teaching assistant. Good endings are important and allow the child to move on with a positive frame of mind.

Although we weren't able to give Molly and Kit a leaving party, the delay had given me time to buy them a leaving card and gift each – children's toy mobile phones. When the buttons were pressed, they played little tunes and taught the alphabet, counting, nursery rhymes and so on. Molly's was more sophisticated than Kit's, as she was that bit older, and included simple sums and word recognition. I was sure they were going to be delighted with them, as they were both fascinated by my mobile phone. Lucy, Adrian and Paula kept their phones with them, but if I left mine unattended and within reach of Molly or Kit, one of them was sure to appear with it before long. Molly tended to press the keys, while Kit often made us laugh as he held the phone to his ear and, with a very earnest expression, walked around the house babbling, presumably mimicking me when I took a call.

Once the children were in bed that evening, I wrapped their gifts and we all signed the card. I put them out of sight under my bed with their half-packed suitcases. I then wrote up my log notes, aware there was a very good chance I'd be writing the final entry tomorrow after they'd gone.

Both children slept well but were awake very early, as if sensing change might be in the air. I managed to persuade Kit to play in his cot, and Molly to stay in her bedroom, while I had a quick shower and dressed. By 7.15 a.m. the three of us were downstairs, an hour earlier than usual. We were having breakfast as Adrian, Paula and Lucy appeared. It was a week-day, so they didn't have time to talk or play with the children as they did at weekends; however, they all made a point of saying goodbye and giving them a big hug and kiss before they left. I assured them I'd text as soon as I heard from Tess. It was all very unsettling, and as 9 a.m. approached and the social services' offices opened I felt my anxiety levels step up another notch. Edith was due to arrive at eleven o'clock and I wondered if perhaps she'd bring the news I was waiting for.

I sat with the children in the living room and played various games and activities with them as I waited. While I was partly resigned to them leaving – it wouldn't be the shock it had been when Tess had first told me – I would need time to explain to them what was happening and pack the rest of their belongings. Given that they had contact in the after-noon, I was assuming the move would take place in the morn-ing, but we were running out of time.

Just after 10 a.m. the house phone rang and I snatched up the handset in the living room. 'Cathy, it's Tess.'

'Yes?'

'How are Molly and Kit?' she asked sombrely.

'OK, they're here in the living room with me, playing.'

'Can you move away so they can't hear you?'

'Just a minute.' I took the handset into the hall, wondering what on earth Tess had to tell me. 'I'm out of earshot.'

'Good.' She paused as if summoning herself for what she had to say. My mouth went dry and my heart beat loudly. 'I have the test results we've been waiting for and I'm afraid to say it appears we have a case of FDIA. Are you familiar with that term?'

'Didn't it used to be called Munchausen syndrome by proxy?'

'That's right. FDIA – Factitious Disorder Imposed on Another – or Munchausen syndrome by proxy. It's when a person pretends that someone they look after is ill when they are not. In extreme cases they make the person ill. It would appear that is what Aneta has been doing.'

'What?' I gasped.

'Yes, I know, shocking. But there's little doubt, Aneta has intentionally been making her children sick.'

CHAPTER TWENTY

BEYOND BELIEF

It took a moment for what Tess had told me to sink in. 'Aneta has been making her children sick?' I said numbly. 'But how? They've been ill here too.'

'That's one of the reasons we didn't make the connection. When Filip came to see me, he brought in a bottle of fluid that we've now had tested. It contained linctus, which induces vomiting.'

'What?' I gasped again, in utter disbelief. 'What sort of linctus?' I'd never heard of anything like that.

'It's usually used for medicinal purposes to make someone sick if they've ingested a poison. It appears that Aneta was using it regularly to make her children sick. She was able to buy it on the Internet.'

'But they were sick here too. How did it get into my home?' I asked, struggling to understand.

'It was in the drink Molly and Kit brought home from contact, including the pineapple juice we took from the Family Centre to be tested.'

'Oh.' My head spun.

'The police have been informed and will be interviewing the parents later today.'

'Both parents?'

'Yes. Although, from what we know, it's likely Aneta was solely responsible. But that's for the police to decide. In the meantime I'm suspending contact from today. I've informed the parents and the Family Centre. Can you tell the children, please?'

'Yes, but what shall I say?'

'Blame it on me,' Tess said decisively. 'Say I have made the decision to suspend contact for now. I'll leave the exact wording to you. But don't tell them one or both of their parents has been making them sick.'

'No, I won't.' I was still struggling to take it all in.

'I'll need to come and see them next week. I'm not sure which day yet. I'll let you know. You haven't got any other food or drink from contact still there? The police asked.'

'No. I threw it all away when I thought it could be responsible for making the children ill. I was thinking it must have gone off, never in a million years …' My voice trailed away. 'So Aneta added this linctus to the juice?' I asked, still unable to believe it.

'Yes. I've given the food diary to the police. They may want to speak to you about it.'

'They don't think I had anything to do with making the children sick?' I asked, horrified.

'No, but they may need to clarify some of your entries. Your writing isn't that clear in places and the diary may be used in evidence.'

'Sorry, I scribbled down notes as I went, never thinking it would lead to this.'

'Also, can you confirm that Molly and Kit haven't been ill since food and drink was banned from contact.'

'That's right, they haven't,' I said. 'But the rash and breathing difficulties that Kit developed – when I had to take him to hospital – how does that fit in?'

'It's likely to have been caused by repeated doses of the linctus she was giving them. It gradually poisons the system. It could have killed them both.'

I went cold as I remembered how I'd given Kit the juice drink the day he'd been very ill, lots of it. He'd wanted juice and, unaware it contained the poison, I'd given him as much as he wanted, unwittingly making him worse. My anger flared. Aneta had been using me as a tool to continue her evil actions, but why had she done it at all?

'Why would anyone want to make their children ill?' I asked. 'I don't understand.'

'FDIA is a mental illness,' Tess said. 'The care-giver exaggerates the child's illness or intentionally makes them sick in order to gain attention and sympathy. The victim is usually a child. FDIA is relatively rare but difficult to identify, so cases can easily be missed. It is most commonly found in parents of small children. One in ten victims dies as a result.'

I shuddered. 'Good grief. It could have killed Molly and Kit.' I felt weak at the knees. Then my thoughts turned to the miserable childhoods they'd endured – always being sick. 'Those poor children,' I said. 'They've been ill for most of their lives and needn't have been. I can't believe this.'

'I know. We're struggling here too. Kit and Molly will be staying with you for now.'

'You've decided that?'

'Yes, I've spoken to my manager. In view of what's come to light, the probability is that Aneta made up the allegations about you to deflect attention away from herself. The police are of the same opinion.'

'That's a relief. My family and I were very upset at the suggestion we could have intentionally harmed the children.'

'Filip has apologized. He has asked that the children remain with you for now, as they are settled. I'll notify Edith so she can inform the other carers.'

'She's due here soon,' I said. 'Shall I tell her?'

'Yes, please. She can phone me if she has any questions. But I can only tell her what I've told you. I'll know more once both parents have been interviewed by the police. Thank you, Cathy.'

'For what?'

'Keeping a very detailed food diary and making the connection.'

'It was you who suggested the food diary,' I pointed out. 'I was logging everything, thinking I was going to be able to identify a food allergy. It would never have occurred to me it could be this.'

'No. The doctors might have eventually made a connection, but by then it might have been too late. The social services became involved because of Kit's broken arm and other suspected non-accidental injuries. None of us considered FDIA, although personally I thought there was more going on with Aneta than met the eye. But that was a hunch, no more. Thankfully, Filip brought in the bottle of linctus.'

'How did he know what it was? Did he just find it?'

'He told us that Aneta was always giving the children medicine, so he didn't think anything of it. He worked long hours and left the childcare to Aneta. When he saw her adding the linctus to the juice to take to contact, he queried it. Aneta told him you weren't giving the children their medicine and that was why they were sick, so she wanted to make sure they had it. Sometimes she gave them juice at contact – which I'm guessing is when they were sick soon after – and the rest was sent home to you. The contact supervisor didn't notice the packets were already open. There was no reason for her to check. Filip has told us that Aneta kept the medicines in a locked cabinet in their bathroom and she had the key. He only became suspicious when you made the link between the children being sick and the food and drink they were having at contact. When we took the juice and biscuits from the Family Centre to be analysed, he confronted Aneta and demanded the key to the medicine cabinet, where he found the bottle of linctus. He said he was horrified when he read on the label that the medicine was used to induce vomiting.'

'So you don't think he was involved?'

'It's unlikely. He was very upset and remorseful when he came in, and is blaming himself for not spotting sooner that something was wrong. But that's for the police investigation to determine. I'll be in touch with a date to visit you and the children next week.'

'All right. Thank you.'

Stunned from what I'd heard, I returned to the living room and, replacing the handset in its cradle, sat heavily on the sofa.

'Look what we've made!' Molly cried, proudly showing me a construction from building bricks.

'Very nice.'

'Kit helped.'

'Good.'

Aneta had been intentionally making her children ill to gain attention and sympathy! It seemed incredible and beggared belief. I'd heard of the condition FDIA. Indeed, a few years back I'd read an article – a true-life story – that had featured a woman who as a child had been repeatedly made ill by her mother. It had gone undetected for eight years until she'd finally been able to tell a doctor what her mother was doing. The mother had received a prison sentence in a secure psychiatric hospital. I'd never personally come across a case of FDIA until now, and I hoped I never would again.

I remembered Tess telling me when she'd first placed Molly and Kit that Aneta had taken the children to the doctor and hospital dozens and dozens of times. It was horrendous to think what they had been through. All those unnecessary tests, some of which had been very uncomfortable, when the doctors had tried to establish the cause of their illness. It would be upsetting enough to have to put a child through all of that if it was necessary and they were genuinely ill, but it was monstrous if they were not and it was avoidable. Molly's and Kit's young lives had been blighted by sickness, and it was their mother's fault!

As I watched the children playing, my heart sank at the thought that I had added to their suffering by giving them food and drink from contact, which contained the linctus to make them ill. I remembered Molly once saying that my juice was nicer than her mother's. I hadn't thought anything of it at the time, but now I wondered if the linctus had made the juice taste odd. Lucy hadn't mentioned it when she'd had their juice and been sick, but I would ask her later when she came home. I had to admit it was clever of Aneta, adding the poison to the packets of juice and then sending them home. She would have known some of it was bound to be consumed on days when the children didn't have contact, thus deflecting any suspicion away from her. Clever, crafty, cunning, devious and vicious, I thought. Had the children only ever been ill just after contact, I might have made the connection sooner. Although I might have put it down to the emotional upset of having to say goodbye to their parents, as I had done when Molly and Kit had first arrived. I remembered the night

Molly had told me it was thinking of her mummy that had made her sick. I had assumed she meant she was upset and missed her, but now it had a different connotation – as if she'd associated being sick with her mother. The two had become synonymous.

All those times Aneta had protested her innocence and I'd almost believed her and wondered if the social services had got it wrong. Yet shouldn't Filip have spotted something sooner, living in the same house? Maybe not, for, as Tess said, he worked long hours and left the childcare to Aneta.

I was suddenly jolted from my thoughts by a ring on the front doorbell. I glanced at the clock on the mantelpiece. It was nearly eleven o'clock. 'That'll be Edith,' I said, standing. I left the children playing as I went to answer the door.

'Hello,' Edith said, business-like and sombre. 'I'll have to take a statement from you, but I'm aware the children are here. Can they play in another room?'

'Statement?' I asked, confused.

'Yes, in respect of the allegations.'

'Oh. That's all changed. Tess has just phoned. The children can stay with me for now.' I then told her what Tess had said, staying in the hall so that Molly and Kit wouldn't hear.

Edith's face went through a spectrum of emotions: doubt, shock, horror and back to doubt. 'I'll need to speak to Tess to confirm all of this,' she said, and took her mobile phone from her jacket pocket.

'I'll leave you to it then.' I returned down the hall to the living room.

I supposed it was reasonable that Edith would want to check what I'd told her, although the social services had been quick enough to believe Aneta when she'd made the allegations against me.

Molly and Kit were still playing nicely. 'Edith is in the hall using her phone,' I said. 'You two stay here and I'll make you a drink and a snack.' They usually had one about now.

From the kitchen I could hear Edith on her phone. She'd got through to Tess and was mainly listening, interjecting with the occasional 'Oh', 'I see' and 'Really?'

I cut up some cheese into little squares, halved some grapes, sliced a banana and arranged it in bowls for the children's snack. I poured their drinks – Kit's into his trainer cup and Molly's into a plastic beaker – and then set them ready on the table. I called Kit and Molly in and made myself a cup of coffee.

Edith finished on the phone. 'We're in here!' I called.

'You were right,' she said, coming into our kitchen-diner.

I looked pointedly in the direction of the children, reminding her not to let anything slip in front of them. 'Do you want a coffee?' I offered.

'Yes, please.'

I made her a coffee and then, leaving Kit and Molly at the table eating their snacks, Edith and I went into the hall, where I could keep an eye on the children but they couldn't easily hear us.

'Tess confirmed that the allegations against you were unfounded,' Edith said. 'I don't think I need to take a statement from you, but I'll check with my manager when I get back to the office.'

I nodded. Whether Edith had to take a statement or not was the last thing on my mind. 'Have you ever come across FDIA before?' I asked, still reeling from the shock of it.

'Yes. When I worked in child protection – before I became a supervising social worker – we had something similar. A mother made her child ill by crushing up her antidepressant tablets and putting them into the child's food. The child nearly died.'

'That's awful,' I said, horrified.

'I believe there are about two hundred cases of FDIA or Munchausen syndrome by proxy a year in this country alone, as well as more cases of just Munchausen's syndrome, when the person pretends they are ill or makes themselves ill. And that's only the ones that are detected. You remember the case of Nurse Beverley Allitt? She was convicted of murdering infants in the hospital where she worked as a trainee nurse.'

'Yes, it was horrendous,' I said. Most people would remember the case. It had been widely reported in the news and had shocked the whole country.

'She was diagnosed with suffering from Munchausen syndrome by proxy – or FDIA as it's now called,' Edith said.

I shuddered. Dear little Molly and Kit could have easily died.

'Tess has suspended contact,' I said. 'She's asked me to tell the children, but not the reason. She is going to see them next week. It's difficult to know what to say to them, they're so young.'

'Do you want to do it while I'm here?'

'Yes, we may as well.'

We returned to the kitchen-diner where Molly and Kit were finishing their snacks and drinks. 'You are doing well,' I said, sitting at the table and setting down my mug of coffee. Edith sat next to me, opposite the children. There was no easy way to tell them that they wouldn't be seeing their parents. 'Your social worker, Tess, telephoned,' I began. 'She's decided it is best for now if we don't go to the Family Centre.'

'Why?' Molly asked.

'Because Tess needs to sort out some things to make sure you are safe. She has told your mummy and daddy, so they won't be going to the Family Centre either.' I didn't expect Kit to understand, but clearly Molly would.

'What things?' she said.

Edith replied. 'Sometimes social workers have to make difficult decisions. Your social worker has decided that it's better for you and Kit if you don't go to the Family Centre to see your parents for a while.'

'When do we see them?' Molly asked.

'We're not sure yet,' Edith said.

'Tess will tell us more next week,' I added.

Molly seemed to accept this, although I knew she was bound to return to the matter later with more questions. I would answer them as best I could without telling her the real reason contact had been suspended. Having finished eating, Kit began agitating to be out of his chair so I undid his harness and helped him down. We all went into the living room where the children played, while Edith continued with the standard part of her supervisory visit, much as she usually did. She asked how the children were generally, if there'd been any changes in my household – a standard question at each visit – and made some notes. She advised me on further training, checked my log notes and then looked around the house. Before leaving, she set the date for her next supervisory visit but said she would be in touch after she'd spoken to her manager.

Once she'd gone, I felt in dire need of a change of scenery and told the children that as there was no contact we would go out. It was raining, so the park wasn't an option.

'Can we go to the ball pond?' Molly asked.

'Where we went yesterday?' I said.

'Yes.'

'OK.'

She was delighted and went to find her shoes. Kit followed her. Going to the soft-play centre would help take their minds off not seeing their parents and we could have some lunch there too. While the children tried to put on their shoes, I sent a WhatsApp message to the Glass group: *Molly and Kit staying for the foreseeable future. Will explain when I see you. Love Mum xxx.*

CHAPTER TWENTY-ONE

NO CONTACT

'So the witch tried to poison me!' Lucy exclaimed, shocked. 'It wasn't intended for you,' I said. 'But yes, I'm certain drinking Molly and Kit's juice is what made you sick.'

I was telling my family about Aneta making the children ill and FDIA as they came home, always making sure that Molly and Kit couldn't hear. Paula had visibly paled when I'd told her. Now Lucy was upset and angry.

'Evil or what! I might have died!' Lucy cried dramatically.

'I doubt it from one dose, but lots of the poison in small children could have killed them.'

'It's shocking. We covered Munchausen syndrome briefly in my nursery training, but I don't think there's ever been a case at the nursery, certainly not while I've been there.'

'Lucy, did you notice if the juice tasted odd when you drank it?' I asked.

'Now you come to mention it, yes. I thought at the time it tasted a bit different – sharper – than the one you usually bought, but I put it down to it being a different brand. I still can't believe what she's been doing. We could have all been poisoned!'

'Although in a way it's probably just as well you did have some of that juice, as it helped me to make the connection.'

'Glad I was of use,' Lucy said tartly. 'Well, at least Molly and Kit are safe and can stay with us.'

'Yes, absolutely, for now at least.'

Lucy went off to play with them and I continued to make dinner. When Adrian came home – just before dinner – I quietly told him too, and of course he was as shaken as the rest of us.

'All those times the little ones were ill and they needn't have been,' he said, greatly saddened. 'Those poor children, and the worry it caused you.'

'Caused all of us,' I said. For to be honest, since Molly and Kit had arrived and been constantly sick, it had been one long worry for us all. Only once they'd stopped being ill had it become easier and we could enjoy looking after them, and then we'd had the worry of them being moved.

We ate together and then Adrian went to see Kirsty, saying he'd be back late as he didn't have to be up for work in the morning and I shouldn't wait up for him. Once Molly and Kit were in bed, I telephoned my mother. I told her that Molly and Kit were no longer being sick, as the cause had been identified.

'That's good,' she said. 'I thought the doctors would eventually find out what they were allergic to.'

I left it like that and didn't explain further. Mum didn't need to know about FDIA and the horror of a mother intentionally making her children ill – not at her age. It would upset her and play on her mind. Bad enough to know that a parent had repeatedly lashed out and hit a child in anger, or neglected them through drug or alcohol abuse, as had happened to many of the children I'd fostered. But how much worse to learn that a mother had systematically made her children ill over months, if not years? I had to remind myself that it was a mental illness and I shouldn't judge Aneta.

I was still puzzled by the linctus Tess had referred to, which Aneta had bought online to induce vomiting. I'd never heard of such a thing, and with Molly and Kit asleep, Adrian out, Lucy getting ready to go out with her friends and Paula relaxing in her bedroom, I went into the front room and sat at my computer. I typed *how to induce vomiting* into a search engine and a list of websites appeared. I found what I was looking for very quickly. It wasn't called linctus but syrup, and yes, it could be bought easily online. Its original purpose, I read, was for the emergency treatment of certain kinds of poisoning by making the patient vomit. It came with the warning that it should not be used to cause weight loss, and if used regularly it could lead to serious health problems, including rashes, breathing difficulties, seizures and even death. I failed to understand why such an item would be available for the public to buy at all, but then of course you can buy virtually anything on the Internet now. There was a picture of a bottle of the syrup, just like the one Aneta would have bought to make her children sick. I reminded myself again that FDIA was a mental illness and I shouldn't demonize Aneta.

Wanting to know more about her illness so I could try to understand it, I typed *Munchausen by proxy* – as FDIA is more commonly referred to – into the search engine and found a medical website that gave a lot of information. I began to read: *Munchausen syndrome by proxy (MSP), also known as Factitious Disorder Imposed on Another (FDIA), is a mental illness that affects caregivers, especially mothers of small children. Someone suffering from FDIA will act as though their child is sick. They will lie to doctors about their child's health in order to gain attention and sympathy. They may also intentionally make their child sick, resulting in painful or risky medical procedures for the child. Someone who has FDIA may cause symptoms by withholding food or fluid, poisoning, suffocating, giving the child inappropriate medicines or not giving them prescribed medicines.*

Common symptoms and illnesses found in the victims of FDIA are vomiting, diarrhoea, seizures, breathing difficulty and asthma, infections and allergic reactions. This was exactly what Molly and Kit had been suffering from, induced by the syrup. I read on. *Identifying someone with FDIA is difficult. Many have suffered mental, physical or sexual abuse growing up.* I had no idea if that was true of Aneta. *People who have FDIA appear to be attentive parents, concerned with the well-being of their child.* That was also true of Aneta. *Many times, the child's symptoms do not match a single disease.* True again.

One way to confirm suspicions of FDIA is to separate the mother from her child and see if the symptoms disappear. Unless, like Aneta, you continue to poison your children from a distance, I thought bitterly. *Doctors can look at patterns of appointments and hospital attendance. For example, a child who presents with a range of different illnesses in a short time may cause suspicion.* The article ended: *If you believe a child is currently a victim of FDIA, you should contact the police or child protection services.*

In view of what I'd read, I wondered if the doctors should have suspected something was wrong sooner, but that was for the health authority to look into. I answered the emails in my inbox and then, exhausted after a gruelling week, switched off the computer, made a cup of tea and went into the living room to write up my log notes. It was only when I opened my log that I realized it was Friday the 13th. Associated with bad luck and misfortune, it seemed quite fitting, given what had been revealed today. But foster carers are expected to be professional and non-judgemental, so I wrote up my log notes objectively and dispassionately. The weekend beckoned and we had a lot to be grateful for: Molly and Kit were healthy and were being allowed to stay with us. My family and my mother were all doing well, so I needed to stop worrying. Sometimes that's easier said than done in fostering.

During the weekend my thoughts often returned to what Aneta had been doing to her children, but overall it was a good weekend. Probably the best we'd had since they'd arrived. The pressure had eased now they'd stopped being sick, and now I knew they would be with us for Christmas I could plan ahead. On Saturday, Lucy, Paula and I took Molly and Kit into town to do some Christmas shopping. I had a lot to buy for and having the girls there meant they could distract the children while I bought some of their presents. We spent over an hour in the toy shop and then another hour in the toy area of the department store. Many new toys were on display for children to explore and play with (and persuade their parents or carers to buy!). Lucy and Paula also began their Christmas shopping, and we had lunch out. It was such a relief to know Molly and Kit could eat what they wanted and I didn't have to worry about possible allergens the food or drink contained. However, it would take time before I completely got out of the habit of checking labels – I found myself doing it automatically.

When we arrived home that afternoon, I decided to give the children the toy mobile phones I'd bought for their leaving gifts, minus the card. I could have added them to their Christmas sacks, but I thought it would be nice if they had them now to enjoy. We didn't need to keep them amused from then on; they spent most of the time on their phones, pretending to make and receive calls. Kirsty came in to say hello to everyone and then she and Adrian went to see a play at the repertory theatre in a neighbouring town.

The children slept well and I woke to hear Molly on her phone, pretending to talk to Kit. Kit's phone was downstairs. Sunday was a bright, cold day and I took the children to a park a short drive away that had different play equipment. Lucy came with us, but Paula stayed at home to complete some college work, having been out shopping with us for most of the previous day. Later we all had dinner together, and then prepared ourselves for Monday and the start of another working week.

'Are we seeing Mummy on Monday?' Molly asked as I took her to bed.

'No, love, not tomorrow.'

'Can I see Daddy?'

'Not at present.'

'When can I see Mummy and Daddy?' she asked plaintively. I felt so sorry for her.

'I'm not sure, love. Tess is coming to talk to us next week. We will ask her then.'

'I miss Mummy and Daddy,' she said, her little face puckering and close to tears.

'I know, love. It's difficult. But it's important we keep you and Kit safe and healthy – just as you are now.'

An older child might have asked more and delved deeper, but at Molly's age she didn't have the reasoning or vocabulary to do that, although she would intuit what she couldn't verbalize and needed lots of reassurance and hugs, just as Kit did. Despite what their mother (and possibly their father too) had done to them, they loved their parents.

* * *

On Monday Tess telephoned, asked us what sort of weekend we'd had and then said she'd visit us on Wednesday afternoon at two o'clock. She didn't have anything new to tell me at present. When I finished the call, Molly asked me who was on the phone.

'Your social worker, Tess,' I said. 'She's coming to see us on Wednesday. That's not today or tomorrow but the next day.'

'Will I see Mummy and Daddy then?'

'No, love, but we can ask her about that.'

'You ask,' she said.

'Yes, I will.' I gave her and Kit another big hug.

I took the children to our local park on Monday afternoon, and then on Tuesday a fostering friend of mine visited. She was looking after a four-year-old boy who attended nursery five mornings a week. He played nicely with Molly and went out of his way to include Kit in the games, even adapting them for a younger child. He was only three months older then Molly, but his social skills were far more advanced. He was able to organize little games and knew how to take turns and share. I thought again that Molly would benefit from nursery and playing with similar-aged children. She played with Kit sometimes, of course, and my family, and I spent hours playing with both children, but she needed to interact with her peer group. I made a note to raise the matter with Tess. Previously Aneta had objected to the children attending nursery or playgroup on the grounds they were susceptible to germs and it would make them ill. That concern had now been negated. It wasn't germs that had been making Molly and Kit ill, but Aneta. I didn't see any reason why Molly shouldn't start attending nursery for a few mornings a week, even if their mother still objected.

* * *

On Wednesday, five minutes before Tess was due to arrive, I changed the boxes of toys in the living room for fresh ones in the hope that Molly and Kit would be kept amused while Tess and I talked. Unfortunately, Tess was half an hour late, by which time the children had tired of the toys, so I changed them again. I find that rotating toys allows children to come to them afresh. I'd put their mobile phones out of sight as the noise they made, especially when on together, would make it difficult for Tess and me to concentrate or even hear each other properly.

Tess apologized for being late, asked for a glass of water and went into the living room. 'My! You two look well,' she exclaimed as soon as she saw Molly and Kit.

'Can you see a difference?' I asked, pleased.

'Yes, even since the last time I saw them. They look so much brighter.'

'My family and I thought so too, but it's good to hear it from you.'

'So how are you both?' she asked Molly and Kit as she sipped her water. 'You look fine to me.'

Kit carried on playing, while Molly looked to me to ask the question that was on her mind.

'Molly would like to know when she can see her parents,' I said. 'She's asked me a few times.'

'That reminds me,' Tess said. 'I've got a photograph for you.' She delved into her bag and took out a six-by-four-inch photograph of Molly and Kit with their parents. It had been taken at contact, presumably by the contact supervisor on Filip's or Aneta's phone.

'That's great. I'll buy a frame for it and we can put in on the shelf in your bedroom,' I told the children enthusiastically. Most children in care have at least one family photograph, some have many. It helps to keep the memory of their parents alive while they are separated from them.

Molly looked at the picture and then at me again. I knew why: Tess hadn't answered my question.

'So is there no contact at present?' I asked Tess.

'No, but Mummy and Daddy both send their love,' she told the children. 'You and Kit are being well looked after and are happy here with Cathy, so there is nothing for you to worry about. Christmas is coming. You'll have lots of fun. What do you want Father Christmas to bring?' While Molly thought about this, Tess said quietly to me, 'Aneta is in –' and she named the psychiatric unit in the city hospital. I nodded. 'Their solicitor has been in touch. Filip is asking for contact, just for him. We're considering it, but I want to hear from the police first.'

I nodded again.

'Can I see Mummy and Daddy?' Molly asked.

'Not for now,' Tess said. 'Cathy will tell you if that changes.' Clearly Tess had decided not to tell Molly their mother was receiving psychiatric care and I thought that was the right decision. Mental illness can be difficult for adults to understand; it would be virtually impossible to explain it to a three-year-old, and Molly didn't need to know. 'OK?' Tess asked Molly, and she gave a small nod. I thought it was time to change the subject.

'I was thinking it would be nice if Molly went to nursery a few mornings each week,' I said. 'I could take Kit to a toddler group so they both get used to playing with other children.'

'Excellent idea,' Tess said positively, and smiled at Molly. She took a notepad and pen from her bag and made a note. 'Do you have a nursery in mind?' she asked me.

'There is a good one attached to our local infant school, but I know they have a waiting list.'

'Looked-after children can usually be found a place,' she said. 'Give me the details and I'll speak to them.'

I told her the name and address of the nursery, then as she wrote I quickly googled their contact number on my phone and read that out. 'They also run a toddler group one afternoon a week where the parent or carer stays. There isn't a waiting list, I checked. I was thinking of taking Kit to that. Obviously, Molly would come too.'

'Fine with me,' Tess said, and made another note. 'Anything else?' she asked. Both children were playing again.

'Yes,' I said. 'I've received this letter from the allergy clinic at the hospital.' I passed her the letter. 'You remember a referral was made that time I had to take Kit to the hospital and he was kept in overnight?' She nodded as she read the letter.

'He doesn't need to go to this, does he?' she asked me, looking up.

'No, I don't think so. He's not allergic to anything.'

'Other than vomiting linctus,' Tess said cuttingly.

'Exactly. If you are OK with it, I thought I'd phone and cancel the appointment.'

'Yes. The children have been through enough unnecessary medical tests, they don't need any more.'

She handed back the letter and I put it to one side to deal with later.

'Can we have our mobile phones?' Molly now asked me.

Tess looked at me, horrified.

'Toy ones,' I clarified.

She laughed. 'For one moment I thought –'

'I know. But surely no one gives a child aged three a real one?'

'You'd be surprised.'

'Can we have our phones?' Molly asked again.

'Yes, OK, but we'll put the volume on low,' I said.

I retrieved the toy phones from the cupboard and turned down the volume on both before handing them to the children. They began pressing buttons and the recorded messages, sounds and music played as Tess and I talked. She asked me about the children's routine, their development, general health and well-being, which was a standard part of most social worker visits, and took notes. Finally, she said, 'All that's left is for me to have a look around.' It's usual for the social worker to check the foster carer's house when they visit, just as the supervising social worker does. 'Are you going to show me your bedroom?' she asked the children.

'Yes,' Molly said, and took it as a sign to turn up the volume on her phone and on Kit's. It didn't matter. Tess and I had finished talking.

Tess took Kit's free hand and I took Molly's and the four of us walked around the house, in and out of the rooms, to the nursery rhymes coming loudly from Kit's phone and the voice counting to twenty from Molly's.

CHAPTER TWENTY-TWO

LOVE THE CHILDREN

After Tess had gone, I quickly zipped the children into their winter coats and took them to the High Street to choose a frame for the family photograph Tess had brought with her. On our return, Molly watched as I put the photo into the frame and then set in on a shelf in her bedroom. Kit could come in and see it whenever he wanted to, although he wasn't showing the same interest Molly was. She spent some time repositioning it and then asked again when she would see her mummy and daddy. I told her Tess had said she'd let us know, and reassured her that her mummy and daddy were fine and she mustn't worry about them.

'I miss Mummy and Daddy,' she said as we returned downstairs.

'I know you do, love.'

But I also knew from fostering other children that the pain of separation usually eased the longer the child went without seeing their parents, until eventually they were ready to bond with a new forever family. Sad though it is, some children can't ever return home and are either fostered long term, adopted or looked after by another family member. The main reason for Kit and Molly coming into care had been the suspicion of non-accidental injury, and the care plan had been a full care order with the likelihood they wouldn't return home. I assumed this was still true. Although care plans can and do change, nothing had come to light to say they would be safe at home – far from it.

On Thursday afternoon, Tess telephoned, having spoken to the head of the local nursery. 'They can offer Molly a place for two mornings a week.'

'That's fantastic,' I said. 'Thank you.'

'The Head is Alison Dene. I've given her some background information and she's expecting you to phone her. She'd like you to take Molly in for a preliminary visit before she starts.'

'Thank you so much. I'll phone her now. This will be great for Molly.'

'Let me know how it goes,' Tess said.

'I will.' I thanked her again and we said goodbye.

I'd taken the call in the living room where Molly and Kit were playing and I stayed there while I telephoned the nursery. There was nothing they shouldn't overhear.

'Could I speak to Alison Dene, please?' I said as a woman answered.

'Speaking.'

'Hello, I'm Cathy Glass, I believe Tess –'

I didn't get any further. 'Yes. Hello. The children's social worker called earlier. I'd be happy to offer Molly a place for two mornings a week, starting next week. It would have to be Tuesday and Thursday, as we're completely full on all the other days. Is that all right with you?'

'Yes. That's perfect.'

'We always like an introductory visit before the child starts, so I suggest you bring Molly here tomorrow morning at eleven o'clock if you can manage it. I know how busy you foster carers are.'

'Yes, we can make that.'

'Excellent. I'll show you around, give you the information pack, and you can fill in the registration form. We like parents and carers to stay with the child for the first week while they settle in.'

'I'll have Molly's younger brother with me. Is that OK?'

'That's fine. See you tomorrow then at eleven.'

'Yes.'

She sounded a lovely lady and very enthusiastic. I was excited for Molly. I replaced the handset and immediately told her.

'Will Mummy and Daddy be there?' she asked.

'No, love, it's for children. You'll have a great time. You'll do lots of fun things and will be able to play with other children your age. We're going for a visit tomorrow.'

'Is Kit coming?'

'Yes, for tomorrow and next week, then we'll take and collect you. Nursery is for big children like you.'

'Will you stay?'

'To begin with, yes.'

'Will I have to sleep there?' she asked, worried.

'No, love.' I gave her a hug. Going to nursery is a big step for most children, but I knew once she'd been a few times and was settled she'd love it. 'It's just for two mornings a week,' I said. 'I have a book somewhere that explains about going to nursery.'

I hunted through the bookshelf and found what I was looking for: *Ned Goes to Nursery*. It was for children about to start nursery and told the story of Ned, a teddy bear, and his first days at nursery. It was beautifully illustrated and addressed many of the worries young children might have at the prospect of going to nursery. Kit wanted to see the book too, so I sat on the sofa with a child either side of me and read the story as they looked at the pictures. I watched Molly's face and could see she was identifying with Ned and being reassured as his concerns were allayed. She wanted me to read it again, and by the time I'd read it a third time she was looking less anxious about nursery.

When Paula, Lucy and Adrian returned home that evening I made a big thing about telling them that Molly was going to start nursery, and they joined in my praise and enthusiasm. When Lucy told Molly that she worked in a nursery just like the one she would be going to, Molly wouldn't leave her side. By the time Molly went to bed, she was looking forward to visiting nursery the following day and telling Lucy all about it.

That evening I looked online again at the details of the playgroup for toddlers I wanted to take Kit to. It was held at the school, but in a separate room to the nursery, every Wednesday 2–4 p.m. The website said a little about the aim of the group, the activities they organized and that they charged £1 per child towards the cost of a drink and a snack. There wasn't a waiting list, but the organizer asked parents and carers to get in touch first, as numbers were limited because of health and safety requirements. I emailed info@ saying I would like to start bringing the child I was fostering, aged twenty months, and I'd need to bring his older sister with me too. Five minutes later an email came back.

Hi Cathy, it's Kate Evans. Remember me? Yes, I did, although I hadn't seen her in a long while. She lived a few roads along from me and had a boy a similar age to Adrian. They'd been in the same class and good friends during primary school, but as far as I knew didn't see each other now. Kate had been a childminder back then, so she was very experienced in childcare. It was lovely to hear from her. She asked how we all were, said she'd heard I was still fostering and confirmed I could take the children on Wednesday, and looked forward to catching up. I emailed back, thanking her, saying we were all well, that I hoped she and her family were well too and I'd see her on Wednesday.

I was pleased both children would soon have the benefit of attending a pre-school group where they could mix with their peers. While Kit was of an age where he could have gone to nursery, I thought it would be too much for him at this point, as he'd had so little experience of being with other children, and had had to cope with the disruption of leaving his parents and coming into care.

The following morning, Molly was awake very early. I heard her cry out at 5.30. Not fully awake, I grabbed my dressing gown and went round the landing to her bedroom. She was sitting up in bed, leaning forward and clutching her stomach. 'I feel sick,' she moaned.

In a flash all my old fears returned. I thought I must have given her something to eat that she was allergic to, or Aneta had poisoned her. Then I realized it was because she was worried about going to nursery – the Monday-morning tummy ache many school children complain of.

'Molly, love,' I said, sitting on her bed, 'you're fine. You won't be sick.'

'I will. I'll be sick like with Mummy.'

I hesitated and looked at her. She had a good colour and apart from frowning and looking anxious she didn't appear ill. 'I am sure you're not going to be sick. You haven't been sick in a long while. It's all stopped now. I think if you have a tummy ache, it's because you are a bit worried about going to see your nursery today.'

'Why?' she asked.

'Because it's all new to you. Lots of children and adults have funny tummies if they have to do something new that they are not sure about. It's sometimes called having butterflies and will pass.' She looked at me doubtfully. 'You'll be fine once you've seen your nursery and have spent some time there,' I continued. 'It's a bit early to get up yet, so I'd like you to lie down and try to go back to sleep. If you can't, then look at some books quietly while I get ready, and please don't worry about nursery. You'll enjoy it.' I placed some books on her bed.

'Will I be sick?' she asked.

'No.'

'What if I am?'

'You won't be.'

I persuaded her to lie down and left her looking at a book while I showered and dressed. I was usually up shortly after six o'clock anyway, so it wasn't worth going back to bed. When I checked on Molly after I'd showered she was asleep again. She slept for another hour, but as soon as she was awake she asked, 'Will I be sick at nursery?'

'No.'

'Are you sure?'

'Yes.'

I guessed it would take some time before the constant worry of being sick completely left her, if it ever did.

Molly didn't want much breakfast, but I wasn't worried. She was still a little anxious, and she could make up for it at lunch once the anxiety of her first visit to nursery was behind her. We left the house just after 10.30 a.m. with Kit in the stroller and Molly walking slowly beside me. She was quiet, but Kit kept up a steady flow of chatter. His latest expression was 'Whatsthat?' – all run together into one word – and he said it as he pointed to virtually everything we passed. I told him: 'That's a house'. 'A blue car'. 'A tin can'. 'A dog'. 'A lamppost'. 'A dog weeing up a lamppost.' Finally, Molly laughed.

We arrived at the nursery just before eleven o'clock. I pressed the security buzzer and gave my name. 'I'm here for Molly's visit,' I said. While I was familiar with the layout of the school and nursery from when I'd brought my children and some of those I'd fostered, all the staff had changed. Alison Dene, the Head, whom I'd spoken to yesterday, let us in, and was as friendly and warm in person as she had been on the phone. She made a big fuss of Molly and then showed us around the nursery. Most of the children were in the main room where the activities were and looked about Molly's age. They were all occupied – painting, playing in the sand pit, at the water table, in the playhouse and so on. The room was bright with lots of colourful collages on the walls and mobiles hanging from the ceiling. Alison showed us the separate room for babies and infants who still needed a sleep. It was prettily decorated and had four cots, a changing station and a rocking chair.

As we returned to the main room, Alison suggested I put Kit's name on the waiting list for the nursery in case he was still with me. She then gave me an information pack for Molly, which included a registration form, and introduced us to Molly's keyworker, Julie, a young lady who reminded me of Lucy. All the children were assigned a keyworker who they could go to if they needed anything, and who would keep an eye on them. I filled in the registration form, while Molly spent some time with Julie, who talked to her and encouraged her to play with some of the activities.

We stayed until the end of the session and Molly didn't want to leave, she'd had such a nice time. I thanked Julie for looking after her and said we'd see her again next Tuesday. Molly didn't stop talking about nursery all the way home and was looking forward to going again. I was relieved and pleased. However, it must have tired her out because after lunch she fell asleep on the sofa for over an hour. This allowed me some one-to-one time with Kit. Later that afternoon, Molly drew some pictures of her nursery to show Lucy, Paula and Adrian – especially Lucy.

'Fantastic. It's just like my nursery!' Lucy exclaimed as Molly proudly showed her the drawing. In truth it was a typical three-year-old's drawing with lots of different-coloured lines and swirls but nothing distinguishable. It was what Molly wanted to hear, though, and she was delighted.

The following morning, Molly wanted to go to nursery again, so I had to explain that it wasn't held at the weekend and we'd go again on Tuesday – three more sleeps. We had a relaxing day on Saturday and then visited my mother on Sunday, then there were just two more sleeps until Molly could go to nursery again.

On Tuesday I stayed for the whole of the first session, although Molly spent most of it away from me and playing alongside other children. During the second session on Thursday Julie suggested that Kit and I leave the nursery for half an hour to get Molly used to being left, which I did. When I returned, Julie said Molly had asked where I was a couple of times but had been easily reassured. The following week I left her at the start and collected her at the end of the sessions, as the other mothers and carers did, and she was fine. We also began attending the playgroup for Kit on Wednesday afternoon and that went well. Our weeks were now very busy, and with less than a month to go until Christmas I began shopping in earnest. The first weekend in December we put up our Christmas decorations.

Retrieving the boxes of Christmas decorations from the loft and decorating the house is a family tradition, and everyone joins in. Molly couldn't remember last Christmas and Kit had only been nine months old, but Molly said they'd been talking about Christmas at nursery, so she had some understanding of what it meant. Lucy and Paula decided we should approach the task methodically by hanging the ceiling decorations first, then those that went on the walls and doors, then spraying the artificial frost on the windows, and then finally dressing the tree. Adrian, the tallest, went up the ladder, while Lucy, Paula and Molly passed up the decorations, and I tried to keep Kit occupied and out of the way. It was impossible, and happy chaos resulted. Kit pulled garlands, tinsel and baubles from the boxes before Adrian and the girls were ready for them, became entangled in the streamers and then tried to decorate Sammy, who eventually shot out through the cat flap.

It took all afternoon, but by the time we'd finished our house sparkled and shone, ready for Christmas. We switched on the tree lights as soon as it went dark, and it was magical. However, I'd learnt from previous years not to put the chocolate novelties and candy canes on the tree until much closer to Christmas, as they had a habit of mysteriously disappearing, for which Mr Nobody was responsible. I had some illustrated children's books about Christmas which I kept with the decorations and I read them to Molly and Kit for their bedtime stories. Molly was very excited and kept asking questions about Christmas and presents, and going to church on Christmas Eve, which I'd told them all about. My mother would be coming to us for Christmas and we'd see my brother and his family and close friends over the Christmas period. My family and I have always loved Christmas, but we are acutely aware that it can be very difficult for families who are separated. Christmas is a family time and the loss of separation is highlighted by all the images on the television and in magazines of families celebrating Christmas together.

It was now nearly four weeks since Molly and Kit had seen their parents and they were talking about them less and less. The last time Tess had mentioned contact was when she'd told me that Aneta was in a psychiatric hospital and Filip's solicitor was asking for contact for just him, and she was waiting for the outcome of the police enquiry. The following Wednesday Tess phoned. She thanked me for my email updating her about Molly going to nursery and Kit's play-group, asked how they were, and then said, 'We're going to reinstate contact for Filip two days a week, starting this Friday. The police are satisfied that he played no part in making the children ill.'

'OK.'

'I shall observe contact this Friday,' Tess continued. 'It will be Monday and Friday, three till five, so Filip can work the early shift. I won't have a chance to see Molly and Kit before Friday so can you prepare them for seeing their father again, please?'

'Yes, I will. A month is a long time in a young child's life. What shall I tell them about their mother? Molly is sure to ask.'

'If Molly does ask then tell her she is in hospital, which is what Filip will be saying.'

'All right.'

Tess then said she'd just sent out the invitations for the children's next review on 17th December, and we said goodbye. I wasn't surprised that contact had resumed for Filip if he hadn't played any part in making his children ill. He had a moral and legal right to see them, at least until the final court hearing when the judge would decide where Molly and Kit would live permanently, and set any contact arrangements.

I introduced the subject of contact to Molly and Kit that afternoon as we walked to playgroup. 'Tess telephoned me and she said you will be able to see your daddy this Friday afternoon.'

Molly looked thoughtful. 'And Mummy?' she asked.

'No. It will just be Daddy, and Tess will be there too.'

'Why not Mummy?'

'She is in hospital being looked after by doctors and nurses.'

'Mummy likes hospitals,' Molly said, as she'd said before. 'I hope I'm not sick,' she said a moment later, immediately growing anxious.

'No, you won't be. That time has passed.'

'I don't like being sick. I like living with you, because I'm not sick.'

'Good.' I smiled.

'Do you like me living with you?'

'Yes, I do, a lot.' I swallowed hard. I was a professional foster carer and knew that at some point the children could leave me, but that hadn't stopped me growing very close to them, loving them, as did my family. If we ever had to say goodbye, I knew it was going to be heart-breaking for us all.

CHAPTER TWENTY-THREE

DISCLOSURE

I prepared Molly and Kit as best I could for seeing their father again on Friday. Molly, that much older, had a better understanding than Kit. 'Daddy,' he said whenever I broached the subject. I replied, 'Yes, you are seeing your daddy again on Friday.' Molly kept telling him that too.

I was slightly apprehensive at meeting Filip again after all that had happened. I also worried that the children might not show him the warmth they had done in the past and which he might be expecting. Molly and Kit had got used to life without their parents, were bonding with my family and had different lives now that involved nursery and playgroup, where they were making friends. They weren't the quiet, anxious, compliant and sickly children Filip had been used to.

I explained to Molly and Kit that they'd be seeing their father at the Family Centre and I'd take and collect them as I had before. Molly fell silent as we approached the centre, but Kit kept up his usual chatter. 'Whatsthat?' he said as I parked.

'The Family Centre, silly,' Molly replied.

'Molly, he's only little,' I reminded her.

The notice in reception about not taking in food and drink had gone, having served its purpose. The receptionist told me the children would be in Rainbow Room – primarily reserved for babies and very young children. Whether this was by chance or design I didn't know, but I was pleased they weren't in Blue Room. It could have set off many memories, not all of them positive. This seemed to be a fresh start. I signed the Visitors' Book and the receptionist said we could go straight through, as Tess and the children's father were already there.

I took Molly and Kit by the hand and we went down the corridor and through swing fire doors. 'Is Mummy here?' Molly asked, although I'd already told her a few times she wouldn't be.

'No, just Daddy, and Tess, your social worker.'

We had to cross the central atrium to get to Rainbow Room and a boy aged about eight was kicking a football with his mother. She told him to stop to let the kiddies pass. I thanked them and we continued across and down a short corridor. The door to Rainbow Room was decorated with brightly coloured rainbows. I knocked and opened it. Filip, dressed smartly in grey trousers, open-neck shirt and jumper, was standing in the middle of the room with Tess. It was clear they'd been talking. A contact supervisor, a different one from before, sat at the table.

'Molly, Kit!' Filip said as he saw them, and opened his arms wide.

The children hesitated and then Molly shouted, 'Daddy!' at the top of her voice and ran to him. Kit followed. Filip scooped them up and held them close. I saw his face crumple as he dissolved into tears. The poor man was embarrassed and buried his head in his children so we couldn't see him cry. My heart went out to him, and if Tess hadn't placed a comforting hand on his arm I would have done. His shoulders heaved as, head down, he wept. I felt my own eyes fill.

Tess nodded to me that I could go. 'I'll see you at five,' I said quietly, and came out, closing the door behind me.

I swallowed hard as I began back down the corridor. Yes, it had been upsetting and very moving to see Filip so emotional, but I was relieved and pleased Molly and Kit had gone readily to their father. It would have been far more upsetting for him if they'd appeared cool or even rejected him. It was a promising start and I hoped the rest of the contact followed suit. I assumed Tess had talked to Filip and explained that the children might need time to adjust, having not seen him for a month, and were unlikely to be able to simply pick up where they'd left off. I'd had experience of parents who, for various reasons, had been in a similar position, where they hadn't seen their children for a while, and when contact resumed they'd become upset and angry that their children hadn't been able to show them the love and attention they'd been expecting. Sometimes they were angry at the foster carer, whom they felt had been encouraging the children in this. It's not like that. Children bond with their main care-giver, whoever it is: birth parent, adoptive parent, foster carer or relative. It they don't then it's even more worrying, as it suggests they might have an attachment disorder, which if left untreated can have a negative impact on the rest of their lives.

When I returned to collect Molly and Kit I was apprehensive again, hoping it had all gone well. It was exactly five o'clock as I knocked on the door to Rainbow Room and went in. The children were sitting on the sofa either side of their father and listening to a story. He had an arm around each of them and they both had their heads resting against his chest. Molly was sucking her thumb as she did sometimes when she was relaxed. The contact supervisor was at the table, writing, and Tess had apparently gone.

'Is it that time already?' Filip asked, looking up.

'I'm afraid so,' I said. 'Have you all had a nice time?' The atmosphere was calm and relaxed, quite different to the end of some contacts, when Filip had been playing riotous games with Molly and Kit.

'Yes, we have, thank you,' Filip said, and slowly took his arms from his children and closed the book. 'Molly has been telling me about nursery,' he said, standing. 'I hear Kit goes to a group too.'

'Yes, that's right, although I stay with him.'

'Tess explained.' Filip returned the book to the shelf and came over to where I was waiting, just inside the door. 'Molly's quite the young lady,' he said. 'She's talking a lot more and Kit's got some words too, so that's good.' Although what he said was positive, there was sadness in his eyes. 'You know where Aneta is?' he asked me quietly.

'Yes. Tess told me.'

He nodded slowly. 'I see her most days after work.'

'How is she?'

'Making progress. Tomorrow I'll tell her I've seen Molly and Kit and they are doing well. She will be pleased. She knows what she did was wrong.' He stopped. Molly and Kit had come over to us now. 'I'm sure these two have grown since I last saw them!' he exclaimed, and picked them up. 'They'll be as tall as me soon!'

I smiled. He kissed and hugged them goodbye, and set them down again. 'Molly plays nicely with Kit now,' he remarked.

'Yes, I think mixing with other children at nursery is helping.'

He looked thoughtful. 'They didn't really mix before. Aneta didn't ...' Aware the children would hear, he let his words fall away. 'Anyway, you're doing a good job.' But his eyes were sad.

'Thank you. We'll see you on Monday then. Have a good weekend.'

'And you.'

He said goodbye to the children again and we left, the children parting easily from their father. They were quiet as we left the centre, but as I drove away Molly said, 'Daddy was different. Unhappy.'

'He's been through a lot,' I said, glancing at her in the rear-view mirror. 'He was very pleased to see you both. That will make him happy.'

'I told him about my friends at nursery and he's going to tell Mummy.'

'Good.'

'Why can't I tell Mummy?' Molly asked.

'Because your mummy is in hospital.'

'That's what Daddy said. When can I see Mummy?'

'I don't know, love. What did your daddy say?' I guessed she'd asked him, and parents are often made aware of arrangements before the foster carer.

'Daddy said he didn't know. But someone must know!' she declared adamantly and tutted. I smiled to myself.

'We will be told if anything changes,' I said.

'Whatsthat?' Kit said, pointing to a large red bus that had just pulled out in front of us.

'It's a bus, silly,' Molly told him.

'Don't call him silly,' I lightly admonished. 'We all have to learn.'

'But he is.'

Calling Kit silly had increased since Molly had started nursery, so I thought that while mixing with her peers had generally been positive, it had also produced some behaviour we could have done without, just as school often does.

While I drove, Molly talked about the games they'd played with their father. She also said their mother was in hospital, being made better by the doctors, which I assumed was what Filip had said. But then, as I parked outside the house, she suddenly said, 'Cathy, you know Kit broke his arm?'

'Yes, love, but it's all better now.'

'It was my fault.'

I turned in my seat to look at her. 'What do you mean?'

'I was playing with him at the top of the stairs and I pushed him and he fell. I didn't know he would fall all the way down and break his arm. I'm sorry, I didn't mean to.'

'And you can remember that?' She nodded. 'Where was Mummy?'

'In the bathroom, brushing her teeth. She told me not to play on the stairs, but I did.'

'OK, love. It was an accident. You didn't mean to hurt him.'

'He was crying and I was upset he was hurt.'

'I know. It must have hurt him a lot. But you wouldn't do anything like that again, would you?'

'No. I was sorry. I love Kit.'

'I know. Good girl. What made you tell me now?'

She thought for a moment and then said, 'Mummy is in hospital. It made me think about it.' Which rang true. Children often remember traumatic events more acutely than happy ones. Kit's broken arm was the last trauma she'd been through before coming into care and it had resulted in them all going to hospital. Of course, what Molly had said was highly significant as the injury had been considered non-accidental.

I reassured Molly that Kit was fine now and his arm was completely healed, and once indoors I asked Paula to look after the children while I wrote up my log. I needed to do so while it was fresh in my mind and I used Molly's exact words. Kit's broken arm, suspected non-accidental injury caused by their mother, had been the deciding factor in bringing the children into care. I didn't know what other injuries they had suffered prior to this that were thought to be non-accidental, but if what Molly had said was true – and I had no reason to doubt her – then Aneta wasn't responsible for Kit's broken arm. Some time ago Aneta had claimed she was innocent and it was Molly's fault, and it seemed in this instance she was right. However, Molly, at her age, couldn't be held responsible, as she wouldn't have fully understood that pushing Kit could result in him being seriously injured. What bearing Molly's disclosure would have on the child-protection case I didn't know, but as soon as the children were in bed I emailed Tess, typing exactly what Molly had told me from my log notes.

Saturday morning, the invitation to the children's review on 17th December arrived with booklets for the children to complete. As before, I filled in Kit's and then sat with Molly and wrote down her answers. She wanted to draw a picture in the space at the end of the form for further comments and I gave her crayons. She drew a box and filled it with lots of different-coloured lines and circles, which she told me was a house with Mummy, Daddy, Kit, her and all of us living in it. I wrote what she'd said beside it.

On Sunday we went to see my mother, minus Adrian, who was going to Kirsty's for lunch, and once again Molly and Kit enjoyed the special attention that a grandparent can give. All their questions, comments and needs, regardless of how trivial, were responded to immediately. My mother loved to spoil the children we looked after, and Molly and Kit took it in turns to sit on her lap for a cuddle and to be made a fuss of. Molly told Mum about nursery and also that she used to push Kit, but she didn't any more because it was unkind and hurt. I guessed that pushing Kit downstairs was still very much on her mind. Mum told Molly that we have to be kind to those younger than us and look after them, reinforcing what I'd been telling her. Molly also told my mother that her mummy was in hospital, and she was only seeing her daddy.

On Monday morning, Tess telephoned. She thanked me for my email and asked if I thought Molly was telling the truth about pushing Kit downstairs or if she was being loyal to her mother by taking the blame. I said I thought she was telling the truth, partly because of the childlike way she'd described it. Tess said she'd read the contact supervisor's report for Friday and the incident on the stairs hadn't been mentioned, so it wasn't Filip who'd suggested she take the blame. Apparently, he'd told Molly her mother was in hospital and had answered her questions, but that was all. I know of instances at contact where a parent, desperate to have their child returned or to escape a criminal prosecution, told their child to lie to their foster carer and social workers and take the blame for events that led to them coming into care, not appreciating that what they were saying was being written down by the contact supervisor and would find its way to their social worker.

On Monday afternoon the children saw their father again and I took in another batch of photographs of Molly and Kit for Filip to keep. I gave them to him at the start of contact and he was very grateful. He seemed a bit more relaxed than he had on Friday and asked if we'd had a nice weekend and what we'd done. He said he'd worked Saturday and Sunday mornings and had visited Aneta in the afternoon. At the end of contact he thanked me again for the photographs and asked about the soft-play centre and the various parks that were shown in them. 'I'll show them to Aneta,' he said. 'I'm going there now, straight after contact.'

'Have a good evening,' I said.

'Thank you, and you. Will you be at the review on Thursday?' he asked.

'Yes. I'll see you there.'

As I came away I wondered as to the wisdom of showing Aneta the photographs when she'd been so opposed to me taking the children out. However, foster carers are expected to give the parents photographs, sometimes video clips, as well as including photos in the child's Life Story Book. I could hardly have told Filip not to show Aneta. It was his decision, he was in regular contact with his wife, knew how she was progressing and had clearly forgiven her for harming their children far more readily than I was doing. I was struggling to come to terms with what she'd done, and couldn't help thinking of all the times she'd made little Molly and Kit sick while at home and after coming into care.

On Thursday, the day of the review, Molly went to nursery as usual in the morning. When I collected her, I had to do a quick turnaround to be at the review for 1.30 p.m., so I had a sandwich lunch ready for them at home. I'd asked Maggie to babysit again and she arrived fifteen minutes early, but without Keelie.

'She's in school!' Maggie declared triumphantly as she came in. 'She's finally woken up to the fact that she'll need qualifications to have a career in childcare. In part, that's thanks to you. Or rather these two little darlings …' We'd gone through to the kitchen-diner where Molly and Kit were seated at the table, having their lunch. Maggie kissed the top of their heads. 'Thanks to you two treasures Keelie wants to become a nanny.'

'Wonderful,' I said. 'I'm sure she'll be very good at it.'

'Yes, although she only wants to be a nanny in a very rich family in Dubai where she'll have her own flat, car and swimming pool, and be taken on holidays all over the world!'

'Well, she's aiming high,' I laughed.

'You can say that again!'

I couldn't stay to chat as I had to leave, so, saying goodbye to Molly and Kit, I left them to it. As I went down the hall I heard Molly ask Maggie when she would see Keelie again and Maggie replied, 'This Saturday, at the fostering Christmas party.'

'Great!' I called, and let myself out of the front door.

CHAPTER TWENTY-FOUR

THE WONDER OF CHRISTMAS

The Guardian ad Litem and Edith weren't present at the review. There was no obligation for the Guardian to attend, as there was for the social worker and foster carer, and Edith was ill, I learnt. They would be sent copies of the minutes when they were circulated. Filip said he'd come straight from work and Tess arrived carrying a mug of coffee, saying she'd come straight from another meeting. The Independent Reviewing Officer (IRO) was the same one as last time – Mary Bridges. She opened her laptop, thanked us for coming, noted apologies for absence and then asked us to introduce ourselves. 'Your wife won't be joining us then?' she asked Filip.

'No. She's still in hospital.'

She nodded. 'So this is the second review for Molly and Kit and I see quite a lot has happened since the last one. Cathy, would you like to start by telling us how the children are now, please?'

I had my notes ready on the table in front of me. The IRO was right when she said a lot had happened since the last review, but it wasn't for me to cover it all, and I chose my words carefully. 'Kit's broken arm has healed,' I began positively, 'so he no longer has to wear a splint, and there are no more follow-up appointments.' I paused to allow the IRO time to type. 'Both children are well and up to date with their health checks,' I continued. 'Kit was hospitalized at the end of October when he was very sick and developed a rash and difficulty breathing. I called an ambulance and he was admitted overnight, but he recovered by the follow morning. It was at a time when both children were being sick – throughout September and October. They stopped being ill at the beginning of November when it was discovered what was causing them to be sick.' I paused again to allow the IRO to catch up. I wouldn't mention Aneta's FDIA unless asked. Tess would cover that if she felt it appropriate, and the IRO would have been made aware of it prior to the review.

'Molly and Kit are both doing very well,' I continued. 'Molly is attending nursery two mornings a week and is really enjoying it.' The IRO smiled as she typed. 'She's learning how to share and is making friends. I take Kit to a playgroup one afternoon a week where I stay, and he likes playing with the other children.'

'How are Molly and Kit getting along with each other?' the IRO asked.

'Molly sometimes has to be reminded that Kit is younger and smaller than she is, and she mustn't push him, but generally she's more aware of her actions. Apart from a little sibling rivalry, they get along like most brothers and sisters their age.'

'Do they still sleep in separate rooms?'

'Yes, Molly has her own room and Kit's cot is in my bedroom. Both children eat well and generally sleep well,' I continued. 'They are healthy and happy.'

'Do they have any allergies?' the IRO asked.

'No.'

'Do they take any regular medication?'

'No.'

'And the food diary? Are you still keeping it?'

'No. The police needed it.' I kept my eyes away from Filip.

'Any accidents or injuries?' she asked. It was a standard question.

'Only the usual falls from playing in the park or garden, so a few bruises on their knees but nothing serious. I make a note of all accidents in my log.'

The IRO nodded. 'What do the children like to do in their spare time? Can you give an example of a typical day?'

I described an average day and talked a bit about the activities they liked to do at home and also the outings we went on.

'Thank you. Contact has just been re-established; how is that going?' she asked.

'It was only resumed last Friday, but it's going well so far. The children haven't seen their mother. Contact is just with their father at the Family Centre.'

She nodded as she typed. 'And the children can stay with you until the final court hearing?' It was another standard question.

'Yes.'

Filip shifted in his seat and made as if to say something but stopped.

'Is there anything else you would like to add?' the IRO asked me.

'I don't think so.' I glanced at my notes. 'Just that the children are doing well and are a delight to look after.'

'Good,' the IRO said, and then asked Tess to give her report.

Tess began by confirming the care plan was up to date and that she was in regular contact with me and visited the children at least every four weeks. She said both Molly and Kit had continued to suffer bouts of sickness after they'd come into care, but that these had stopped with the diagnosis of Aneta's FDIA, also known as Munchausen syndrome by proxy. She had to spell it for the IRO. She then said Aneta was receiving psychiatric care as a voluntary patient, and gave the name of the hospital and the date she was admitted.

'Do we know when she is likely to be discharged?' the IRO asked.

'No,' Tess said. 'Not at present. I am hoping to speak to the psychiatrist next week.' She then said that there were no plans for the children to see their mother at present or to increase contact with their father. 'However, Filip has applied to have the children returned home,' she said.

'Really?' the IRO asked, clearly as unaware of this as I was.

I looked at Filip, who was concentrating on Tess, his expression serious.

'Yesterday we heard from their solicitor,' Tess said. 'Filip is asking that the children be returned home, and he will put in place childcare until his wife is well enough to be discharged from hospital and look after them. It's likely we will oppose the application.'

'Has a court date been set for that hearing?' the IRO asked as she typed.

'No, not yet. We'll need time to prepare for it: a psychiatric assessment for Aneta, general medicals, the police report, DBS checks and parenting assessments for both parents.'

I glanced at Filip again, but his expression gave nothing away. I was surprised he'd applied to have the children returned to his care. I thought he didn't have a chance. Apart from the practicalities of arranging childcare around the hours he worked, he'd had virtually no experience of bringing up his children before they'd come into care. Also, as far as I knew, Aneta still faced the possibility of police prosecution, and she was a voluntary patient at a psychiatric unit. Supposing she discharged herself before she was well and went home? Little wonder Tess had said the social services would oppose Filip's application.

There was some discussion between the IRO and Tess about the timing of the various court hearings and then the IRO asked her if there were any complaints that needed to be noted. Tess said there were and briefly outlined the complaints Aneta had made during September and October, some of which I was aware of. I saw Filip shift uncomfortably in his seat.

The IRO thanked Tess for her report and then said to Filip, 'Would you like to speak now?'

'Yes, please.' He drew himself up and took a breath. I guessed then that whatever he was about to say he'd given a lot of thought to – he didn't have any notes. 'I don't sleep at night for thinking about what my wife did to our children,' he began, his voice tight. 'I blame myself for not noticing the harm she was causing them or that she was mentally ill. At the time I thought I was doing the right thing, working seven days a week to give my family a reasonable standard of living, but clearly I was wrong. Had I been at home more I might have seen what was going on. It crucifies me to think how Molly and Kit suffered – constantly being sick and having to undergo all those needless tests at the hospital. I let my children down badly, more so than Aneta, who was mentally unwell.' He paused and took a deep breath, trying to contain his emotion.

'It's all right. Take your time,' the IRO said.

He nodded. 'Thank you. My wife hasn't always been like this. She can be loving and caring. We both wanted a family and she was overjoyed when she found out she was expecting. But she was very anxious and being a mother brought back many dark memories of her own childhood. I am not making excuses for what she did, but you should know she was badly abused as a child by her mother. She hasn't seen her since she left home at the age of sixteen. She didn't ever want to talk about what happened, but she probably should have done. She's talking about it now to the psychologist at the hospital. Aneta is not a bad person. She's ill and the doctors are making her better.' He paused again to compose himself.

'I have spoken to the doctor and I've also attended a therapy session with my wife. She is being helped to identify the feelings from her past that caused her to act as she did. She is also learning to change her behaviour and to see that healthy relationships don't rely on someone being ill. I believe she is recovering and that in time she will be able to look after our children again, or rather we both will. I intend to do more. The doctor is positive and has treated other people with FDIA. I see Aneta every day and she always wants to know what Molly and Kit are doing. She is pleased they are well and happy, and bears no grudges, but, like me, she believes the children should be at home. I waited a long time to marry and have children, and I love Molly and Kit just as Aneta does. I couldn't bear it if I never saw them again. I'll do whatever it takes to bring my children home.' His voice broke and his eyes filled. 'Sorry,' he said, embarrassed. 'Can you give me a minute?'

'It's all right,' the IRO said sensitively. 'It's a very emotional time.'

There was silence as Filip took a cotton handkerchief from his pocket and wiped his eyes. I was choked up. He came across as a good, kind man, and what he'd said had been heartfelt and sincere. I thought that Aneta was very lucky to have him as a husband and the children to have him as a father. But I doubted how much of what he'd said would sway the social services or a judge. Their priority was to keep the children safe and make sure they were well looked after. They would need to be certain that if the children were returned home they wouldn't be in any danger. The evidence for that would come largely from the reports Tess had mentioned, and they would take many months to complete.

'Is there anything else you'd like to add?' the IRO gently asked Filip after a few moments, when he was more composed.

'Only that I have every faith my wife will make a complete recovery, and I would ask the social services to do the same. We love our children and need to be together again as a family as soon as possible.'

'Thank you,' the IRO said. 'We wish your wife well.'

The IRO then asked Tess a few questions about the legal aspects of Filip's application and the timing, and drew the meeting to a close by setting the date for the next review in June – in six months' time. When children first come into care they have a review within the first twenty days, then three months after that, then every six months unless something happens in the interim.

As I drove home, Filip's words rang in my ears. I felt sorry for him, and although I was sure he was sincere in what he'd said I doubted his family would be reunited any time soon. The next review was set for six months later and I was sure Molly and Kit would still be with me then, and for many reviews to come, possibly stretching into years.

The house was quiet and orderly when I arrived home, unlike when Keelie was there. Maggie had time for a cup of tea before she left and we chatted a bit about the Christmas party, which was one of the highlights on the fostering calendar. I'd bought the children new outfits to wear – a smart little tuxedo with a bow tie for Kit and a sparkling party dress for Molly, which she'd chosen. Maggie said Keelie had a new costume too and showed me a photo on her phone of Keelie dressed as an elf. We laughed, but I greatly admired Keelie's sense of fun – not many girls her age would dress up like that. Lucy and Paula would be dressed fashionably, but Adrian had his work's Christmas party on the same day. When they were younger, we all went.

The following day, Friday, we had contact in the afternoon. Filip was waiting as usual in the room when I arrived with Molly and Kit. He came over, smiling, kissed the children and gave me an envelope with a card inside. 'It's from Aneta,' he said. I thanked him, although if it contained anything valuable I'd have to give it back. Foster carers aren't allowed to accept gifts from the child's family in case it sways their objectivity when reporting any disclosure the child might make about their home life. I wished them a nice time, said goodbye and waited until I was outside the centre to open the envelope. It was a handmade thank-you card decorated with pretty flowers. Inside, Aneta had written: *Thank you for looking after my children. Aneta x.* There would be no problem in me keeping it, but I would let Edith know the next time I spoke to her.

That weekend was busy, pleasantly so. On Saturday we did the last of our Christmas shopping. Adrian, Lucy and Paula went together to a large shopping centre out of town and I took Molly and Kit locally to buy gifts for their parents. It's usual for the foster carer to buy gifts for their child's family for special occasions, including Christmas, birthdays, Mother's and Father's Day. Kit soon grew bored with shopping and fell asleep in the stroller, while Molly took her time choosing presents for her parents. Eventually she settled on a gift box of toiletries for each of them. She also chose a Christmas card. *To Mummy and Daddy with Love* was on the front in glittery lettering. There were lots of nice words inside about how much they were loved. I could picture Filip reading the card alone on Christmas morning and I knew he'd be touched. I assumed he would be visiting Aneta at some point on Christmas Day and would take the card and her present with him.

The fostering Christmas party on Saturday night was great fun. It was held, as it was most years, in a village hall, and volunteers had spent most of the day decorating the hall with garlands, balloons and a very big Christmas tree. There was a children's entertainer and a disco with disco lights that sent moving coloured patterns across the floor, which the younger children chased and tried to catch and stamp on. Lucy and Paula danced with Molly and Kit while I chatted to friends, some of whom I hadn't seen for a long time. There was a buffet supper, games with prizes for all ages of children and more dancing. The atmosphere was light, festive and gay, where fostering families could come together and leave their problems behind. Towards the end of the evening, the music was halted, sleigh bells were heard in the distance and Father Christmas appeared. He had a sack full of presents over each shoulder, and beside him, ready to help, was a large elf with a white beard, dressed in a red hat and a tight-fitting red-and-green costume with matching sheen tights. We all cheered and clapped, while some of the older lads whistled and whooped. 'I told Keelie she needed the next size up,' Maggie whispered to me, and I smiled.

Father Christmas sat on the chair put out ready for him and the children began going up one at a time to receive a gift. Elf Keelie took the gift from a sack and passed it to Santa, who gave it to the child, wishing them a Merry Christmas. When it was Kit's and Molly's turn Lucy and Paula took them up, and when they came back Molly whispered in my ear, 'I think that elf is Keelie.'

'Really?' I said, surprised. 'Well, fancy that. I guess it's part of the magic of Christmas.'

Sunday was largely spent wrapping Christmas presents. I helped Molly and Kit to wrap theirs and write their card to their parents. Lucy, Paula and Adrian wrapped their presents in their bedrooms, taking turns to use the scissors and sticky tape, and the wrapping paper I'd bought. By the end of the day a mountain of presents had appeared under our Christmas tree. There was even one for Sammy. I took photographs of Molly and Kit sitting in front of the tree to give to Filip. I would take many more photos of them over Christmas and of my family too.

Christmas fell on a Friday this year, but there wouldn't be any contact on that day as the Family Centre would be closed. I therefore took Molly's and Kit's presents for their parents with us to contact on Monday afternoon – the last contact before Christmas. Filip clearly hadn't been expecting presents and as the children gave him their gifts and Molly said, 'Happy Christmas, Daddy,' his eyes filled.

'Thank you so much,' he said, and kissed and hugged them both, then looked embarrassed. Taking a few steps to me so the children wouldn't hear, he said quietly, 'I hadn't thought about Christmas shopping with everything that's been going on. Aneta did it all last year. I didn't realize until now that this would be the last contact before Christmas. If I go shopping tomorrow can I drop off their presents at your house?'

'You can drop them off at the social services and I'll collect them from there,' I suggested. Aneta and Filip purposely hadn't been given my contact details. 'Phone Tess tomorrow and explain. It's not a problem. I've collected presents for children from there before.'

'OK, thank you,' he said, relieved. 'I should have thought about it sooner.'

'Don't worry. You've had a lot on your mind.'

When I collected Molly and Kit at the end of contact Filip was clearly still thinking about this. 'I'll phone Tess first thing in the morning,' he said to me. 'I'll go shopping straight after work. Will you put the children's presents by their beds so they have them on Christmas morning? That's what we did last year.'

'Yes, of course. They'll have ours too.'

'Pretend they're from Father Christmas,' he said. 'And take some photos.'

'Yes, I will.' I could see he was getting emotional again, so, wishing him a Merry Christmas, we said goodbye and left.

Tuesday was the last day of nursery for Molly before Christmas and she came away with a gift, which we put under the tree. There was no playgroup on Wednesday afternoon. Molly's excitement built over the next day as Christmas grew nearer and nearer. Kit was caught up in the excitement too, although at his age he wasn't sure why. It was Thursday morning, Christmas Eve, before Tess telephoned and said that Filip had taken in two large sacksful of Christmas presents for the children and could I collect them. Thankfully Paula and Lucy were at home and stayed with Molly and Kit while I drove to the social services' offices. Adrian was going straight from work to collect my mother. Once home, I smuggled in the sacks and hid them in my wardrobe with the other bags of presents I had for Molly and Kit, and for Adrian, Lucy and Paula, who hadn't yet grown out of wanting to wake up and find presents by their beds.

Adrian arrived home with Mum and after dinner we all went to church for the family carol service, where we met friends and neighbours, many of whom Mum remembered from previous years. After the service we chatted over mulled wine and sweet mince pies. It was about nine o'clock by the time we returned home and Kirsty, who'd come with us, left as she was spending Christmas Day with her parents. Adrian was going to her house on the 26th – Boxing Day. We wished her a Merry Christmas and swapped presents.

Molly and Kit were tired and went off to sleep quite quickly. Paula had given up her bed for my mother and was sharing Lucy's room. We all went up around eleven o'clock, but I could hear Lucy and Paula laughing and giggling well past midnight. Eventually, worried they might wake Molly and Kit, I went round to their room and told them that if they didn't go to sleep Father Christmas wouldn't come. They laughed more loudly than ever but did snuggle down. By 1 a.m. everyone was asleep and I got out of bed and crept from room to room, leaving the sacks of presents by their beds. Six in all, as I had one for my mother, who, like my father, had never lost her childlike enthusiasm for the wonder of Christmas. I think it's her attitude to life that keeps her young.

It was our second Christmas without Dad, but I felt he was close. He'd been a wonderful father, the best, not only to my brother and me, but to his grandchildren and the children we fostered. He was a sensitive man who valued family life, and it had upset him to learn of the neglect and abuse some children suffered. He always went that extra mile for the children we fostered and I knew that had he still been with us he would have adored Molly and Kit. As I turned over ready for sleep I said quietly, 'Night, Dad. Love and miss you. Merry Christmas.'

And from somewhere in the calm and serenity of Christmas Eve came his gentle reply, 'Night, my darling daughter. Sleep tight, and look after those children for me.'

'I will.'

CHAPTER TWENTY-FIVE

ANETA

The build-up to Christmas seems to go on for ever, and then suddenly it's all over and you're facing a new year. We'd had a wonderful Christmas – just as we'd hoped it would be – and although it was hard work and Molly got a bit overexcited and cross sometimes, my family all helped, so I enjoyed it too. Adrian had Monday, 27th December, off work and after lunch he took Mum home, while I took Molly and Kit to contact. Lucy was at work, but Paula's college was closed for the week.

Molly and Kit were wearing new clothes that Filip had given them for Christmas. I thought it was sensible of him to have included some clothes as well as toys in their sacks. The children were excited and looking forward to seeing their father again. I signed the Visitors' Book and we headed towards Rainbow Room. The Christmas decorations were still up, as ours at home were, but somehow after Christmas they never look the same and seem to lose some of their sparkle. I wondered what sort of Christmas Filip had had, and hoped he hadn't been lonely. I appreciate how isolating the Christmas period can be for those who are by themselves.

Filip was in Rainbow Room with the contact supervisor and seemed to be in good spirits. 'Hello, my wonderful children!' he cried. 'You look very smart.' Smiling broadly, he spread his arms and Molly and Kit ran to him. 'The clothes fit perfectly then,' he remarked to me.

'Yes, good choice.'

'I must admit I showed them to Aneta before I wrapped them. She's got such an eye for knowing if something fits just by looking at it.'

I smiled. 'Did you have a nice Christmas?' He seemed very upbeat.

'Wonderful, thank you. Aneta was allowed home for a few days. I collected her Christmas Eve and took her back this morning.'

'Mummy's home?' Molly asked, picking up on some of what her father had said.

'She was, precious,' he replied. 'She's in hospital now, but I'm hoping she will be spending more time at home, then you'll be able to see her again.'

I thought it unwise to tell the children this until it was definite.

'When? When can I see Mummy?' Molly asked excitedly.

'I don't know yet. I need to talk to Tess. Soon I hope.'

'Mummy?' Kit asked, confused, and he looked round as if his mother might appear.

'I'll see you later then,' I said. 'Have a nice time.'

I knew that any contact between Aneta and the children would need to be approved by Tess and carefully supervised at the Family Centre. Hopefully I would be told in advance so I could prepare the children, I thought as I drove. I wondered if Tess was aware that Aneta had been well enough to go home for Christmas. My question was shortly answered. As I pulled up outside the house my mobile rang and it was Tess.

'Did you have a nice Christmas?' she asked.

'Yes, thank you, did you?'

'Very nice, although first day back and I've hit the ground running. Are Molly and Kit at the Family Centre?'

'They are. I've just dropped them off.'

'Aneta has requested contact, but don't tell Molly and Kit. She went home for Christmas and her solicitor has been in touch. I wanted to hear your thoughts. The children have been through a lot. Do they talk about their mother?'

'Not as much as they used to. Kit says "Mummy" sometimes and Molly occasionally asks where she is. They talk more about their father now.'

'Kit's too young to understand what went on, but does Molly know her mother was responsible for making them sick?'

'I don't think so. She's never said anything and I certainly haven't told them. I doubt Filip has either.'

Tess paused. 'At this stage in the proceedings, if Aneta is well enough to see her children she has a right to, as their solicitor pointed out. I'll need to speak to her doctor first. Do you think the children would cope with seeing their mother?'

'If I'm honest, yes.'

'Thank you. I'll let you know what we decide. Nothing will happen until the New Year, though.'

It was nice to be asked my opinion. Foster carers aren't always. Yet while I thought Molly and Kit could cope with seeing their mother, I didn't necessarily think it was for the best. The care plan was for the children to remain in long-term care, so any contact after the final court hearing would be drastically reduced. Was it in the children's best interests to re-establish the bond between them and their mother, only to have it broken again? It happens with looked-after children.

But Aneta was their mother and, as their solicitor had told Tess, she had a right to see her children.

When I collected Molly and Kit at the end of contact they were hyped up from being chased around the room by their father in a 'catch me if you can' game. They completed another couple of circuits, screaming with excitement, before Filip stopped the game and, picking up their coats, said, 'Time to go now.'

'Do we have to?' Molly moaned.

'I'm afraid you do,' Filip said, trying to calm them down so he could persuade them into their coats. 'We'll see each other again soon. I promise you it will be more than twice a week.'

'I want to see you lots!' Molly cried, stamping her foot.

'You will,' Filip said. Again, I thought he really shouldn't have told her that until he knew for certain more contact would be allowed.

The nursery Molly went to followed term times, so it was closed until after the New Year, unlike the private nursery where Lucy worked, which had just closed for Christmas Day and Boxing Day, as had Adrian's office. So while Lucy and Adrian went to work each day from Christmas to the New Year, Paula was at home. Having completed her college work, she helped me with Molly and Kit. The children had so many toys from Christmas to play with that keeping them amused was easy and great fun. We also went out each day for a breath of fresh air and to let them run off some energy.

The next contact was on Friday, New Year's Eve, and that morning a member of staff at the Family Centre telephoned me at 10.30 to say the centre was closing early, so the children's contact had been brought forward to 12–2 p.m. As the children would miss lunch, I gave them a quick snack before we went and left Paula clearing up. When we arrived at the centre Filip was in reception, not one of the rooms. He was complaining to the receptionist that he should have been given more notice of the change in time, as it had caused him a problem at work. Then to me he said, 'I've got to go back to work after contact to make up the hours. I won't be able to collect Aneta for the weekend until much later now.'

I sympathized. I appreciated how disruptive last-minute changes to contact were, but I knew from experience that it happened from time to time for various reasons and often at short notice. I went with Filip and the children into the room, where I left them with the contact supervisor. When I returned Molly, Kit and their father all had their coats on, ready to leave. Filip said a quick goodbye to the children and left ahead of us.

'Daddy has to go to work,' Molly told me on the way out, her face serious. 'He can't take Mummy home until later.'

'I know, love, but it will be OK,' I reassured her.

'When can I see Mummy?' she asked.

'I don't know yet. Tess will tell us.'

'Daddy says it will be soon.'

'It's for Tess to decide.'

'Why?'

'Because she's your social worker.'

That night, Adrian went to Kirsty's house to see in the New Year, Paula went to a friend's house and Lucy went to a party. I saw Molly and Kit into bed and then sat on the sofa with Sammy beside me and watched a film. I stayed up until midnight and saw in the New Year to the chimes of Big Ben on the television. Fireworks began exploding outside, which woke Molly and Kit, and I spent the next hour resettling them. By 1 a.m. it had quietened down and they were asleep again. Adrian and Paula were both sleeping out that night, and Lucy had pre-booked a taxi to bring her home. At 3 a.m. I heard her come in, then heard her footsteps on the stairs and pass my bedroom door as she went to the bathroom. 'Happy New Year, Mum,' she called quietly.

'Happy New Year, love,' I said equally quietly so as not to wake Kit. 'Did you have a nice time?'

'Yes. Fantastic. Love you.'

'Love you too.'

On Sunday, Adrian and Paula went out with their father for lunch and then later we all took down the Christmas decorations and stored them in the loft for another year. How quickly the years passed, I thought. It felt as though we'd just put the decorations away when it was time to get them out again. When I took Molly and Kit to contact on Monday I asked Filip if he'd had a nice weekend – it seemed polite to do so. He told me in front of the children that Aneta had come home but had been upset because she wasn't allowed to see the children and he was speaking to his solicitor. I realized Filip probably needed to share what was going on, but it really wasn't appropriate when the children could hear.

'Did you see Mummy?' Molly asked anxiously, tugging on her father's arm.

'Yes.'

'Best not discuss it here,' I said quietly to him.

He nodded. 'Mummy is fine and sends her love,' he told Molly. 'She's made a card for you and your brother.'

He went over to where his bag lay on a chair and took out an envelope. This was their time, so I said goodbye and left. Later, when I collected the children, Molly came away with the card and was eager to show me. It was beautiful. 'Mummy made this?' I asked.

Molly nodded.

On the front Aneta had painted a bird in flight, its azure blue and green wings so detailed and vibrant you could almost see it flying. 'She has talent,' I said. I looked inside, where she'd written in a delicate cursive script:

Think of me as this bird.
I am flying home to you.
We will all be together again soon.
Love you, Mum xx

It was a beautiful card with very emotional words, but were they realistic? Molly certainly thought so. 'Mummy is getting better,' she declared, carefully returning the card to its envelope. 'Daddy said we will be going home soon.'

I doubted it. But what I really struggled with was how someone who could create such a beautiful card could also intentionally harm her children by making them sick. I reminded myself again that Aneta had a mental illness, and people with mental illness did recover.

Molly kept the card with her all evening and proudly slid it from its envelope to show Paula, Lucy and Adrian as they came home. She sat on the card during dinner and at bedtime she wanted to sleep with it under her pillow. I could see it was getting creased, so I suggested she stood it on the shelf in her bedroom next to the photographs of her parents, which she did. She climbed into bed and chatted happily about nursery. She was looking forward to returning to nursery the following morning and seeing her friends again. Once she'd been there a little longer, I was planning on asking some of her friends to lunch as I had with my children and those I'd fostered.

Kit's playgroup resumed on Wednesday and later that afternoon I received an email from Tess saying she would be visiting us the following Tuesday at 2 p.m. I was expecting a visit from Edith before long, as I hadn't heard from her since she'd sent her apology for absence to the review before Christmas.

On Friday, when I took the children to contact, Filip told me, out of earshot of Molly and Kit, that there was a good chance Aneta would be discharged the following week. He said she was coming home for the weekend, he was taking her back on Sunday evening, then on Monday morning they had a meeting with her psychiatrist when it would be decided.

'You'll be pleased,' I said, smiling.

'So will the children,' Filip replied.

Although Molly and Kit hadn't heard this conversation, when I collected them from contact it was clear the matter had been mentioned, for Molly greeted me with the words, 'Mummy is coming home.'

'We hope so,' Filip corrected.

Once outside, Molly told me again, 'Mummy is coming home.'

'That is good news,' I said.

'Daddy said the doctors have made her better.'

'Excellent.'

'When will we see her?'

'When Tess says,' I replied.

'When will that be?'

'I really don't know, love. Tess is coming to see us tomorrow, so we can ask her then.'

The following day Molly had nursery in the morning, then after lunch I arranged lots of toys and activities in the living room to keep her and Kit occupied during Tess's visit. She arrived promptly at 2 p.m. and spent some time talking to the children, admiring their toys and asking them about Christmas. Then as they played she said to me, 'Aneta is being discharged today.' I nodded. 'Their solicitor is applying to court to have the children returned to their care. We have a court date for the end of March. The social services are opposing the application, but we have agreed to Aneta having supervised contact. She will join Filip at the Family Centre on Monday, Wednesday and Friday, three o'clock to five o'clock. We've added an extra day.'

'So Kit won't be able to go to playgroup,' I said, thinking aloud.

'No, but it can't be helped. Contact takes priority.' Which I knew. Contact takes priority over most things, including the foster carer's family arrangements. One year I hadn't been able to see my mother on Mother's Day as the child I was looking after had to see theirs.

'When do the new arrangements begin?' I asked.

'Tomorrow. I'll talk to the children about seeing their mother in a moment.'

Molly glanced over at us but carried on playing.

'Will Aneta be prosecuted?' I asked Tess quietly, for I thought this would have a bearing on the child-protection case.

'No. The police have decided it isn't in the public interest to prosecute her. She has a diagnosed mental disorder and has been receiving treatment. They'll be returning your food diary.'

'OK.'

Tess didn't say any more about the police's decision not to prosecute, nor about Filip and Aneta's application to court to have the children returned, and it wasn't for me to ask. I should be told what I needed to know.

'Tess, on another matter,' I said, 'Kit's cot is still in my bedroom. He will be two in February and at that age he is no longer allowed to share the carer's bedroom.'

'Oh dear,' Tess said, recognizing there could be a problem.

'I was thinking of returning his cot to Molly's room. If you remember, I had to separate them after Aneta said that Molly had intentionally harmed Kit, but Molly is over that now and I'm not sure it was ever as bad as Aneta portrayed.'

'I agree. I can't tell you all the doctor told me, but Aneta has admitted that while Molly was responsible for Kit falling downstairs, it was an accident. And that apart from some rough play when Molly might have pushed him, she never intentionally harmed him.'

'So why say it? To shift the blame from her?'

'Aneta maintains she didn't harm the children – apart from making them sick, of course, which was a result of her condition.'

'So it's OK to put Kit's cot in Molly's room?' I confirmed.

'Yes.'

Molly looked over again. 'Can I see Mummy?' she asked.

'Yes,' Tess said. 'Tomorrow afternoon.'

Turning to Molly and Kit, Tess then explained in simple, child-appropriate language that their mummy had been unwell, but she was better now, so they would be seeing her again at the Family Centre with their father. Molly didn't show the happiness she might have done and I appreciated, as Tess would, that she must have been struggling with many conflicting emotions, which she couldn't put into words. 'Do you have any questions?' she asked.

Molly looked bemused.

'If you think of any, you can ask Cathy,' Tess said.

'I do ask Cathy,' Molly replied seriously. 'But she says we have to ask you.'

Tess and I smiled. 'Yes, when I don't know the answer to something we ask Tess,' I explained.

'Mummy,' Kit said, picking up on some of the conversation.

'We are seeing Mummy tomorrow at the Family Centre,' Molly told him, repeating what Tess had said. 'Daddy will be there. Why didn't we see Mummy?' she now asked Tess.

'Because she has been ill,' Tess replied.

'What was wrong with Mummy?' Molly asked. I was pleased it was Tess she was asking and not me.

'Your mummy had an illness that caused her to do things that might have hurt you and Kit,' Tess said. 'That's why you and your brother came to live with Cathy and her family.' Although of course there was no *might* about it. Aneta's FDIA *had* hurt Molly and Kit, although at her age Molly didn't need to know that.

'Is Mummy better now?' Molly asked Tess.

'Yes. We think so,' Tess replied.

'Good. I love my mummy,' Molly said, and then looked at me. 'I love you too, Cathy. You are like my other mummy.'

'That's nice,' I said, and I felt my eyes fill.

CHAPTER TWENTY-SIX

PERMANENT?

I wasn't looking forward to meeting Aneta again. I was sure it was going to be difficult, but during my fostering career I'd had to face many situations far more difficult than this one, so I told myself I just had to get on with it. As we got ready to leave that Wednesday afternoon Molly went very quiet, but when I asked her if there was something wrong she shook her head. It must have been strange for her to be seeing her mother again after all these weeks. Kit was his usual mischievous self and ran off with his shoes rather than letting me put them on him. I hadn't moved his cot yet. I needed help to take it from my room, round the landing and into to Molly's room, so we'd move it at the weekend. There was no rush. Kit wasn't two until February. Had Tess not agreed to him sharing Molly's room I would have had to sleep on the sofa bed downstairs, as the rules on looked-after children sharing a bedroom are strict.

In the car I fed the nursery-rhyme CD into the player and headed for the Family Centre. Molly was holding a card I'd helped her and Kit make for their mother. It wasn't anywhere near as good as the one Aneta had made for them, but they'd done their best with glue, glitter and felt tips, and all parents appreciate their children's artwork, don't they? Whatever the standard.

As I parked outside the Family Centre I felt my pulse step up a notch. I wasn't sure how I was expecting Aneta to be with me, but given her previous animosity I naturally felt some reluctance and anxiety at meeting her again, especially now that what she'd been doing to the children was out in the open.

The receptionist said the children's parents and social worker were there and waiting in Blue Room. My heart sank. It was the same room the children had seen their mother in before. Wouldn't it bring back unpleasant memories for them of being sick after contact? Molly made the connection. 'Blue Room is where we were with Mummy,' she said quietly as I signed the Visitors' Book. I half expected her to add something about being sick. She didn't, but she held my hand very tightly as the three of us went along the corridor to Blue Room.

The door was open and Kit rushed in while Molly stayed by my side, still holding my hand. Aneta, Filip and Tess were standing in a circle in the centre of the room and appeared to have been talking. The contact supervisor was at the table. 'Hello, son,' Filip said, picking him up, for he'd run around his mother to get to his father.

'Hello,' I said to everyone. Aneta was looking at Molly, who was still standing beside me, holding my hand. 'Give Mummy your card,' I encouraged her.

'You give it to her,' Molly said, and buried her face in my coat. Tess looked over, slightly surprised, and I knew – as I think Tess did – that we should have prepared Molly better for seeing her mother again. Aneta was looking upset.

'We'll give Mummy the card together,' I told Molly, trying to save the situation.

Molly gingerly raised her head from my coat but still gripped my hand as I took her over to her mother. 'Molly and Kit made this card for you,' I said.

Thankfully, Molly passed the card to her mother, but she stayed close beside me. Aneta opened the card, nodded but didn't say anything. Kit was busy trying to climb onto his father's shoulders for a ride.

'I'll see you later then,' I said. As unobtrusively as I could, I released Molly's hand, turned and walked away, hoping that she wouldn't try to run after me, which would have upset Aneta even more.

As I left I heard Tess say to Molly, 'Let's find you something to play with.'

I closed the door behind me, relieved that the first meeting was over. Apart from Aneta being very uncomfortable and upset at Molly's reaction, she had looked well, with colour in her cheeks. I wondered what she would be thinking, seeing her children again. Now recovering from FDIA, she must realize what she did was wrong, so I assumed she must feel guilty. Had she and Filip discussed it? I guessed so, possibly in therapy. Would they tell the children that their mother was responsible for making them ill? I doubted it, and they were probably young enough not to need to know.

When I returned to the Family Centre I met Tess on her way out. 'How is it going?' I asked her. Feedback from contact is always helpful for the foster carer, although we seldom receive it.

'It's settled down,' she said. 'I've just left Aneta reading Molly a story. Aneta is better now, but she was upset at the start of contact, as she felt the children had rejected her and only wanted their father. I took her out of the room for a while to calm her down and we had a chat. She was worried that you might have told Molly she was responsible for them being ill and turned them against her.'

'Of course I haven't,' I said indignantly. 'Certainly not.'

'I know. I reassured her that wouldn't be so. She was worried that the children's coolness towards her might count against her when the case goes back to court in March. I think she was expecting too much from them at the first contact after the gap. She's coping better now.'

'Good.'

'Filip's relationship with the children has improved,' she said. 'He relates to them far more easily now. He's come a long way.'

'Yes,' I agreed. 'He has.'

'Has the Guardian been in touch with you?' Tess now asked.

'Not recently.'

'She will be. She telephoned me yesterday. She'll be seeing the children again before we go back to court.'

'OK.'

Tess said goodbye and I continued into the Family Centre and to Blue Room. I knocked on the door and went in. Aneta was sitting on the sofa with Molly beside her and reading her a story. Kit was 'helping' his father tidy up the toys, although as fast as Filip put them away, Kit took them out again. 'You're not much help,' Filip laughed.

I smiled and waited in my usual place just inside the door. Eventually Aneta looked up from the book. 'You have to go now,' she said quietly to Molly.

Without being told a second time or protesting about having to leave, Molly stood and came towards me.

'Give Mummy a kiss goodbye,' Filip told her.

Molly dutifully returned to her mother and planted a kiss on her cheek. Aneta hugged her, but Molly didn't return the hug. She straightened and, taking her coat from her father, she brought it to me to help her put it on. I could see Aneta was hurt. As Tess had said, perhaps she was expecting too much, but it would help the children if they saw their mother and me getting along. It was for me to build the bridges.

Instead of coming away, I took a few steps further into the room and said to Aneta, 'It was Molly's idea to make the card. Did you like it?'

She looked up, surprised, and then said, 'Yes, I did. Thank you.'

'She loved your card,' I said. 'She wouldn't be parted from it. It's on a shelf in her bedroom so she can see it last thing at night and when she wakes in the morning. You've got real talent. I couldn't make anything like that, no matter how hard I tried.' I could see Filip watching our exchange.

'Art was my best subject at school,' Aneta offered. 'While I was in hospital they encouraged us to draw and paint and make things.'

'It's a lovely card,' I said. 'And thanks for the one you sent me.'

'You're welcome.' She managed a small smile.

The ice broken, it was time for us to leave. 'I'd better get these two some dinner then,' I said to Aneta. 'We'll see you on Friday.'

'Yes, thank you.'

'Say goodbye then,' I told the children. 'You'll see Mummy and Daddy again soon. Two more sleeps.'

'Bye,' Molly said, then she suddenly ran back to her mother and gave her a kiss and a hug. Kit copied her and Aneta hugged them both. Tears sprang to her eyes and the look of gratitude and appreciation on her face was pitiful. Whatever she'd done in the past, and whatever the outcome of the care proceedings, Aneta was their mother and it was important Molly and Kit had a positive image of her.

Tamara Hastings, the Guardian ad litem, telephoned the following morning while Molly was at nursery and wanted to come to see us that afternoon at two o'clock. After lunch I refreshed the toys in the living room and told Molly and Kit that the Guardian would be coming shortly and she would want to talk to us. Molly seemed to remember her from last time and asked if it was about Mummy. Since they'd seen their mother the day before, Molly had been talking more about her, while Kit had been saying 'Mummy', fetching his shoes and looking hopefully at the front door whenever she was mentioned. He was also wanting more hugs and to sit on my lap, which was an indication he was feeling unsettled and needed reassurance. It must be very confusing for him to have the woman he loved and called Mummy disappear from his life and then suddenly and briefly reappear. Molly had a better understanding and knew she would be seeing her again the next day. Kit sometimes called me mummy and I always corrected him and said, 'I'm Cathy.' But of course it was quite possible there could come a time when he would be calling me or another woman mummy. If the children didn't go home, which seemed the most likely outcome, at their age they would be placed for adoption and their new parents would become their mummy and daddy. Would I put myself forward to be considered? Yes, they were settled and my family and I loved them.

* * *

'So you saw Mummy and Daddy yesterday,' Tamara, the Guardian, said to Molly and Kit a little after 2 p.m. as she settled into an armchair in the living room. 'How did that go?'

Molly stared at her, while Kit said 'Mummy 'n' Daddy' and then picked up his toy fire engine and dumped it in her lap.

'That's a lovely fire engine,' Tamara said. 'Was it a Christmas present?'

'Yes,' said Kit, although he replied yes to most questions.

Molly continued to sit by the toy boxes, looking warily at the Guardian, and I threw her a reassuring smile.

'Did you have a nice time yesterday when you saw your mummy and daddy?' she tried again.

Molly nodded, while Kit took back his fire engine as she wasn't playing with it and brought it to me.

'What did you do when you saw Mummy and Daddy?' the Guardian asked Molly.

She shrugged.

'How do you think it went?' the Guardian now asked me. 'I'll be speaking to Tess tomorrow for an update.'

'I think it went quite well considering they hadn't seen each other for a while,' I said. 'Molly had some questions afterwards, which I did my best to answer. Kit didn't really understand and seemed a bit confused.'

'That's understandable,' she said, and made a note on a pad she took from her bag. 'What questions do you have?' she asked Molly.

Molly shrugged again.

'Mainly about their home, if Mummy is better and whether they will be living with her and Daddy again,' I said.

'We don't know that yet,' she told Molly.

Tamara continued by asking Molly about her feelings towards her parents, if she was happy with me and why she thought her mummy had been in hospital. Molly nodded and shrugged her responses, while Kit sat on my lap and looked around hopefully every time he heard the words 'mummy' or 'daddy'. It was sad.

Tamara made some notes and was with us about an hour. By the time she'd finished I was no closer to knowing what her recommendation to the court would be on the long-term plans for the children. Sometimes the Guardian tells the foster carer and sometimes it's possible to pick up the way it's likely to go from what they say, but that wasn't so here. I supposed she might not have yet decided, although she'd need to soon, as her report would be due in court well ahead of the hearing.

On Friday morning I spent time preparing the children for seeing their mother again, as I didn't want a repeat of their first meeting when Aneta had looked upset and rejected. We sat at the table and drew pictures of Blue Room with their parents and them in it, and of course the contact supervisor was there sitting at the table. 'She does a lot of writing,' Molly remarked.

'She does,' I agreed.

'Mummy said it was about us.'

'Yes, but it's nothing for you to worry about. Just enjoy your time with your parents. How do you think your mummy might be feeling?'

'Happy and sad with a funny tummy, like when I first went to nursery,' Molly said.

'That's a good description.'

Molly wanted to make another card for her mummy and daddy and I helped her, while Kit sat beside me enthusiastically scribbling with jumbo crayons on a separate sheet of paper. 'Mummy 'n' Daddy,' he said.

I smiled. 'Yes, good boy. You'll be seeing them later.'

Contact that afternoon was less awkward right from the start. Aneta seemed more relaxed and said 'Hello' and smiled as we entered the room. It was Blue Room again, but no one seemed to mind. Molly only showed a little hesitation in going to her mother and then ran over and gave her the card.

'For me?' Aneta exclaimed, pleased. 'It's lovely. Thank you, darling. I was thinking we could do some drawing together today. Would you like that?'

'Yes,' Molly said. Kit had gone straight to his father again and gave him the picture he'd made, which Filip admired.

I wished them a nice time, said goodbye and left.

When I returned to collect the children from contact Molly presented me with a picture. 'Mummy helped me,' she said.

'Fantastic. Thank you.' It was of a beautiful picturesque country scene with a cottage, a river, and cows and horses grazing in the meadow. 'I'll put it in our living room so we can all enjoy it,' I said.

Aneta picked up the children's coats, gave Kit's to Filip to help him put it on and then went to Molly. She allowed her mother to help her into her coat. 'You have to keep warm, it's cold out there,' Aneta said. 'Have a nice weekend and I'll see you on Monday.'

Both parents kissed the children goodbye and we left.

'Mummy! Daddy!' Kit suddenly cried as we went down the corridor and began agitating to go back into the room, which wasn't a good idea.

'You'll see Mummy and Daddy again soon,' I said. 'Three

more sleeps.' He tugged on my arm to return, so I picked him up and carried him out of the building and to the car.

'Mummy, Daddy,' he said, straining to look out of the window as I drove away.

'Three more sleeps,' Molly told him and held his hand.

'Good girl.'

On Saturday Adrian helped me move Kit's cot into Molly's room and that evening the children took a long time to get off to sleep. I didn't mind. They were very excited to be sharing and there was a lot of laughing and giggling, and Molly kept getting out of bed. While I didn't think she would intentionally harm Kit, I was concerned there might be an accident, and I checked on them regularly until they were both asleep a little after 10 p.m. At 6.30 a.m. I woke to the sound of them laughing and squealing again and Kit jumping up and down in his cot. I went in and found him trying to climb out. I knew it wouldn't be long before he needed a proper bed.

We saw my mother on Sunday and then the week flew by with contact on three afternoons and Molly at nursery for two mornings. I was also planning a birthday party for Molly and Kit. Their birthdays were in February and only a week apart: Molly would be four and Kit two. I decided on a joint party and we gave out invitations to Molly's friends at nursery. I also invited someone I'd been chatting to at the playgroup Kit had gone to, who had a similar-aged boy. My mother, Paula, Lucy, Adrian and possibly Kirsty would be coming too. Molly asked if her mummy and daddy could come, and I had to say that wasn't possible, but they'd have another birthday party at contact, which she accepted. I knew that parents usually made a little party for their children during normal contact hours, when they also gave them their presents.

A colleague of Edith's telephoned and said that Edith was off sick, having had an appendectomy, and I should contact her if I needed anything urgently. I emailed Edith wishing her a speedy recovery and then copied her into emails I sent to her colleague and Tess, so she was kept up to date for when she returned. Molly would start school in September and I provisionally reserved a place for her at the school on the same site as the nursery, where my children had gone.

Molly's and Kit's birthdays obligingly fell on days when they had contact – Molly's on Monday and Kit's the following Wednesday – and Aneta told me she was planning party teas. I dressed the children in some of the new clothes Filip had bought, and they were excited. Aneta and Filip had set out party food on paper plates and there were balloons and a birthday cake on both days. They gave them presents: Molly a bike with a basket and bell and Kit a tricycle that had a loud horn on the front. They were lovely presents, and at the end of contact Filip and Aneta came out to my car to help put the bikes in the boot, and then waved us off from the car park.

The party I threw for Molly and Kit was on the Saturday between their birthdays, 2–5 p.m., so they had three parties in all. I made a birthday tea with little sandwiches, cocktail sausages, thinly sliced carrots and cucumber, crisps, jelly and ice cream. Mum made cupcakes and I'd also bought a birthday cake for each of them. The parents of the children from nursery and playgroup stayed and had a glass of wine, so we had a house full. I think the adults enjoyed themselves as much as the children. I know I did. I arranged party games, which we all played, the parents shouting and laughing and just as competitive as the little ones. The party ran on and it was 7 p.m. before all our guests had gone. Mum and Kirsty played with Molly and Kit while the rest of us cleared up.

Later that evening, when the house was tidy and the children were in bed, Mum and I sat in the living room talking over a cup of tea and another cupcake. She was staying the night. Adrian was taking Kirsty home and the girls were relaxing in their bedrooms.

'Molly and Kit have come on so much,' Mum said. 'When I think back to how they were when they first arrived – pasty and withdrawn – they're different children now. You've done a good job.'

'Thank you. It wasn't difficult. They are little treasures.'

'You'll miss them if they have to leave,' she said.

'We all will,' I agreed. 'But I'm almost certain that's not going to happen. The social services are opposing the parents' application to have them returned and I think the Guardian's recommendation will support that.'

'Will they stay with you permanently then?'

'I hope so.'

CHAPTER TWENTY-SEVEN

JUDGE'S DECISION

The rest of February was bitterly cold, with a heavy frost each night but no snow. The children loved their new bikes and we took them to the park each weekend. I took lots of photographs and gave a set to their parents at contact. February gave way to March, the evenings drew out and daffodils bloomed, suggesting spring wasn't far away. I was assuming Molly and Kit would be with us long term, so I measured their bedroom and started looking at beds. It wasn't a big room, and the present bed was rather large, so I thought I would buy two small single beds rather than a bunk bed, which would be safer. I could imagine Kit climbing up and jumping off a bunk bed, and we certainly didn't want an accident and another visit to A&E!

The court case loomed. Scheduled for three days at the end of March, it wasn't mentioned by Aneta and Filip when I took the children to contact or collected them, although it must have been playing on their minds. Indeed, I doubted they thought about much else. This was their chance – possibly their only chance – to win back their children, and my heart went out to them. Clearly the children's welfare was paramount, but for any parent to lose their children is horrendous. Although they didn't say anything, I could see the strain taking its toll as they tried to put on brave faces for the sake of Molly and Kit.

The week before the court hearing Tess visited us and said she'd asked Filip and Aneta not to discuss the proceedings in front of the children. She also said there would be no contact on Wednesday and Friday the following week as Filip and Aneta would be in court. She was with us for about an hour, talked to and played with the children, with and without me present. She looked around the house and when we went into the children's bedroom I told her my plans for replacing the beds and she agreed it was a good idea. Molly and Kit were with us and Molly was excited that Kit was going to have a 'big bed' as she put it. 'Mummy's getting one too,' she said, which was the first I'd heard of it. I looked at Tess and she nodded.

'I advised them to wait until after the hearing,' Tess said quietly to me.

Was buying a bed wishful thinking on the part of the parents or did they have a reasonable chance of winning the court case and having the children returned? Clearly Tess didn't think so, and from what I knew, neither did I.

When I took the children to contact on Monday – the last one before the court hearing – Aneta and Filip were very subdued, unsurprisingly. The next time we saw them the decision on their children's future would have been made. If the judge decided the children should remain in care then contact would be swiftly and drastically reduced down to once or twice a year to allow Molly and Kit to bond with their permanent family. Did I think they would be allowed to stay with me? Yes, I thought there was a strong possibility, as the children were settled with us. Against me was my age. Children as young as Molly and Kit were usually adopted by young childless couples in their thirties. I already had three children and was in my fifties. I would be in my seventies before Molly and Kit were young adults and could reasonably be expected to live independently if I died. This would be a factor, but I could change my will and appoint Adrian, Lucy and Paula as Molly and Kit's guardians should I die while they were minors. Another factor was the number of bedrooms in the house. Molly and Kit could only share for another year and then, when Molly was five, she would need a bedroom of her own. There was a chance Adrian might be living with Kirsty by then – I felt it was only a matter of time – and if not, perhaps Paula and Lucy could share or I could extend the house. I had it all worked out.

When I collected Molly and Kit at the end of contact on Monday Aneta and Filip held them close and gave them lots of extra kisses. 'Wish us luck,' Filip said as we left.

'Luck,' Kit repeated.

Although the children weren't aware – as far as I knew – of the enormity of what their parents were facing, Molly, at least, had picked up on their anxiety. As we got into the car she suddenly cried, 'I feel sick!' And just for a moment I wondered if Aneta had tampered with their food and drink at contact, but then I realized that it was more likely nerves.

'Take a few deep breaths,' I told Molly. 'There is nothing to worry about. Mummy and Daddy are fine and you'll see them next week.' She did as I said and the feeling of nausea passed.

The weeks usually fly by, but that week seemed very long. I thought a lot about the court proceedings that would seal Molly and Kit's fate. I could picture Aneta and Filip in court, dressed smartly but very nervous, their solicitor and barrister with caseloads of paperwork, the Guardian ad Litem, Tess, the social services' solicitor and barrister with their paperwork – all taking turns to present their evidence to the judge. Tess had said the case had been allocated three days, so I was assuming the earliest I would hear from her would be the following Monday. However, it was possible a decision might not be made and the judge would adjourn the proceedings and ask for further reports. It was a nail-biting wait.

With no contact for the rest of the week, on Friday after lunch I took the children with their bikes to our local park. We made slow progress on the way there with them pedalling and me steadying the bikes and keeping them away from the kerb. Usually we took the bikes to the park at weekends when I had the help of the girls. It was just after two o'clock when we entered the park and my mobile began to ring. To my surprise it was Tess. 'Where are you?' she asked, her voice tight.

'In the park.'

'You need to get the children to contact for three o'clock.'

'Do I?' I asked, panic setting in. 'I thought contact had been cancelled and you were in court.'

'We were. I've just come out. The judge has made his decision. The children will be returning home.'

'What?' I asked, shocked.

'I know. I'll phone you on Monday with the details, but the judge wants contact to take place this afternoon. It won't be supervised, but take the children to the Family Centre anyway and they can go out from there.'

'Not supervised?'

'That's right. Contact is in the community. The parents can take the children out. I would have liked more time to prepare them, but that's not going to happen. Their barrister pushed for contact today and the judge agreed. I'll phone you on Monday, but I need to go now. Make sure they are there for three o'clock,' she said.

'I will.'

My mouth went dry and my legs felt like jelly. I continued walking in a daze a little behind the children. Unsupervised contact, the children were going home – I was as shocked as Tess had sounded. No, I was more than shocked, I was stunned. But the judge had made the decision and it needed to be acted on.

'Molly! Kit!' I cried, catching up with them. 'We have to go back straight away. You're seeing your mummy and daddy this afternoon.'

They stopped pedalling. Molly looked at me, confused, while Kit repeated, 'Mummy 'n' Daddy.'

'Yes, come on. We have to go to the Family Centre.' I turned their bikes around and we headed back towards the house, my heart drumming loudly as I struggled to come to terms with the judge's decision. While I'd been involved in other cases where the judge had ruled against the social services, I couldn't ever remember it happening when they'd been so convinced the judge would uphold their view. I assumed the Guardian's report had recommended the children were returned home, as the judge usually accepted their recommendation. But the judge must have been convinced it was the correct guidance and the children wouldn't be in any danger.

Did I feel any bitterness or resentment towards the parents? No, but I was devastated at the prospect of losing Molly and Kit. As a family that fosters, we'd had to say good-bye to many children in the past, but never had it been so unexpected and abrupt. I didn't know the timescale of Molly and Kit moving home – Tess would tell me on Monday – but given that we'd gone straight to unsupervised contact I knew it wouldn't be long.

I left the bikes in the hall to put away later, hurried the children into the car and drove straight to the Family Centre. Aneta and Filip must have been waiting in reception, for as I parked they rushed out and down the path.

'You're coming home!' Filip cried, opening the rear door, while Aneta burst into tears.

The children looked anxious.

'Not today, but soon,' I told them as I got out. This wasn't the way to prepare children for leaving.

'Next weekend you're coming home,' Filip said joyfully.

Seeing their father so jubilant and their mother crying was worrying Molly and Kit.

'It's OK,' I reassured them as we stood on the pavement. 'Mummy and Daddy are happy.'

'Because you're allowed to come home!' Filip cried, and lifted Kit high into the air. Aneta hugged Molly.

'I understand you are taking them out today and then we meet back here at five o'clock,' I said, trying to firm up arrangements.

'Yes,' Filip said. 'We'll go to the park, but if it gets too cold we'll come back early and go inside.'

'OK, so I'll meet you here then. Tess said she'd phone me with the details for next week.'

'I can tell you what they are,' Filip said exuberantly. 'Monday and Tuesday will be the same as today. Then on Wednesday, Thursday and Friday we can take the children home.' He gave Kit another spin in the air. 'I think you have to drop them off and collect them from our place, and then on Saturday they will move back with us! That's what our lawyer pushed for and that's what we got! Well done, Mr Coles!' Who I assumed was their lawyer.

Molly and Kit looked more confused than ever, so I told them they were going to have a nice time in the park with their mummy and daddy, and I'd come back here later to collect them. I said goodbye and left. As I pulled away, I glanced in the rear-view mirror and saw the four of them crossing the road, heading towards the park. Aneta was holding Molly's hand and Kit was on his father's shoulders, a family about to be reunited.

Paula arrived home shortly after I did and I told her of the judge's decision. She was as surprised as I was but said sensibly, 'The judge would have had all the evidence and must believe it's safe for Molly and Kit to go home.'

'Yes, absolutely,' I agreed.

'Do judges ever make mistakes?' she asked.

'Sometimes. But let's not go there.'

'I'll miss them a lot.'

'I know, we all will. Hopefully we'll be able to keep in touch.' Although Paula knew as I did that that would rely on Molly and Kit's parents. Not all parents wanted to keep in touch and be reminded of a time they'd rather forget.

When I returned to collect Molly and Kit they were waiting in reception with their parents, having only just returned from their outing to the park. The children were fine, more relaxed, and had roses in their cheeks from the cold.

'We found a café in the park,' Filip told me, 'and had a hot chocolate.'

'Lovely,' I said. 'My favourite.'

Then Aneta suddenly gained confidence in her role as mother and began advising me. 'Make sure Molly and Kit keep their hats and gloves on, it's cold today.'

'I will,' I said. 'I always do.'

'They might not want their dinner yet, as they had cake as well as hot chocolate, so you can give it to them later.'

'Yes, OK,' I said. 'Thanks for letting me know.'

Aneta and Filip brought Molly and Kit to the car and Filip lifted them into their seats in the back.

'Make sure their seatbelts are properly done up,' Aneta told him.

He double-checked. 'See you Monday,' he said, kissing them goodbye. 'Remember, you move home for good in a week, so not long.'

Aneta gave them both another kiss. 'Not long now,' she said.

I got into the driver's seat and the parents stood on the pavement and waved until we were out of sight. The children were very quiet.

'Did you have a nice time?' I asked them.

'How long is a week?' Molly asked. 'Daddy said we can go home in a week.'

'Seven sleeps,' I said. And that was all that was said for the rest of the journey.

Lucy was in when we arrived home. Paula had told her of the judge's decision. 'I hope their parents look after them properly this time,' Lucy said.

'Yes, I'm sure they will,' I replied. I had to believe it.

Both girls then spent the rest of the evening playing with Molly and Kit, wanting to make the most of their time together. When Adrian came home I told him of the decision.

'I didn't see that coming,' he said, surprised.

'No. Neither did I.'

'So the mother was innocent?'

'I guess so. She had FDIA. I'm hoping to learn more from Tess on Monday.'

That evening I telephoned my mother to tell her of the judge's ruling. She was shocked to begin with and then said stoically, 'Well, I suppose he knows what he's doing.'

'We hope so,' I said. I then asked her if it was all right if we visited her on Sunday so she and the children could say goodbye.

'I'd like that,' she said, her voice catching.

It would be upsetting for her to have to say goodbye, as it would be for us when the time came, but goodbyes are important and allow everyone to move on, especially the children who would be leaving us. I hoped Molly would have the chance to say goodbye to her friends at nursery, but I wouldn't know until Tess told me the exact arrangements for the following week.

That evening, once the children were in bed, I went round the house collecting up their toys and returning them to the toy boxes as I did every evening. I tried to picture what it was going to be like once they'd gone, and it was impossible. They were such a part of our home, lives and family, I couldn't imagine life without them. Foster carers bond with the children they look after, but they also have to remember that the children aren't theirs and at some point they will very likely go home. Fostering is different to adoption, which is permanent, and the child is legally theirs. If a child is staying with a foster carer long term then, with the agreement of the social services, they can apply to the family court for a residence order, which gives them parenting rights and more permanency.

Now I had to accept that I'd done my job, fulfilled my role, and Molly and Kit were being returned to their parents, difficult though that was going to be for me and my family.

CHAPTER TWENTY-EIGHT

SAYING GOODBYE

When Tess telephoned on Monday morning she sounded brighter, having recovered from her ordeal in court. I was in a better frame of mind too. We'd had a pleasant afternoon at my mother's the day before and Mum had stayed positive and had hidden her tears when the time had come for her to say goodbye to Molly and Kit. Tess now told me the arrangements for the week ahead, which I wrote down: the children would have unsupervised community contact today and tomorrow, 3–5 p.m., and I would take and collect them from the Family Centre. On Wednesday, Thursday and Friday I had to take them to their parents' home for 11 a.m. and collect them at 5 p.m. Filip was having the week off work. On Saturday I would move them home, again arriving at about 11 a.m. Tess suggested I took some of their belongings on each trip. This would help Molly and Kit gradually transfer their feelings of home from my house to theirs, and on a practical level all their belongings wouldn't fit in my car in one go. Tess said she would visit the family on Monday and then each week for the first month.

'The children have been returned on a supervision order,' she said. This would allow the social services to monitor the family for a year, which could be extended if necessary.

'I was surprised by the judge's decision,' I said. 'Can I ask what the reasoning was behind it?'

'In a nutshell, the judge was impressed that Aneta recognized what she'd done was wrong and that she'd been suffering from a mental illness, and had put herself in voluntary psychiatric care. The psychologist's report was positive and he was confident Aneta no longer posed a threat to her children. She'll be continuing therapy as an outpatient. Aneta was very remorseful, but maintained she didn't ever harm the children in any other way, and the judge believed her. There wasn't the evidence to prove other non-accidental injuries, and of course Molly had already admitted to accidently pushing Kit downstairs when he sustained his broken arm. Their lawyer was good. He highlighted Aneta's abusive childhood and emphasized how much she and Filip loved their children, and that they had cooperated with the social services. When Filip gave evidence, he said he felt he was to blame for not giving his wife more support. He said he was far more aware and involved with his family now. He is going to continue working the early shift and not take on overtime so he can spend more time at home.' Tess continued to say that the social services were going to put in some help, and Molly and Kit would be going to a nursery that offered parents support five mornings a week.

'Thank you,' I said. 'It makes more sense now.'

Tess wound up by saying she'd phone me mid-week to see how the children's rehabilitation home was going, but that I should call her before if there were any problems.

I replaced the handset and looked at Molly and Kit, who were just finishing their mid-morning snack. They seemed so small and vulnerable. *Their lawyer was good*, Tess had said, by which she'd meant they'd used the evidence to show the parents in the best possible light, as was their job.

Since I've been publishing my fostering memoirs, I regularly receive emails from distraught parents, relatives and friends of a family whose children are in care or are about to be taken into care. Their messages are heart-breaking, but the advice I always give is to seek legal help and try to cooperate with the social services. I appreciate this can be difficult when feelings run high, and it's easy to blame the social worker and make them an enemy. But it doesn't help the children or the parents. Their legal team will advise the family of their rights, lead them through the court proceedings and appoint a lawyer to represent them in court. While the children's safety and welfare will always be paramount, when the case goes to court the parents' lawyer will make a strong argument for having the children returned to them, while the social services' lawyer will try to show the opposite. The judge weighs up all the evidence and gives his or her ruling on what is in the best interests of the children.

So the decision had been made for Molly and Kit. Whether I thought it was the correct one wasn't for me to say. The judge had all the evidence, I did not. All that was left for me to do now was to settle the children back home.

Aneta's and Filip's excitement was obvious from the moment I parked outside the Family Centre on Monday afternoon. They were waiting on the pavement ready, coats buttoned up and gloves on. The centre was only being used as a meeting point, so they no longer had to go inside. Filip opened the rear door of the car as soon as I cut the engine.

'Hello, my beautiful children,' he said, unfastening their belts and lifting them out.

'Nice weekend?' I asked, as I joined them on the pavement.

'Yes, thank you,' Aneta replied stiffly.

'Are you going to the park?' I asked, making conversation.

'We can take them wherever we like,' she returned sharply.

'I know. I was just wondering.'

'Yes, we shall be going to the park,' Filip replied more civilly. 'Could you bring their bikes tomorrow so they can ride them in the park?'

'Sure, good idea. You could take them home with you after. I doubt we'll have time to use them this week and it will be one less thing for me to bring.'

'Fair enough,' he said.

Aneta took Molly's hand and Filip hoisted Kit onto his shoulders, ready to cross the road and head towards the park. I said goodbye and that I'd see them later, and then returned to my car. I felt that Aneta's sharpness towards me probably stemmed from resentment, partly because I'd been parenting her children, and also, I think, because it was me who had raised the alarm on what she'd been doing to the children's drinks. Ironically, it was only because I had that she'd been able to receive the help she needed to get better, allowing their family to be together again. I hoped her attitude would improve as the week progressed.

When I returned to collect Molly and Kit, both parents were cool towards me but not hostile. Clearly they'd all had a nice time, and Molly and Kit separated from their parents without too much trouble. The following day it was different. When I collected them from outside the Family Centre they wanted to stay with their parents. Molly clung to her mother and said she wasn't coming with me and wanted to go home, then Kit copied her. While this was all to be expected, and clearly pleased Aneta, we had to follow Tess's timetable, and Molly and Kit needed to see us all working together.

Aneta found that difficult. 'My poor darlings,' Aneta lamented. 'I know you don't want to go with her,' she kept saying, smothering the children in kisses. I waited patiently on the pavement, and eventually Filip realized his wife's behaviour wasn't helping Molly and Kit, so, taking over, he helped me to persuade them into my car.

'When are we going home with Mummy and Daddy?' Molly asked moodily as I drove away. 'Mummy is cross it's taking long.'

'You're going to spend tomorrow with them at home,' I said. 'Then you come back with me to sleep.' She groaned. 'Wednesday, Thursday and Friday are the same,' I continued. 'Then on Saturday you go home for good.'

Molly went very quiet. The transition period when the children are between homes is always difficult, especially when they are young and don't really understand. I would explain it again later and as often as was needed.

The next day, Wednesday, following Tess's instructions, I took Molly and Kit to their parents' for 11 a.m. with some of their possessions. While Molly remembered her home from when she'd lived there, Kit, at his age, didn't. It would have been appropriate for the parents to invite me in, as it would have given the children a positive message and been more relaxed, but that didn't happen. Aneta took them from me on the doorstep and disappeared into their ground-floor maisonette, while Filip helped me unload the car. He said goodbye, that he'd see me at 5 p.m., and then closed the door.

When I returned to collect Molly and Kit they'd obviously had a lovely day, and didn't want to leave, which again was only to be expected. I waited on the doorstep while Aneta and Filip made a half-hearted attempt to persuade them into their coats and shoes, but the children kept running off. 'They may as well stay,' Filip said.

'I can't just leave them,' I said. 'We need to follow Tess's timetable.'

'And if we don't?' he challenged.

'You could find yourselves back in court.'

'Stay there, I'll get them,' he told me brusquely, and went inside, closing the front door.

A few minutes later the door opened again. Aneta was smirking conspiratorially, and she and Filip spent some time helping the children into their coats.

'You take them to her car,' she told Filip. 'Make sure she does up their seatbelts properly.' I ignored the slight.

The children were subdued now, having picked up the atmosphere. 'I'm going to speak to Tess about these arrangements,' Filip said sternly to me as we went to the car. 'I'll get our lawyer to change them.'

I didn't tell him that wasn't going to happen. It was only a few days and there is good reason for gradually rehabilitating the children home, which I knew Tess would have explained to him and Aneta. He returned indoors and Aneta was nowhere to be seen.

'Why is Daddy upset?' Molly asked as I pulled away.

'He and Mummy want you home now, but we have to wait until Saturday. It's not long. Three more sleeps.'

Molly and Kit were both restless that night, which was only to be expected with so much going on.

Tess telephoned the following morning, having just spoken to Filip, not his lawyer. She asked me how it was going and I gave her a detailed update. She said she had explained to Filip why the children needed this period of readjustment and that the timetable was still appropriate. When I took Molly and Kit home that morning both parents came to the door, cold but not confrontational. Molly and Kit went inside with Aneta, while Filip helped me unload the car. Then, as had happened the day before, he said goodbye on the doorstep. When I collected Molly and Kit at 5 p.m. their parents were more cooperative and told the children they needed to go with me today. 'Two more sleeps,' Aneta said, adopting the phrase I used. 'Then you come home to Mummy and Daddy for good.'

Meanwhile Adrian, Lucy, Paula and I were gradually coming to terms with the children leaving. There wasn't the opportunity for Molly to say goodbye to her friends at nursery, but I telephoned the Head and explained why she wouldn't be returning and thanked her for all she'd done. Neither was there time to give Molly and Kit a leaving party. It was 6 p.m. by the time we returned each day, and they were exhausted and just about managed to stay awake long enough to have some dinner before going to bed. I brought them a leaving gift and we all signed the card.

On Saturday morning, the day of Molly and Kit's departure, Paula, Lucy and Adrian forwent their usual lie-in so they could see them off. It's bittersweet when children leave. You're pleased they can return home, but at the same time you know you're going to miss them dreadfully and life won't be the same for a long time to come. My family put on brave faces. Lucy and Paula helped the children into their coats and shoes, while Adrian helped me load the last of their belongings into the car, including the soft toys they slept with. I checked the house for any stray items, and then it was time to say goodbye.

'Give me a high-five,' Adrian said to Kit. He laughed and slapped the palm of Adrian's hand. 'Bye, Molly, look after your brother,' Adrian said to her. She wanted a high-five too.

He stood aside to let Paula say goodbye. 'I'll miss you both lots and lots,' she said, and hugged and kissed them in turn.

Lucy's eyes glistened with tears as she said goodbye, for she knew better than the rest of us what it was like to be returned home. It had happened to her many times before she'd come to live with us. 'Your mummy and daddy are very lucky to have you back,' she told them as she cuddled and kissed them. 'Remember, if you have any problems, tell your social worker.' Which is what she'd been told to do.

All that remained now was to get the children into the car. Kit wanted to ride on Adrian's shoulders. Since his father had been giving him rides like this, he often wanted Adrian to do it too. Adrian lifted him onto his shoulders, while Lucy and Paula held Molly's hands, and we went down the path to my car. Adrian, Lucy and Paula gave them a final hug and then helped them into the back seat, where Lucy gave them another kiss and hug. I could see Molly's face start to pucker and Kit was looking worried. 'Time to go,' I said positively, and closed their car door.

My family stood on the pavement and waved until we were out of sight.

'Can we see you all again?' Molly asked.

'I certainly hope so,' I said brightly.

The children were quiet. Parting from my family had been difficult for them, but now they needed to look forward to their future with their parents. 'Soon be home,' I told them.

As I pulled up outside their home the front door flew open and Aneta and Filip, full of smiles, rushed out. Filip opened the car door and lifted out the children. Aneta smothered them in hugs and kisses. She took them indoors, while Filip and I unloaded the car. There wasn't a huge amount, as I'd brought most of it on the previous trips.

'I think that's everything,' I said. Filip took the last bag from me and placed it in the hall. 'If I find anything, I'll drop it off.'

'Thank you,' he said coolly.

I was now expecting him to invite me in or call the children to the door so we could say goodbye. Adrian, Lucy and Paula had said their goodbyes at home, but I hadn't, assuming I'd do it here. I looked past him and down the hall. I could hear Molly's and Kit's voices coming from inside, but I couldn't see them. 'Can I say goodbye to the children?' I asked him.

Filip glanced over his shoulder and then looked at me. 'They're busy,' he said. 'I'll tell them you said goodbye. Thanks for bringing them.' And with that, he closed the door.

It was the most heartless goodbye I'd ever experienced in fostering, and as I returned to the car my eyes filled. Filip and Aneta wouldn't have lost anything by allowing me to say goodbye properly to Molly and Kit. It would have meant a lot to me and probably to the children too. I wouldn't tell my family, as they would be upset and angry on my behalf. I knew then that Filip and Aneta wouldn't be keeping in touch, so it was unlikely we'd ever see Molly and Kit again. I hoped the children had some fond memories of the time they'd spent with us and knew we'd loved them.

AFTERWORD

Once a child has left a foster carer, there is no provision to keep the carer informed of their progress. Sometimes we hear updates by word of mouth from another foster carer or social worker, and sometimes the family or the child themselves (if they are old enough) keeps in touch. It's always wonderful when they do, and as a foster carer I never forget the children I've looked after, ever. Sometimes years go by without any news and then suddenly the child makes contact. Only time would tell if that would be true for Molly and Kit.

For the latest on Molly and Kit and the other children in my books, please visit www.cathyglass.co.uk

AFTERWORD

SUGGESTED TOPICS FOR
READING-GROUP DISCUSSION

———————

Near the start of the book Cathy says that no one wants to take children from their parents, but sometimes there is no alternative if they are to be kept safe. Discuss.

We learn that sometimes children can be placed in care voluntarily. In what circumstances do you think that might be possible? Why is it generally considered preferable to a court order?

Molly and Kit had only recently come to the attention of the social services. Should they have done so sooner?

Fostering involves the whole family. Discuss the roles of family members, including Cathy's mother.

How do you see the role of the Guardian ad Litem in child-protection cases?

Describe the characters of Aneta and Filip. Cathy initially has empathy for them. Is it misplaced?

Cathy is upset and angry when she finds out what Aneta has been doing but manages to remain professional. How difficult might this have been?

Discuss the nature of FDIA (Munchausen syndrome by proxy) and what could lead to a person developing the illness.

Aneta makes allegations against Cathy. How vulnerable are foster carers to unfounded allegations by angry parents?

The judge returns Molly and Kit home with a supervision order. Do you think it was the correct decision? Why?

Cathy Glass

————

One remarkable woman, more
than **150** foster children cared for.

Cathy Glass has been a foster carer for
twenty-five years, during which time she has
looked after more than 150 children, as well
as raising three children of her own. She was
awarded a degree in education and psychology
as a mature student, and writes under a
pseudonym. To find out more about Cathy
and her story visit **www.cathyglass.co.uk**.

Finding Stevie

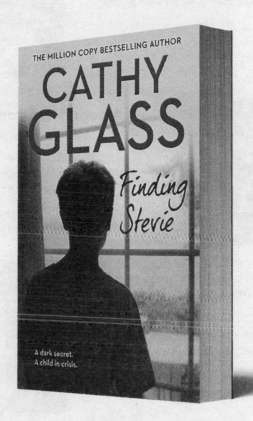

THE MILLION COPY BESTSELLING AUTHOR

CATHY GLASS

Finding Stevie

A dark secret.
A child in crisis.

Fourteen-year-old Stevie is exploring his gender identity

Like many young people, he spends time online, but Cathy is shocked when she learns his terrible secret.

Where Has Mummy Gone?

When Melody is taken into care, she fears her mother won't cope alone

It is only when Melody's mother vanishes that what has really been going on at home comes to light.

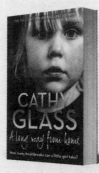

A Long Way from Home

Abandoned in an orphanage, Anna's future looks bleak until she is adopted

Anna's new parents love her, so why does she end up in foster care?

Cruel to be Kind

Max is shockingly overweight and struggles to make friends

Cathy faces a challenge to help this unhappy boy.

Nobody's Son

Born in prison and brought up in care, Alex has only ever known rejection

He is longing for a family of his own, but again the system fails him.

Can I Let You Go?

Faye is 24, pregnant and has learning difficulties as a result of her mother's alcoholism

Can Cathy help Faye learn enough to parent her child?

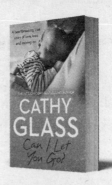

The Silent Cry

A mother battling depression. A family in denial

Cathy is desperate to help before something terrible happens.

Girl Alone

An angry, traumatized young girl on a path to self-destruction

Can Cathy discover the truth behind Joss's dangerous behaviour before it's too late?

Saving Danny

Danny's parents can no longer cope with his challenging behaviour

Calling on all her expertise, Cathy discovers a frightened little boy who just wants to be loved.

The Child Bride

A girl blamed and abused for dishonouring her community

Cathy discovers the devastating truth.

Daddy's Little Princess

A sweet-natured girl with a complicated past

Cathy picks up the pieces after events take a dramatic turn.

Will You Love Me?

A broken child desperate for a loving home

The true story of Cathy's adopted daughter Lucy.

Please Don't Take My Baby

Seventeen-year-old Jade is pregnant, homeless and alone

Cathy has room in her heart for two.

Another Forgotten Child

Eight-year-old Aimee was on the child-protection register at birth

Cathy is determined to give her the happy home she deserves.

A Baby's Cry

A newborn, only hours old, taken into care

Cathy protects tiny Harrison from the potentially fatal secrets that surround his existence.

The Night the Angels Came

A little boy on the brink of bereavement

Cathy and her family make sure Michael is never alone.

Mummy Told Me Not to Tell

A troubled boy sworn to secrecy

After his dark past has been revealed, Cathy helps Reece to rebuild his life.

I Miss Mummy

Four-year-old Alice doesn't understand why she's in care

Cathy fights for her to have the happy home she deserves.

The Saddest Girl in the World

A haunted child who refuses to speak

Do Donna's scars run too deep for Cathy to help?

Cut

Dawn is desperate to be loved

Abused and abandoned, this vulnerable child pushes Cathy and her family to their limits.

Hidden

The boy with no past

Can Cathy help Tayo to feel like he belongs again?

Damaged

A forgotten child

Cathy is Jodie's last hope. For the first time, this abused young girl has found someone she can trust.

Run, Mummy, Run

The gripping story of a woman caught in a horrific cycle of abuse, and the desperate measures she must take to escape.

My Dad's a Policeman

The dramatic short story about a young boy's desperate bid to keep his family together.

The Girl in the Mirror

Trying to piece together her past, Mandy uncovers a dreadful family secret that has been blanked from her memory for years.

About Writing
and How to Publish

A clear, concise practical
guide on writing and the best
ways to get published.

Happy Mealtimes
for Kids

A guide to healthy eating
with simple recipes that
children love.

Happy Adults

A practical guide to achieving lasting
happiness, contentment and success.
The essential manual for getting
the best out of life.

Happy Kids

A clear and concise guide to
raising confident, well-behaved
and happy children.

Be amazed
Be moved
Be inspired

Discover more about Cathy Glass
visit www.cathyglass.co.uk

If you loved this book
why not join Cathy on

facebook and **twitter** ?

Cathy will share updates on the children
from her books and on those she's currently
fostering – plus, you'll be the first to know
as soon as her new books hit the shops!

Join her now

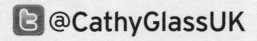 /cathy.glass.180

@CathyGlassUK